Praise for John Cowan and *Hold to a Dream*

"How many of us have wished we could have "that conversation" with someone who inspired us in our particular field of endeavor? If you're a musician, the answer to that is probably all of us. My friend John Cowan has done the hard part for the rest of us by way of a wonderful collection of personal conversations he's enjoyed with some of the most iconic musical artists of our time. I highly recommend this heartfelt and enlightening read." —*Michael McDonald*

"John Cowan is one of the most talented and unique singers I've ever heard. The way he was able to bring a singing style mostly heard in rock or contemporary music into bluegrass and please that audience was an amazing thing. I've loved his voice since I heard it the very first time. He's a humble and thankful man. I'm a fan!" —*Ricky Skaggs*

"John Cowan is tapped into the musical life force. It's hard for him not to thrill you. With his skyscraping voice and his thunderous bass, he was the perfect foil to the equally powerful Sam Bush in the legendary New Grass Revival." —*Tim O'Brien*

"John's interviews allow us to feel like we're sitting in the same room enjoying the conversation, enjoying backstories and obscure details. This book could be recommended reading for college classes focused on American popular music." —*IBMA Foundation*

"John Cowan introduced the bluegrass community to a level of vocal virtuosity it had never dreamed of, along with a sense of fun and curiosity that is to this day as infectious as it is inspiring." —*Chris Thile*

"What a joy. John Cowan's beautiful, strong, lilting tenor, fine songwriting and playing only helps us appreciate life a little more. Thanks, John, for a peek inside your incredible journey." —*Chris Hillman*

"John Cowan's soul-of-the-earth bass playing and voice made in heaven was not only an integral part of New Grass Revival's one-of-a-kind sound but of the modern-day Doobie Brothers as well. Ditto his own discography. I've certainly appropriated his shining timbre in order to make my records sound better. But most important to me is the ever-evolving man himself. He's my friend. I love him." —*Rodney Crowell*

"Cowan's voice, for me, will always be the voice of the Telluride Bluegrass Festival. No one sings like John Cowan and the sound of his voice, and now this memoir, bring back decades of incredible musical memories. His band New Grass Revival changed the lives of many, mine included." —*Craig Ferguson, president,* **Planet Bluegrass**

"There are not many singers who can be referred to as the voice of a musical genre. After joining New Grass Revival in the mid-1970s, John Cowan clearly became the voice of newgrass. In this book, Cowan chose to reveal himself by allowing readers to experience his conversations with musical icons from nearly every genre of American music. To these stellar individuals, he is a trusted friend, a highly respected musician and singer and a fellow influential traveler along life's musical highway. As a result, these conversations are personal, relaxed and reveal much more about the artists on both sides of the conversation than one could expect from a conventional interview or memoir." —*Dan Miller,* **Bluegrass Unlimited**

"John Cowan was one of the first people I met when I first visited Nashville. I've been blown away by his voice for over four decades, and somehow, he keeps getting better." —*Victor L. Wooten*

"I've known John for over fifty years and no matter what he does, you can't unfriend him." —*Tom Britt*

"Man, you're a monster!"—*Jerry Garcia*

HOLD TO
A DREAM

HOLD TO A DREAM

A NEWGRASS ODYSSEY

JOHN COWAN
with
JIMMY SCHWARTZ

Foreword by
Wendy Waldman

Backbeat Books

Essex, Connecticut

An imprint of Globe Pequot, the trade division of
The Rowman & Littlefield Publishing Group, Inc.
4501 Forbes Blvd., Ste. 200
Lanham, MD 20706
www.rowman.com

Distributed by NATIONAL BOOK NETWORK

Copyright © 2024 by John Cowan and Jimmy Schwartz

All the interviews in this book were recorded by John Cowan and producer Jonathan Shaffer at Mr. Cowan's personal expense, in various locations around Nashville, Tennessee, unless stated otherwise. Each interview aired once in 2012 on WSM radio as part of John's monthly radio show, *I Believe to My Soul*, for which he received no compensation. All interviews have been edited for clarity.

All rights reserved. No part of this book may be reproduced in any form or by any electronic or mechanical means, including information storage and retrieval systems, without written permission from the publisher, except by a reviewer who may quote passages in a review.

British Library Cataloguing in Publication Information available

Library of Congress Cataloging-in-Publication Data Available

ISBN: 978-1-4930-8458-6 (cloth: alk. paper)
ISBN: 978-1-4930-8459-3 (ebook)

♾️™ The paper used in this publication meets the minimum requirements of American National Standard for Information Sciences—Permanence of Paper for Printed Library Materials, ANSI/NISO Z39.48-1992

*To my brother, Doug Cowan,
who didn't sign up for patriarch of our family
but sure did one hell of a job.*

Getting ready to play with the HercuLeons. We were joined by my good friend, the great songwriter Darrell Scott (background). *Courtesy Madison Thorn*

CONTENTS

FOREWORD by Wendy Waldman — xi
PROLOGUE: Whitey and Me — xvii
MINERVA, OHIO, 1953 — 1
INTERVIEWS AND INSPIRATIONS — 31

PLAYING IN THE BAND — 33

1. In a Place Where There's No Space and Time
   A Memory of Leon Russell — 35

2. Jamming with Sam Bush, Godfather of Newgrass — 45

3. Béla Fleck Throws Down His Heart for the Five-String Banjo — 69

ALL FOR A SONG — 87

4. "Always Nice to Get a Letter from Home, Isn't it, Kris?"
   Me and Bobby and Kris Kristofferson — 89

5. "You Can't Tell Nothin' in a Movie"
   High on the Mountaintop with Miss Loretta Lynn — 101

6. Rodney Crowell and a Blessing for the Unfinished Song — 123

BIRDS OF SONG — 133

7. "We Knew How to be Great. Famous Will *Kill Ya*."
   The Unsinkable Bonnie Bramlett — 135

8. "You Know We Can't Copy Them Jordanaires!"
   A Closer Walk with the Legendary Gordon Stoker — 149

9. Touching the Soul of the Great Sam Moore	167
PACIFIC STANDARD TIME	**179**
10. A Byrd, a Burrito, and a Squirrel Barker Walk into a Bar The Cosmic Life of Chris Hillman	181
11. God's Own Singer of Songs Just Might Be Bernie Leadon	205
12. A Producer. A Picker. A Pioneer. Pickin' up the Pieces with Poco's Jim Messina	227
PROG AND PROGENY	**249**
13. Chicago's Robert Lamm Knows Exactly What Time It Is	251
14. I'm Just a Singer with Justin Hayward of the Moody Blues	263
15. By and By, John Carter Cash Keeps the Circle Unbroken	271
EPILOGUE	291
ACKNOWLEDGMENTS	293
DISCOGRAPHY	295
A FEW PERFORMANCES ONLINE	297
INDEX	301
ABOUT THE AUTHORS	315

FOREWORD

Wendy Waldman

There are moments in the history of any art form, stretching back to antiquity, when special things happen. For a time, artists are drawn together, and experimentation begins on a concentrated scale. Perhaps there's a receptive community "scene" in a given society, or other cultural factors that come into play. You can see these moments in history: Paris in the late 1800s into the early 1900s was one such scene for painters, England in the late 1500s into the middle 1600s for writers, Los Angeles from the 1930s to the 1990s for the golden age of film composition, and the United States and the United Kingdom from the 1950s to the 1990s for the explosion of vast new kinds of pop, folk, rock 'n' roll, and world music. Those big movements yielded other movements, offshoots, splinters, and new directions on the heels of the big ones, very much the way universes spin off new stars and galaxies from themselves. The net result of all this physical, cultural, and artistic migration is that new genres of art are forged. You're wondering why I'm talking about such a global and expansive topic, but this is, in fact, the backdrop for the story of my friend John Cowan and his role in the forging of a new American music genre.

In the 1970s and '80s, a convergence happened here in the United States, prompted by the exponentially exploding role of popular music media. Several "American ethnic" music movements had been running on parallel tracks at that time, loosely listed here:

Old-time music, hailing from the rural parts of the eastern and southern United States, with its roots in music brought over by the English, Irish, and Scottish immigrants from early days, with early black gospel and blues with roots in slave music in the southeast.

Bluegrass music, the shiny new invention with its roots in old-time music and much cleaned-up black rural music, played faster and more precisely with a clean, conservative aesthetic.

Jazz and Western swing, which had recently been excised from "country and western" and left to go its own way.

And, on another track, rock 'n' roll, which had its roots in all of the above, as well as urban pop music of the '50s and '60s, including the great British reinvention and reimportation of all of that American music, set to electric instruments.

There was, as well, the enormous accompanying counterculture of rock 'n' roll.

On top of *that* came the birth of the singer-songwriter movement that exploded when the great writer from Minnesota, Bob Dylan, began writing new, relevant, poetic lyrics to existing, much earlier folk music forms, primarily exemplified by Woody Guthrie, who had been doing the same thing a generation earlier.

This was all fueled by a vibrant and golden era of FM rock and folk radio in the United States and Europe.

As a result, musicians, writers, and producers were starting to work in all these aforementioned genres: musicians from San Francisco, Boston, New York, Los Angeles, and the United Kingdom. But one particular "offshoot" was finding its feet in the South and eastern United States. Nashville eventually became ground zero for this new movement from the late '70s onward. The background setting for this dynamic change was the explosion of the commercial country music business in Nashville with many studios, higher national visibility, sales, and an influx of new musicians. Along with people coming to work in the newly refurbished country music, some younger, more experimental musicians who were closer to Tennessee physically and spiritually also found their way there. In the shadow of the commercial giant, a brand-new genre based on the convergence of all these musical rivers began to take shape.

Many of these newcomers were people who were already world-class players because of the discipline required to play mandolin, fiddle, guitar, banjo, and bass in these highly technical, traditional musical fields. The skill required to play bluegrass is equal to the skill required to play any form of classical music. But these kids, unlike the generation from whom they learned their intense craft, were influenced by pop radio, rock 'n' roll, world music, and jazz, the songwriters as well. And they were beginning to toy with combining the music they'd played in families and traditional gatherings and contests with the music they were consuming from all the new channels of media available to them. They were also attracted to other musicians on the West Coast and Northeast who were experimenting with the same combinations, so a lot of interaction took place.

Ohio native John Cowan, too, was making his way at this time, having joined the band New Grass Revival in Kentucky in 1974. NGR was a band featuring several world-class players with roots in traditional music who had also grown up with all genres of contemporary music, and one member who had exposure to classical music as well.

There has been much documentation about New Grass Revival, which is still considered the apex of the new movement of high post-bluegrass music. It is said that the Telluride Bluegrass Festival in legend, if not in fact, was created around them. This movement, which was at first small and followed by dedicated "serious" fans and musicians, eventually gained steam, interacting with the explosion first of country music and those artists who wanted to incorporate these values into their commercial work, then blending with the "jam-grass" world of rock bands like the Grateful Dead, and giving rise to many such bands. Over the years, "newgrass" has become a world movement, interacting as much with jazz and classical music as its original acoustic-festival, cultlike beginnings. Although we can list many of the acts who have been influenced by NGR, that's not really the focus of this piece. But it is important to have a historical context as a backdrop to understand John Cowan's contribution.

Cowan became the bassist of NGR before they heard him sing, or so the story goes. Clearly, once he opened his mouth, and the members heard the astonishing range and texture of his voice, the die was cast. Add to that John's innate curiosity and openness to all kinds of music, and New Grass Revival had the perfect lead singer and collaborator. John never claims that he came out of bluegrass music at all; rather, his influences were urban and quite different. This made him the perfect lead singer for this highly experimental band, as he brought a heavy dose of pop music, progressive rock, and jazz to the mixture. More than any of the other members, Cowan was the most connected to those influences. The genius of the blending of styles gave rise to something completely different. The band always tips its hat to those who came before, such as Tony Rice, David Grisman, and others, but my contention is that until John showed up as a member of New Grass Revival, none of the others had ever pushed the envelope into blending rock and pop with the already existing blend of jazz and bluegrass. This dynamic was solidified by one other major difference: John Cowan was and still is an unparalleled rock and soul singer. Therein lies the secret in the sauce.

John Cowan, with his deep and wide musical breadth, when added to New Grass Revival, helped the band indisputably break open the genre of post-bluegrass music and turn it into a world genre of much weight. NGR was, and continues to be, a major influence and North Star in the shaping of this music, which now includes the likes of Yo-Yo Ma, James Taylor, and

Robert Plant. John was the only rock artist in those days with that broad knowledge of musical genres and the skills and talent to collaborate and perform such high-demand tunes. His iconic voice, like no other in that field, his fearless bass with a style that is unique and recognizable as his alone, and the vision to push all the boundaries helped earn New Grass Revival its leading role as founders of the "newgrass" genre. Without John Cowan, this might've been a different picture.

I've had the honor of working with John now for 35+ years. I was privileged to produce the last New Grass Revival album in captivity, *Friday Night in America*, as well as to produce two solo projects and the brilliant collaborative project with Andrea Zonn, the HercuLeons. It's always an adventure, and always very satisfying in the playback, to say the least. I'd like to add a few personal observations about the man himself.

In the way old days of pop music, very few singers were writers themselves, or wrote sparingly, as they were focused on finding music to sing and build their repertoire. They were great interpreters. I have been lucky to work with a handful of these singers, among them Linda Ronstadt, Jonathan Edwards, and John Cowan. What struck me when I started working with Cowan was that, like Ronstadt, he had the uncanny ability to find absolutely incredible tunes—I like to say, from anywhere, even under a rock! I had learned that about Ronstadt early on. These very rare singers have a nose for a great song that many others would have missed. I think I first heard Ralph Vaughan Williams's "The Lark Ascending" at John's house, as well as connecting with Yes's "Long Distance Runaround" through John's interpretation, far more than I ever had been able to from the original version. From Miles Davis to Loretta Lynn, with a little English classical music thrown in for good measure, I have loved seeing, every time we go into the studio, what John has found that he wants to show the world.

What fascinates me but doesn't surprise me about this memoir is the assertion here that to know whom John admires can reveal so much about the man himself. Although that's a valid and humble way to approach him, there's so much more. An educated fan of film and modern culture in all its forms, John never ceases to amaze me with the places he goes as he engages with his colleagues as an artist and a fan himself. This book shows a glimpse of that. He is his own kind of music historian and deeply knowledgeable. It's a conversation you want to have with him if you ever get the chance. Until then, please enjoy these conversations, as I have, with influential friends and artists who happen to be some of the most foundational figures in American music.

Another thing that many local friends of his know, but his wider audiences may not, is that he is a leader in giving to mental health, drug and alcohol addiction recovery programs, a nonstop crusader, healer, counselor, and example for countless people who have suffered. He has made an enormous difference in the lives of so many, but this is never discussed. Cowan is a wonderful, humble, and inspired human being who also sports a wicked and sophisticated sense of humor. The public at large needs to know this guy, who is a treasure, and as you can see, someone I cherish and love very much. It has been my complete joy and honor to work with him these several decades.

More than seventy artists have recorded songs that Wendy Waldman either wrote or cowrote, including Linda Ronstadt, Robert Smith of the Cure, Kim Carnes, Cee Cee Winans, Randy Travis, Percy Sledge, Kenny Rogers, Kathy Mattea, Judy Collins, Rita Coolidge, and Bette Midler. Among her biggest hits are "Save the Best for Last" (the top-selling record of 1992) by Vanessa Williams, "Fishing in the Dark" by the Nitty Gritty Dirt Band, "Baby, What About You?" by Crystal Gayle, "I Owe You One" by Aaron Neville, and "You Plant Your Fields" by New Grass Revival. As a producer, she's also been the rarest of talents: a living, breathing female record producer in Nashville.

PROLOGUE

Whitey and Me

I got my bass guitar, "Whitey" in 1975 at the Doo Wop Shop on Bardstown Road in Louisville, Kentucky. When I joined New Grass Revival (NGR) in 1974, I was playing a Plexiglas Dan Armstrong bass. Once I'd been in the band a couple of days, I started playing a Fender Precision that belonged to our banjoist, Courtney Johnson. Up to that point, I had played with my fingers, tap style, like John Entwistle and Jack Cassidy, or with a pick or plectrum. Sam Bush suggested I play with my fingers like an upright bass and actually pull/pluck the strings. Being eager to please my bandmates, I gave it a try and never looked back. The Precision bass was cool but a little unwieldy in my hands. Hence the trip to Louisville to the Doo Wop Shop. I played the 1962 Olympic White Fender Jazz Bass and immediately fell in love. To this day, it had the thinnest neck I've ever seen on a Fender Jazz Bass. When I inquired how much they were asking for it, they said a whopping $225. I didn't have that kind of cash, but I *did* have the Dan Armstrong. Thank goodness they agreed to trade them straight up, and I left the shop with Whitey. Our life together started then, and it ain't by any means over.

When NGR was Leon Russell's band in '78, '79, and '80, we played the Illinois State Fair on a blistering, hot-ass day. After the show, our "crew," Kathy Bush, Hazel Johnson, Liz Cowan, and the four of us, Curtis Burch, Courtney Johnson, Sam Bush, and I, were tearing around the stage, unplugging stuff and loading it into our van. After one of the trips to the van, I went

My trusty companion, "Whitey," taking a break onstage at the Chicago Theatre in 2022 next to a Doobie Brothers set list. *Photo by Jeremy Denton/Courtesy Karim Karmi, Full Stop Music Management*

back on the stage and noticed that Whitey was gone. At first, I'd assumed that one us had taken it and put away. After asking around, we realized that it had been stolen off the stage. I was completely devastated and heartbroken. Our next gig was in Los Angeles, outdoors. Upon arriving in LA, Leon called his "Wrecking Crew" partner, the great Carol Kaye, and asked her if she would lend me a bass and that we'd come get it. Carol said, "Nonsense, I'll bring it out myself." Of course, I already knew of her. She was royalty to any serious bassist worth their weight.* She showed up with a brand-new cherry red Fender Precision. Keep in mind, I'm all of twenty-five years old, talking to Carol Kaye, and now playing her bass. Jeez.

Through luck, or spirit, or my late dad watching over me (I liked to imagine him being responsible for the good turns my life took), the person who'd stolen the bass was found, and the State Fair called us. We told the police that if he'd return the bass, we wouldn't press charges as he was just seventeen years old.

In 2008, if you recall, the U.S. economy went down the tubes. My wife got laid off from her job in December, we had four kids of various ages under our roof and mounting financial needs. I had pared my band down to Jeff Autry, myself, and Shad Cobb. It was *rough*. We were driving all over the country playing for either low guarantees or "door deals." At this point, I decided that the best thing to do to help us out was to sell Whitey.

So, I called up my old friend George Gruhn and asked him if he'd sell it as a consignment. First thing he said was, "Are you sure?" I gritted my teeth and said, "Yeah, man, family first!" Whitey sat there at Gruhn Guitars for a good while with barely any nibbles. At some point, both deflated and relieved, I went down there and took him back. Not long after that, at the

---

* Carol was the Queen. She was the first woman in the A-Team of LA session players and played on an estimated 10,000 sessions from the Beach Boys *Pet Sounds*, Motown, Sinatra, Sam Cooke, Stevie Wonder, Phil Spector, you name it. I feel like Carol played on practically every pop song that reached us out in the hinterlands. I think because she started out as a jazz guitarist, she brought a lot of much-needed melodic structure to pop songs.

IBMA (International Bluegrass Music Association) convention in Nashville, I ran into Sammy Shelor, banjoist extraordinaire and founder/leader of the Lonesome River Band. Sammy told me he had a friend who wanted to buy my bass. His name was Johnny Green, and Johnny was an NGR fan. We talked, and he was as much a guitarist as a bass player, and otherwise, just an angel. He said, "Look, I'll buy this from you and hold on to it and when you can, I'll sell it back to you, but I won't get rid of it or anything." Much relieved and deeply grateful, I agreed and went on my way. I had other basses to play, but they ain't Whitey.

My oldest sibling was Richard Douglas "Doug" Cowan. When my father passed away, I was twenty-one years old, and Doug was thirty-three. He watched and supported me as a kid with an "against-all-odds" dream that I fought to make reality. When I told brother Doug what happened with Whitey, he said, "I'm sending you a check, and I want you to get your bass back. You pay me if you can, when you can."

My brother passed away in December of 2021. I love him more than I can express. He was proud of me for, I think, the right reasons. He saw my struggles with addiction and my recovery. He reinforced my belief in family first by his own examples and the value of having lifelong friends that you have to maintain for both parties no matter what.

Yes, one of the reasons I love my 1962 ol' piece of wood is that it reminds me so much of my own history: the songs, the words, and the hearts of everyone we've encountered along the way.

Love 'n' stuff,

Johnny C.

MINERVA, OHIO, 1953

I was born to Richard and Cleo Cowan on August 24th in Minerva, Ohio (Stark County), causing the population in 1953 to surge from 1,687 to 1,688. There were a few complications with my entry into the brave, new world, consistent with the touch-and-go Eisenhower presidency. I weighed three pounds, eight ounces. In preemie care, I not only spent my first year in and out of the hospital with pneumonia but, as part of the bargain, I have a birthmark, a rambling port wine stain, that covers two-thirds of my upper torso. I've always referred to it as God's tattoo.

When I was three, my father, Richard, an accountant, was transferred to a new job in Cleveland; and soon he, along with my mother, Cleo; my brothers, Douglas and Steven; my sister, Sue; our grandmother, Blanche; our

Photo by Jeremy Denton/Courtesy Karim Karmi, Full Stop Music Management

dachshund, Fritzie; and I were settling into our new 1,692-square-foot first home in Solon, Ohio, twenty miles southeast of downtown.

NFL Football, and the Cleveland Browns specifically, were very much a part of our lives then. Aunts, uncles, cousins, and family gatherings frequently convened around our colorful Brownies, scrimmaging in the center of our living room on a black-and-white television with a rabbit ears antenna that my dad would arrange according to the whims of the weather. Other Sundays, I distinctly remember holding my father's hand at age five, walking wide-eyed up the ramp to our seats at cavernous Cleveland Municipal Stadium. Football is what held my interest full-time. After games, most of the kids in our neighborhood would gather in our yards to try to re-create what we'd seen on TV that day.

But that wasn't all that was on TV.

As a nation, we were staggering through the assassination of President John F. Kennedy. We became eyewitnesses to sons and brothers being cut down in Vietnam, right there on the six o'clock news. On that very same black-and-white TV, you could now watch fellow citizens of color being beaten, subdued by fire hoses, and attacked by police dogs while following coverage of the Civil Rights Movement. Everyone was confused, and everyone had an opinion, even us kids. We just weren't supposed to express them out loud. I felt voiceless in my own home.

Then, on February 9th, 1964, the most remarkable thing happened. A comet slipped through the ether from the bonds of the galaxy (or was it Liverpool?) and into the side door of the Ed Sullivan Theater, depositing four humanlike beings onto Ed's stage and into my living room. The debut of the Beatles that night—John, Paul, George, and Ringo—combined with an audience of shrieking, hyperventilating girls, changed the trajectory of my life forever. I knew what I wanted to do. I just had no idea how to start. But for the first time in my life, I had a dream to hold on to.

Minerva, Ohio, 1953

I'd grown up singing in church just like my dad did, and I loved music. I may have been afflicted with a distinct lack of an attention span, but I didn't have trouble focusing on music. Strolling through our neighborhood one spring afternoon, I met a young man about my age sitting on his front step playing a Sears Silvertone guitar plugged into his guitar case that had a little speaker in it. I don't think I thought in phrases like this then, but if I had, I'd have said something like, "What the *fuuuuuuck?*" He was cool. We struck up a conversation and, of course, with all the bluster I could muster, I acted like seeing this was a perfectly normal occurrence, and I was all about it. His name was Gerry Gillespie, and fifty years later, we are still good friends. Gerry told me that a guy a few blocks down the street, Tom Shields, had an actual drum set. We talked for at least an hour, and *he played me songs! He could actually play and sing!* We talked about our favorite bands and naturally arrived at the Beatles as our first frame of reference. In my hea*d—at that mome*nt—I was marching home and asking my folks for a guitar.

Now, up to that point, my only true interests had been football and girls, and all my report cards reflected that. Soon after meeting Gerry, though, I pestered my parents to the point of my dad escorting me to a pawn shop downtown and buying me my first bass: a Univox Beatle Bass and an Ampeg B-12 Bass Amplifier. Associated promises and head nodding about chores and study were extracted from me, and I did my best to follow through. To my parents' utter astonishment, I spent every waking moment practicing the bass and singing. By the next year, Gerry and I had coerced the drummer, Tom Shields, and a friend from school, Nicky Ulrich, who sang and had a Fender electric twelve-string guitar, into forming a band.

There were two things I immediately noticed about band life. First was that my gridiron ambitions were wearing thin. I'd played Pop Warner football and even junior varsity football, but now I really didn't want to go to summer

The dream begins: me in front of my garage playing my first bass. *Author's collection*

football practice in the Kentucky heat and humidity where I'd sit on the bench every game as the backup center. The second thing I noticed was that whenever I sang, the other guys' eyes would get kind of wide and surprised looking. Then one day we were practicing, and one of the guys' cute sisters said, "You sing really good!" Done deal. I traded in my football cleats for Battle of the Bands and the Middletown Sock Hop.

Since our band was a mostly neighborhood band, our parents, much to our pleasant surprise, helped us out a lot. The moms all got out their Butterick patterns and made us matching Nehru shirts. My dad made us two lighting boxes that each held four floodlights, one each red, yellow, green, and blue. He'd also load up our station wagon with our gear and chain-smoke all the way to the gigs and back. I'm sure he snuck in some Falstaff, Iron City, or Oertles '92 for good luck. I still don't know if they thought it was amusing or were just relieved that we weren't spending our energy on the dark arts available to teenage boys. Either way, I look back on it with gratitude and a warm feeling in my heart.

Then came trouble.

Before my senior year of high school, my dad announced that we were moving to Evansville, Indiana. I was devastated. This just *could not be*. With all the teenage torment I could muster, I desperately tried to convince my parents that I could stay in Louisville and find someone benevolent to take me in for the school year. They weren't having it. We uprooted and moved to Evansville in July. I hated it at first, as anyone who has ever moved away from all their friends can imagine. Hey, look! Another transfer kid! As if I was going to just casually insert myself into the lives of other teenagers who'd spent every year since grade school together. Well, once again, music arrived to prove me wrong and save my ass.

Before long, I met some guys who were two or three years older than me and who had a band, the Young Turks, who were well known in the tristate area. So, I soldiered on, kept my head down, and was the bassist and singer. We had an old yellow school bus that carried all of us and our gear in it. As my senior year wound down, we booked a regional tour for the summer in Indiana, Illinois, Michigan, and Wisconsin. It was a blast. We camped at KOAs and got into some good trouble playing music, drinking beer, smoking pot, and enumerating all the ways we owned the world and always would. Then came the rub. At the end of the summer, my parents marshaled me into the living room for what we'll call:

THE DISCUSSION

Them: John, you will be going to college this fall.

Me: Huh? I barely graduated from high school.

Them: We don't care. That's what we want you to do. It's time you got serious about your future.

Me: I *am* serious about my future; I'm going to pursue being a musician.

Dad: Son, no one makes a living playing music. The odds are completely against you. [OK, he was not wrong.] I know you, son, better than you know yourself. You don't have the heart for it. They'll chew you up and spit you out!

Me: What the hell am I gonna study in college?

Dad: *Accounting*, like I did!

I just laughed. Anyone who knows me even remotely knows that when I see numbers and problems presented as mathematics, I reflexively see hieroglyphics. There is nothing more paralyzing to me than the idea of sitting at a desk crunching numbers. This was a very, very bad idea. But, the deal was done. No bargaining, no cajoling, no mercy.

Now, it's no reflection on the good people at Indiana State University, Evansville, to say that my one year there was a waste of my father's money and both of our time. I took an "incomplete" in every course except one, University Choir, where I pulled an A. I've always told people that my college career was one in which I confused GPA with THC. By the end of the second semester, in a year that effectively went up in smoke, I had made some of my biggest mistakes and some of the best friends that I still have to this day.

My father, believe me, was not happy with me wasting his tuition money, and he and I were barely speaking. My mom, as usual, was caught in the middle trying to negotiate like Henry Kissinger with Ho Chi Minh and LBJ. All the same, I knew what I wanted to do, and in the summer of 1973, there was no stopping me. I left, under grievous circumstances. I decided that I'd move back to Louisville, bring two musicians from Evansville, Michael

Boenigk and Tom Britt, grab Gerry and Tom, and start anew. I got a job at the Brownsville Road Car Wash during the day, and nights were full of rehearsal, rehearsal, and more rehearsal. We got some gigs playing in Louisville. I went home to Evansville to visit my folks occasionally, but things were chilly between my dad and me. Semi-pleasantries in passing were about all we had for each other.

On one of my last visits home I noticed that my dad had bought a beautiful leather coat, and I told him how cool I thought it was, and he seemed pleased that I approved of the choice. I had just accepted my first "road gig" for a short run to play for six weeks at a nightclub in Pittsburgh. I had come home to let them know I was taking the job and was there to grab a suitcase for my travels. After saying good night and good-bye, my folks went to bed. I knew my dad would be gone for work by the time I got up in the morning. I had packed the suitcase and set it in the breezeway so I could just get up and drive to the airport in Louisville. When I awoke the next morning, Dad was already gone, so I had some coffee and toast with my mom. I finished and did a quick dummy check to see if I had left anything I'd need later. On my way to the breezeway, my mom asked me if I had seen my suitcase.

I said, "Not since last night."

She said, "You need to open it up."

I asked why.

She said, "Just open it up, son."

I put the suitcase down on the floor and opened it. There, laying neatly folded on the top, was my dad's new coat with a note attached. I opened the note, and it said, "Dear son, I hope you like this coat, be safe and stay warm. I love you, Dad." The following August, my father died. Honestly, I've never really gotten over it.

Two months later, I got a call from Sam Bush, bandleader of New Grass Revival, who was looking for a bass player. A mutual friend, Kentucky guitar legend Kenny Lee Smith, had given Sam my phone number. Kenny had told him I was a great bassist and could sing well. Sam asked if I'd be willing to drive down to Barren County, Kentucky, where they lived, to audition for NGR. I was working in the car wash in Louisville at the time and had seen them perform exactly once. I said, "Sure, of course, I'd love to!"

Folks, I have always believed in the spirit world, whether it's through Christianity, Hinduism, Buddhism, Carl Jung, or Edgar Cayce. I still believe to this day that somehow, some way, my father, after all our struggles, "nudged" me into the New Grass Revival, a band I was about to play and tour the world with for the next fifteen years as bassist and lead singer. New Grass Revival became one of the most celebrated and influential bands of the 1980s. Over time, our name came to represent an entire music genre, and NGR was ultimately elected to the Bluegrass Hall of Fame in 2020. But in the beginning, in those first moments, as a rock kid who'd only ever played in local garage bands, I was completely out of my element. At least I was smart enough to say, "I have no idea what I'm doing. You're going to have to help me." All Sam Bush told me was, "Take I-65 South to the Cave City/Glasgow exit, get off, and go to the Shell station and call us. Courtney and I will come get you." The funny thing is he didn't say, "Go get our album and learn these songs," or *anything*.

NEW GRASS REVIVAL, 1974: CHROME REVERSE WHEELS AND GLASSPACK MUFFLERS

My best friend, Tom Britt, drove down there with me from Louisville. I'm pretty sure I heard Courtney Johnson's '68 cranberry-colored Super Sport Chevelle before I saw it. It sounded *good*, that deep-throated rumble from glasspack dual exhausts. (Yes, of course, he had chrome reverse wheels on it.) Now, I grew up in the suburbs of Cleveland, Pittsburgh, Louisville, and

Evansville, where the steel belt plays chicken with the Bible Belt. Courtney's house was almost literally a shack in an unincorporated little village called Hiseville, Kentucky (population 240 in the 2010 census), about eleven miles east of the interstate. It was agrarian, mostly tobacco farms, but plenty of fowl, beef, dairy, and hogs to accent the breeze. The house, where he and his South African wife, Hazel, lived, had three rooms. It did have running water, but they did not have heat, except for a cast iron woodstove. Through the front door was the modest living room, featuring one couch, a table and chairs, and behind that, a kitchen and a bathroom. The upstairs, a space I would come to know well, was unfinished and dark.

Courtney Johnson, banjo master from south Georgia, was a chain-smoking, coffee-"suppin'" redhead with a beautiful, flowing beard, generous smile, and twinkling eyes to match. Curtis Burch, the brilliant guitarist, was tall, about six feet, and skinny, with exaggerated facial features and an unruly mess of big ol' Georgia hair. Sam, he was Sam. He already looked like Robert Plant.

A "REAL BASS PLAYER"

The first day I auditioned, there was a drummer from North Carolina in the band named Michael Clem, who had been with them for a couple of years. I slept in Courtney's farmhouse that night, and the next day when I woke up, Michael was on the front porch loading up his car and fighting back tears. I asked him what was going on, and he told me, "They fired me! The other guys decided that since they now had a 'real bass player,' they were gonna go back to just being a four-piece unit."* Everyone said their good-byes, and Michael drove away.

My first few months and the early years that followed, I know now, were a hallowed gift to me. I moved into Courtney and Hazel's upstairs space.

---

* See the Sam Bush interview for more details of the "How-the-new-bassist-John-Cowan-unwittingly-got-a-really-nice-drummer-fired" story.

My bed was the warmest sleeping bag I could afford. As each winter night approached, and the last logs in the woodstove turned to embers, I'd put on two pairs of socks, a T-shirt, a flannel shirt, and a toboggan hat pulled down tight to cover everything but my mouth, slip into my sleeping bag, zip it up, and blissfully sleep.

But, oh man, the days. Curtis and Sam would arrive around ten or eleven a.m. Courtney, up since dawn, had drunk about a pot of "Looziane" coffee with chicory. Someone, usually Courtney, had a couple of joints rolled up. We'd get started, generally, by passing a joint among us and listening to a record and talking about it. Sometimes it was John Hartford's *Aereo-Plain*, or the Dillard's *Copperfields*, Norman Blake's *The Fields of November*, the Allman Brothers Band's *Live at Fillmore East*, Jimi Hendrix, Doc & Merle Watson, Seatrain, the Mahavishnu Orchestra, Cream, or the Grateful Dead. Other than being a proud owner of the Nitty Gritty Dirt Band's *Will the Circle Be Unbroken* album, I knew absolutely nothing about bluegrass music. When I

Sam Bush, Curtis Burch, me, and Courtney Johnson on Sam's porch in Bowling Green, Kentucky. *Photo by Leo Fernandez/Courtesy Leo Fernandez Estate*

joined the band, I was twenty-one, and Courtney was already thirty-six. I was so out of my element.

I would eventually come to learn the entire NGR repertoire, song by song, day by day, at Courtney's. It was so foreign and beautiful to me. I knew I was in heaven musically, but I paid a great deal of attention to my role as a bassist in a band without a drummer or percussionist because it was my job to keep the train on the tracks, so to speak. I also knew it wasn't going to work for me vocally to try to sing like Bill Monroe, John Duffey, or Bobby Osborne. That wasn't in me.

One day, I said, "Do you mind if I sing a song?" Sam agreed, and we played J. D. Crowe's "Some Old Day," and I sang it in my high tenor, with full gospel voice and vibrato. At the end of it, Sam looked at me and said, "John, I *used* to be the lead singer. Now *you* are."

Sam was always encouraging, and the more I sang, the more I developed my own voice. These guys were all very kind and supportive of me in this situation, treating me as a partner, not someone they were mentoring, though in so many ways, they surely were. We were called New Grass Revival because, as Sam would say, "We were trying to revive a new bluegrass that had already been invented by bands like the Osborne Brothers, the Dillards, and Jim & Jessie. We were only hoping to further the progressiveness." Because I was a big progressive rock fan, experimenting with jamming on traditional instruments over songs from different genres was right up my alley.

"CHAIR-SNAPPIN' TIME"

We drove all over the country playing festivals and small clubs; and whether the traditional bluegrass world cared for it or not, NGR was building our own loyal audience. We were a "musician's musicians" band, much like Little Feat, a group we revered. At many shows, we started noticing other musicians about our age hanging out and watching us from the side of the stage. Occasionally, some inspired promoters tried to bill us as "The Grateful Dead of Bluegrass" because of our long, roaming jams and improvisation. Sam had to insist in our contracts that we not be billed that way to avoid any possibility of Deadheads showing up hoping to hear their favorite tunes.* So, a lot of times, they'd put us on around 11 p.m., after Lester Flatt or Jimmy Martin, or whomever, because, to a lot of old-guard fans, we were reprehensible. We were plugged in. Everybody's got an amp. We'd play "One Love" by Bob Marley or "Great Balls of Fire." And, maybe the last straw, we now had a lead singer who was accused of sounding like Robert Plant.

But the joke among us, and the dark reality was, that we began to refer to our sets as "chair-snappin' time" because the fans who brought their coolers and portable chairs to enjoy Lester Flatt or Ralph Stanley, or J. D. Crowe or the Country Gentlemen, would hear about ten or fifteen bars of our first song, and you could see it and hear it from the stage: *Snap! Snap! Thump! Whap!* Folks began leaving in droves for their cars while our fans, who looked and dressed a lot like us, hung around for our set. Like almost everything else going on in 1975 and 1976, there was a cultural chasm between the young and old guard and, in the bluegrass world, it was often tough going. Sometimes it cost us money.

We once had an opportunity to share a bill with Bill Monroe, the "Father of Bluegrass," until he told the promoters that if they hired New Grass Revival, "Don't expect me to be there."† This happened a lot. I believe we didn't work certain shows that other people did because of the nature of what we were doing musically. Traditional bluegrass royalty thought our music was sacrilegious. They thought that rock and roll had no place in bluegrass music.

---

* We didn't do any.
† Sam has joked that, "If Bill was the Father of Bluegrass, then I must be the mother, because Monroe would say, 'Here comes that mother now.'"

Nor did jazz. Nor did rhythm and blues. Our hair and clothes were undoubtedly a factor because we all looked like hippies while they were up there with their cowboy hats, crisp suits, and tie pins that were often the American flag or a crucifix. Every artist I've ever known is insecure to some degree. This was really something different.

Another time, we were playing a summer festival out in a farm field in Nebraska, sharing a bill with Jimmy Martin, the self-proclaimed "King of Bluegrass Music,"* and it was hotter than blazes. Back then, if you were hired at a festival and only played one day, you were obliged to do two shows. Jimmy was just finishing his first show when we pulled into the parking lot in what we affectionately called our "bread truck" (an old yellow and blue dry-cleaning van that looked to most folks like the colors of Bunny Bread), and we parked it next to his bus. We got out and were just hanging out. Jimmy, who appeared to my eye to be thoroughly inebriated onstage (and spitting!), saw us and began sermonizing to the crowd, "Y'know folks, there ain't no place for rock and roll in bluegrass music!" We were well aware that he was talking about us. And Jimmy, well-oiled, just kept going. It was the first time any of us had ever witnessed such a public lack of respect by one artist toward another. Knowing that we were the target of his contempt was both upsetting and infuriating as hell.

---

* Jimmy Martin, once a member of Monroe's Bluegrass Boys, was a brilliant artist with enormous God-given talent, but he had an angry, self-destructive nature. He famously managed to get himself thrown off the Grand Ole Opry for drinking and other erratic behavior. In his mind, he competed with Bill Monroe, "Father of Bluegrass," to the point of designing and installing his own six-foot headstone years before his death with the self-titled inscription, "*King* of Bluegrass Music."

LEON RUSSELL AND MAHALIA

In the fall of 1978, NGR was booked to play a small theater, the Apollo Delman in Tulsa, Oklahoma. Unbeknownst to us, Leon Russell, who Sam and the band had played with before,* had moved back to Tulsa from Los Angeles after going through a divorce from his wife, Mary. He'd been lying low, had done a live record with Willie Nelson, and that was about it. Our mutual friend, Emily Smith (the inspiration for Leon's wonderful song "Sweet Emily"), was chauffeuring Leon around Tulsa one day when they passed the theater and saw "New Grass Revival" on the marquee. Emily yelled, "Look Leon! It's the New Grass boys. We should go see 'em." Damned if they didn't show up in her Cadillac right around sound check. I, of course, didn't know Leon Russell other than him being one of my musical heroes, but they just strolled in unannounced. Much hand shaking, hugging, and grinning ensued.

"How ya'll boys doing!?" he asked.

"Well, we're good, *really good*!" said Sam. "We got rid of our drummer and hired this guy John who sings and plays his ass off!"

"Hmm," said Leon. "Y'all got an extra guitar I can play?"

I didn't quite poop in my pants, but nearly. We played "Jambalaya" and maybe "Prince of Peace." He loved it, and we were all smiles. Leon came back for the show that night, and after the show we all retired to Emily's house. It was just a loose, joyful little party where we swapped songs and off-color road stories and laughed. Me? I just tried to act like I belonged there and tried my best not to stare at Leon too much.

Somehow, over the next few days, a piano appeared, and we simply kept playing music together while teaching Leon bluegrass songs. At some point, Mr. Leon Freaking Russell, who three years earlier was one of the biggest stars

---

* Also see the Sam Bush interview, coming up shortly, about NGR auditioning for Leon in his bathrobe, at his home in Tulsa.

Minerva, Ohio, 1953

Courtney, Curtis, Sam, and the new kid. *Courtesy Jim McGuire*

in America, asked us if we wanted to go on tour with him. *Um, let us check our calendars. Why, yes, we seem to be available.*

"Do you mean you want us to open for you?"

"No," he replied, "I want you boys to open the show and then be my band for my part of the show."

It was decided then that the tour would be called Leon Russell & the New Grass Revival, Rhythm and Bluegrass. We rehearsed relentlessly. The repertoire included Leon's songs, bluegrass and country standards, some great gospel, some Beatles, Sam & Dave, and some crazy standards Leon threw in like "Don't Let the Stars Get in Your Eyes."

Our first shows were brutal.

We would play for thirty minutes, and although our name was on the bill, and we had some hard-core fans out there, most people came to see Leon Russell and either booed us lustily or screamed "LEON!" through most of our set. By the third show, Leon took to grabbing a microphone backstage and announcing to the audience, "Hey, folks! It's Leon here! Just wanted to tell y'all that we got my good friends here, the New Grass Revival, and they're gonna play a few songs, and then we're all going to do a big show together for y'all. So, please make them feel welcome because I love them a lot!" And then we'd play, and people didn't boo quite *as* much.

Now, I'm not totally sure if Leon was trying to pay off his divorce or just feeling alive again, but we did close to three hundred shows a year for the next three years. His bus was an old Silver Eagle that I think he got from Willie Nelson, decorated inside with what can only be described as the hair of a thousand troll dolls. He called it "Mexican mink."

Leon's bus broke down constantly. When it finally died for good, he decided to buy himself a mobile home. So, I bought a van, Sam bought a van, and Courtney, Hazel, and Curtis got one, too. I believe we may have had the first all-female road crew. Sam's wife, Kathy, ran the sound. Hazel changed strings, which were exploding at the speed of sound that we played. She also helped Sam switch between fiddle and mandolin during the show. My wife, Liz, sold merchandise. As we kept our frantic pace, the band continued to expand: Tom Britt joined on pedal steel and electric guitar. John "Juke" Logan was on Little Walter/Chicago style blues harmonica, Bill Kenner assisted on mandolin, and Ambrose and Shampsi, two wondrous Nigerian percussionists, joined forces as well. We were rolling.

Leon loved to play up-tempo music in Pentecostal style, so my job on bass was literally to double his left hand note for note. It was some insanely powerful shit. I'd never heard anything like it and probably never will. Leon had quit drinking at this point in his life, which didn't agree with him or anyone around him, unless you can imagine (and take a kind of deviant pleasure in) seeing Jimmy Swaggart with cascading silver hair dancing on top of a piano, invoking Jesus's name while singing a song about fornication. As the bass player gazing out into the audience, I can tell you that a whole lot of people did. They will tell their children years from now of "the good old days."

As a singer, I was innately familiar with Leon's voice and phrasing. So, trying to emulate Kathi McDonald, Rita Coolidge, Pam Polland, or Claudia

Minerva, Ohio, 1953

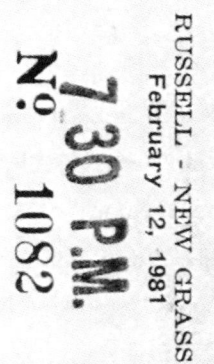
Courtesy Madison Thorn

Lennear* was almost second nature to me. Sam was a huge help because of his own familiarity with Leon's phrasing and timbre. We worked tenaciously on blending with Leon's voice. With every inflection and anywhere he went vocally, we were on him like white on rice. At first, I'd been a little intimidated singing in the style I was developing in the bluegrass world, which usually meant no vibrato. But Leon's music gave me an opportunity to feel more confident in what I was discovering I *could* do. Then, one night, we played in Kansas City, and one of the songs I was featured on was Bill Monroe's "A Good Woman's Love." That song allowed me to lean hard into a more bluesy, gospel style, which was my God-given sweet spot. The next day, a music critic wrote a highly favorable review of the show, adding that my singing "evoked Mahalia Jackson." *Mahalia Jackson*? I could've died right then and been happy with what I'd achieved in this life. In the coming months, other reviews followed, and I was about to find out that it would not be the last time someone wrote or said something flattering about my voice, using words that a kid, just a few years removed from working in a car wash in Louisville, would not have dared to think himself.

---

* These women are four of the most supremely gifted rock and soul singers of all time, all of whom performed with Leon Russell at some point in their careers. If you don't know their names, please write 'em down and look them up and discover why you love so many of the records you do.

THE VOICE OF NEWGRASS

Whether it was the older guys like Bill Monroe or the younger guys like my friend Ricky Skaggs, it was fast becoming clear to me—having known *nothing* about bluegrass previously—that there wasn't anybody out there offering the things that I could do vocally. It was like putting Stevie Wonder or Gregg Allman in a bluegrass band because that's who I listened to and borrowed from and aspired to be as a rock and soul tenor. Nobody could sing high Bs and high Cs and hold the note for sixteen bars. Or maybe nobody else wanted to. But in terms of a progressive sound, it instantly separated New Grass Revival from any other traditional bluegrass band, and it pulled in a lot of young people with it. A player and writer named Jack Tottle did a review of our band for *Bluegrass Unlimited* magazine, and I *think* he thought he was disparaging me when he made a reference to my "Robert Plant screaming." Although I can usually detect a personal dig when I see one, at the same time, all I could think was, "Oh, hell, yes! I like that."

"Y'ALL HAVE A GOOD LIFE"

Our tour with Leon went on for almost three years, and it got to where he would say, "Why don't y'all boys play about twenty minutes, and then we'll do about one or two of your songs in my show with me backing you up?" Little by little, NGR's sets had gone from forty, to thirty, and now twenty minutes. We weren't always sure what that was about and privately started referring to Leon as the "miser of space and time." We loved him, but I believe we'd hit a point where all he really wanted to do is play a show, get paid, and get the fuck out of there and on to the next town. As much as he loved the music, he'd already been on the road for twenty years. He also had a big chip on his shoulder because he'd been a megastar once, America's top concert draw in 1972 according to *Billboard*, and now he wasn't.

Then one day, he finally said, "I'll tell you what boys, let's just do this: y'all come out when I come out, and we'll do "A Good Woman's Love," and you guys can play "Prince of Peace" and maybe one other song, and that'll be the show." And Curtis and Courtney, who rode together, said, "Well, what the fuck, what about New Grass Revival?" They didn't like it, nor did they like our breakneck pace, the drive-play-sleep-drive-play way we were traveling. Next thing we knew, Courtney and Curtis stepped forward to challenge the authority within the band. Since Sam was the guy who managed all our business affairs, Courtney called Sam up and said, "This is bullshit! We're not even playing our music. We're going to have to do something different. You're going to have to go tell Leon that we need to play our own music, or I quit!"

It's worth mentioning here that whenever there was a problem in our ranks, it was usually between Courtney and Sam. Not that they didn't love each other, because they did. But Courtney could be cantankerous. Even when he was thirty-eight, he acted like he was sixty. When Sam called me up to tell me about their exchange, I said, "So, what did you tell 'em?" And Sam said, "I told them, "OK, then, y'all be well,"" which they truly did not expect. They were blown away. "Y'all have a good life," said Sam. "Cow and I are gonna stay on with Leon." And just like that, Courtney and Curtis were gone. Sam and I stayed with Leon an extra year and facetiously called ourselves Two Grass Revival. But that wouldn't last much longer.

BÉLA FLECK AND PAT FLYNN

With deep, abiding gratitude and respect for Ebo Walker, Butch Robbins, Michael Clem, Courtney Johnson, and Curtis Burch, Sam and I agreed, in 1981, to carry on as the New Grass Revival. We were not starting over as much as picking up where we left off with a vengeance and a new focus. Sam already had two people in mind to join the band.

We'd met the brilliant California guitarist Pat Flynn a year or so earlier at the Telluride Bluegrass Festival accompanying Jimmie Ibbotson of the Nitty Gritty Dirt Band. We were knocked out by him, plus he was a gifted songwriter.* Pat lived in Thousand Oaks, California, so we invited him to audition while we were at Leon's house on Sky Hill Drive.† We jammed for a long time, and Pat played and sang his ass off. After he left, Leon, who'd been listening from the next room, was beaming like a proud papa. He stroked his long, snowy beard and said, "I don't know what y'all think, but I think that's your guy right there." Sam and I were giddy and quickly agreed.

Next, Sam told me about a banjo player.

"I just met this kid, Béla Fleck. He's crazy good and younger than we are. I played on his first solo album.‡ He's the best young banjoist I've ever heard in my life. Maybe we should go after him."

At the time, Béla, who was originally from New York City, was now in a great band in Lexington called Spectrum and had invested a lot of time, energy, and miles in their success. Still, when Sam called him, he was curious enough to drive down to Nashville where Sam and I lived, and the three of us just sat in a room and jammed. The whole event felt strangely backward, as if Béla were auditioning *us*. He told us that he'd just recorded "Spain" by Chick Corea and was deeply invested in both jazz fusion and hard-core be-bop. We played and talked more about music with him, and he told us that our repertoire was quite appealing to him. He even joked that once we started "Fly Through the Country," one of our signature jam songs, you could leave after the first verse, go out for dinner, come back, and still catch the last verse. He then suggested that we try some jazz pieces in 6/8, and some walking bass,

---

* Unbeknownst to us, Pat had spent a couple of years learning how to play the mandolin because, he told us later, his dream was to be in the New Grass Revival.

† Both of Leon's Asylum Choir albums, among others, were made there.

‡ That was *Crossing the Tracks*, on Rounder Records. Béla had also been a student of our good friend Tony Trischka and was already starting to develop a reputation as the enfant terrible of the banjo in bluegrass circles.

and the like. I think he wanted to see if we could keep up with him.* We told Béla that if he wanted to be our banjo player, we'd be thrilled to have him. He seemed thrilled as well.

Then he said, dryly, "Does this mean I have to take drugs?"

We thought maybe he was joking, but with Béla you can never really tell. So, Sam said, "No, John and I will take care of all that."

LEAVING LEON RUSSELL

With Béla and Pat joining, our departure from Leon became inevitable. It was fall of 1981, and when we told Leon of our plans, he begged us not to leave. Begged. I know as a band member and bandleader how that feels. It's very threatening once you've grown accustomed to things being a certain way, especially when they are so damn *good*. He was completely torn up. We said, "We love you, Leon, but we've got to go do our deal."

Our last show with Leon Russell was in Columbus, Ohio. I don't remember much about the show except that Leon, for some reason, either to celebrate or to drown his unhappiness, decided to drink after the show. We all did. He paid us each a huge cash bonus on top of our pay, and everyone got *really* drunk and stoned, and some of us were still awake when the sun came up. My wife, Liz, as always, being a little more sensible than the rest of us, went outside and passed out in our van with all of the money in her pants.

"HURRY UP AND GET IT OVER WITH"

The new configuration of New Grass Revival, Sam, Béla, Pat, and I, got signed to EMI/Capitol Records and immediately got a bigger booking agent, a man

---

* We could . . . *then*.

named Jim Halsey.* Jim's offices were in Tulsa, and he managed many of the genuine household names in country music at that time. I'd say between 1981, when we started with Béla and Pat, until around 1986, New Grass Revival opened for *everybody*: Ronnie Milsap. Don Williams, the "gentle giant." We played the Kennedy Center with Loretta Lynn. Dozens of shows with Emmylou Harris, Nanci Griffith, Steve Wariner, and to repeat a theme, at least half of the time, it was a disaster. People didn't know who we were to begin with and, once again, they came to see the big country star. Take Ronnie Milsap, please. It was one of those deals where we'd be sharing a vast stage with the star's main instruments arranged on it, including elaborate lighting and sound rigs, none of it ours, that were all managed by an imposing crew of cretinous assholes. "Just set your shit up in front of us and hurry up and get it over with" was a typical greeting.

So, we'd get out there and do our flawless thing. We played Marvin Gaye songs and Bob Marley songs and our own "Can't Stop Now." We thought we were presenting a pretty homogenized show, for us. But people would just look up at us like, *What the fuck is that?* This was not a bluegrass audience of chair snappers in a cornfield that I spoke of so fondly earlier. We were now facing big arenas of hard-core, mainstream country fans because we had a country music booking agent who was putting us, night after night, in front of their roster of mainstream country artists. Why? To get us work. To get us exposure. And if I'm being totally truthful, because it was their job. But more often than not, it was a train wreck. Many times, they'd get our name wrong. "Ladies and gentlemen, the Bluegrass Revival!" And we'd do our thing and play our instrumentals and do the very finest show we could. To me, it was undeniably powerful, nearly incendiary. When you're playing our kind of music, and the players are in sync spiritually, musically, and emotionally,

---

* Jim Halsey, as a manager and agent, is more deserving of his own encyclopedia than a mere footnote in my book. He has promoted or managed the careers of twenty-nine members of the Country Music Hall of Fame and ten members of the Rock & Roll Hall of Fame.

there was just nothing like it anywhere. And it would just fall on deaf ears. This happened a lot, and it never seemed to us like the booking agents gave a shit. They continued to throw us onstage as the warm-up act for absolutely anybody.

We flew to Ireland to open for Nanci Griffith, and this time, the odds finally seemed to be working in our favor. Béla had already written the tune "County Clare" and was dating the transcendent Irish singer Maura O'Connell, who was from County Clare. Nanci was huge in Ireland and drew enormous audiences of faithful followers who loved her every utterance, as we all did. This time, we were jacked, thinking, quite incorrectly it turns out, that Ireland was going to *love* us. New Grass Revival went out there, blew up the stage as usual, and people literally just sat there. You could almost feel them thinking, *We don't care about you. Can you just get off the stage?* We were dumbstruck and crestfallen.

Yet, despite everything, New Grass Revival, true to our name, started growing a loyal fan base and elevating ourselves from a strictly defined bluegrass world. This was not solely because we applied our inventive bluegrass techniques to rock, blues, gospel, reggae, and jazz, or that, as players, we had made it to what a reviewer in the *Chicago Tribune* once called "the peak of Nashville's virtuoso mountain." It started happening because of video. Evidently, many people thought we were also pretty damn cute.

TNN, The Nashville Network, launched as a basic cable network in 1983 and followed the road map of MTV (1981), with a plan that country artists making videos would now have a platform to put them on. Lo and behold, our first video for "Can't Stop Now," which Sam, Pat, and Béla just mowed down instrumentally, and I believe I nailed vocally, became their "most requested video" and for quite a while sat firmly at number one. In a world where most Americans now had basic cable, New Grass Revival was suddenly performing in people's living rooms in much the same way the Beatles, Aretha, and the

Temptations did for me when I was a kid. "Calling Baton Rouge," a song written by Dennis Linde* and later covered by Garth Brooks, helped us break into the Top 40 charts in the United States for the first time.

Our visionary manager, Ken Levitan, just started pulling rabbits out of his hat.† He got us on the Country Music Awards. We were frequent guests on TV legend Ralph Emery's popular show *Nashville Now*. Ralph, the Dick Clark of country music, loved us. The money started getting better. Suddenly, there were festivals where New Grass Revival was the big deal. At the Telluride Bluegrass Festival, we found twelve thousand people exactly like us. People who looked like us, dressed like us, danced trippy dances to us, and just plain got us. The fifteen-thousand-fan Strawberry Music Festival in Yosemite Park, California, was another. There was a city festival in Nashville called Summer Lights, and they'd always put us on the biggest stage on Saturday night. We had a mighty following in Nashville, in part because we were from there, and people were really proud of us. We were young, joyously eclectic, freakishly talented, and dared to be different. It was 1986, and it just kind of felt like we had arrived.

NEW GRASS SURVIVAL

Another thing that seemed to be going in our favor was what our friend Steve Earle has often referred to as the "country music credibility scare" of the '80s. Lyle Lovett and Nanci Griffith had just signed with MCA records. The O'Kanes were signed to Columbia. Foster and Lloyd were signed to RCA; Earle, himself, to MCA. New Grass Revival signed with Capitol/EMI, who were convinced they could get us on the radio. To their credit, except for one memorably awkward artist and repertoire meeting where they suggested we

---

* Dennis also wrote "Burning Love" for Elvis.
† Today it feels like Ken manages everybody, but New Grass Revival was his first client, followed by Nanci Griffith, Lyle Lovett, Emmylou Harris, Lynyrd Skynyrd, and an empire of other great people.

Minerva, Ohio, 1953

Béla, Sam, me, and Pat at the Nacogdoches, Texas, Bluegrass Festival, 1986. *Courtesy Rick Gardner*

record "Baby's Got Her Blue Jeans On,"* they gave us total artistic freedom and never told us one note to play or sing on our records, thanks to label president Jim Fogelsong.

But the more we tried to honor their proposition of making songs for the radio, the more it undid us as a band. Bless Capitol's heart, they put out our version of Marvin Gaye's "Ain't That Peculiar" and followed it up soon after with the beautiful Gary Nicholson tune "Unconditional Love," a duet with Sam and me. Insert the sound of crickets here. Even the explosive, aforementioned "Can't Stop Now," which Capitol loved, never did on radio what the video did on country music television. Then, suddenly, there was a disturbance in the Force.

Béla told us that he wanted to leave the band.

---

* Sam, Béla, Pat, and I spontaneously burst out laughing after they played the demo for "Baby's Got Her Blue Jeans On." We weren't trying to be mean. It just wasn't even slightly in our universe. It felt as if they'd never heard us play. It was, on the other hand, right up the alley of the late Mel McDaniel, who had a number one hit with it.

In country radio, banjo is generally a color or an afterthought, and Béla had a far more ambitious vision for himself as an artist. He felt deeply conflicted and was literally in tears at times, telling us how much he loved us and the band, but he was just getting musically frustrated. Me, I just thought I'd be in New Grass forever. This was everything I ever wanted, no more, no less. Collectively and personally we all lobbied Béla to stay.* "C'mon, man, we've come so far. Just wait a little longer. We just need to make another record. Look how well our video did." And so, Béla stayed. Looking back on that moment, knowing what I do now, I feel bad thinking that it was our arm-twisting and guilt-tripping that made him stay. But, for the moment, he stayed, and things did get better. New Grass Revival was selling out places everywhere.

We went through the process of recording our next record, *Friday Night in America*, with our new producer, Wendy Waldman. We had no idea that it would be our last. It was simply a great record sonically, artistically, and personally, and it contains some of my all-time favorite deep cuts, as DJ Eddie Stubbs would say: "Any Way the Wind Blows" by Marshall Crenshaw, "You Plant Your Fields" by Wendy Waldman and Donnie Lowery, "Let's Make a Baby King" by Jesse Winchester, "Angel Eyes" by John Hiatt and Fred Koller. We even had Roy "Future Man" Wooten and our hero from Little Feat, Sam Clayton, appear on the title track, "Friday Night in America," written by Pat Flynn and Russell Smith. Wendy, being a gifted songwriter, helped us rearrange the Dennis Linde song "Callin' Baton Rouge"; and the single, to our immense surprise, broke into the *Billboard* Top 40 country charts. Life was good.

Then Béla called a band meeting at McCabe's Pub in west Nashville.

I don't remember being particularly anxious or having any defenses up for this meeting because, in my mind, things were going pretty sweet. But

---

* For more detail about this moment and a peek at Béla's extraordinary career that followed, check out my interview with him coming in part 2.

after we all met up, Béla announced that he was leaving the band and that no amount of cajoling or guilt this time could make him stay. He'd been playing with another group of brilliant musicians who were to become the Flecktones: the otherworldly bassist Victor Wooten (whom I introduced to Béla); Victor's brother and percussionist, Roy "Future Man" Wooten; and multi-instrumentalist Howard Levy, whom we'd all met through Steve Goodman and John Prine.

In New Grass Revival, there were some of Béla's instrumental tunes that he'd have to teach to us in sections, because they'd be in odd time signatures, and he was very patient. But I think when he got Victor and Future Man in the band, he didn't have to do that. He'd just say, "Here's how it goes . . . and *boom*." Béla had found a new band, his new path, and was determined to take it.

I don't remember much after the meeting other than being totally shaken to my core.

HOW DO YOU REPLACE CHARLIE PARKER?

Capitol had planned to release "You Plant Your Fields" as our next single and video, but for a variety of personal and professional reasons, many of which are not mine to tell, we announced through the press that we were breaking up. We even made garish T-shirts with a hefty, singing female Viking and the brilliant headline, "It Ain't Over Till the Fat Lady Sings." But the truth was, it *was* over, and we were exhausted. We knew we couldn't replace Béla. How do you replace Charlie Parker? You can't. And finally, Sam, who had been the band's heart, soul, business manager, and master of ceremonies for eighteen years, just said, "John, I don't want to be a bandleader anymore."

We finished out the year, and it was both beautiful and intensely bittersweet. Our fans knew the end was nigh, and it fueled us to recommit to what

This was our last publicity picture before the breakup. Unbeknownst to me, the birthmark on my left arm was retouched out of this photo without my permission. *Courtesy Peter Nash*

the band stood for and, in our minds, always represented. We made a hell of a lot of supercharged music in those last few months, laying waste to every stage we took. Our friend Tim O'Brien of Hot Rize later said, "You guys were like a fucking *nuclear explosion*!" We admired and challenged each other so much, and we all became better musicians in the process.

New Grass Revival did a good-bye show at The Cannery in Nashville in December of 1989 for fans, family, friends, and the city we called home. I cannot count the number of people, regular fans and musicians, who came up to me to tell me about shows they had seen, or to express their sorrow, or the influence the band had had on them. "You changed my life." "I didn't like bluegrass at all until I heard you guys." "You'll never know what a big fan I was."* Believe me, we did. I remember Sam and me huddling in

---

* That sort of praise has continued to this day. In the past thirty years, every bluegrass fan under the age of fifty has shared similar thoughts, which is beyond gratifying. Have you ever had anyone salaam you? I have.

Minerva, Ohio, 1953

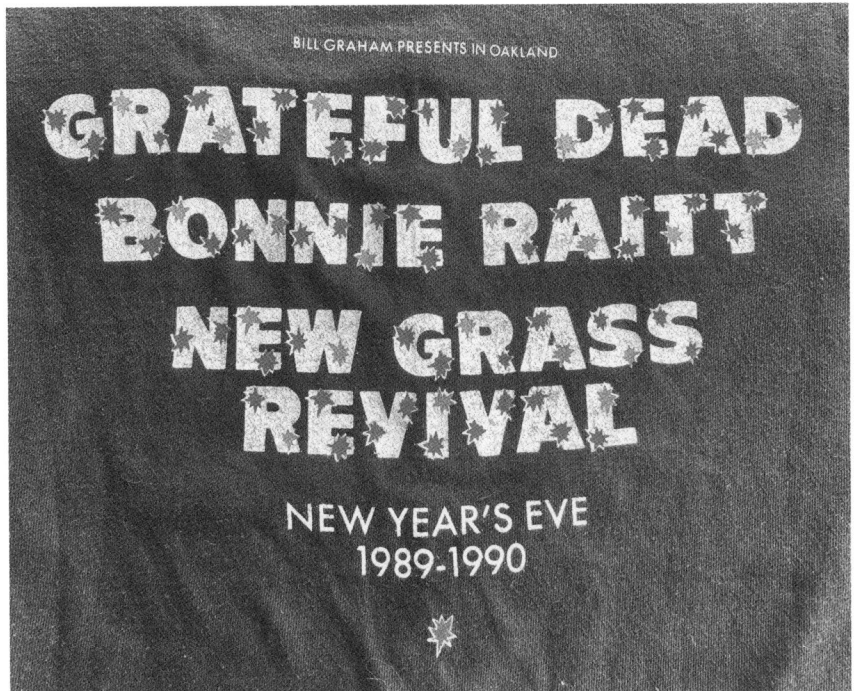

Courtesy of Jimmy Schwartz

Cantrell's backstage area up against the wall in a roomful of people, hugging each other and sobbing like babies. He'd been there from the beginning, a nineteen-year-old kid, and I'd been there since 1974, just twenty-one, and the sense of love and loss was hitting us with the pain of losing a pillar in your family.

There *was* one show after that, however, on the last day of 1989, on New Year's Eve in Oakland. Ironically, after years of trying, New Grass Revival, the band that once asked *never* to be billed as the "Grateful Dead of Bluegrass," finally got booked to open for the Grateful Dead. It was us, Bonnie Raitt, and the Dead. We went out with one hell of a New Year's show, singing and playing our hearts out. After the show, we all met Jerry Garcia, an early bluegrasser himself once, and he said, "You guys are unbelievable. We should do this more!" That's when somebody told him that we were breaking up. "Oh, that's terrible!" he said. "I'm so sorry." Not nearly as sorry as I was. As I turned to walk down the stairs and off the stage, Jerry stopped me and said, "Man, you're a monster!"

JC

INTERVIEWS AND INSPIRATIONS

Courtesy Brian Smith

PLAYING IN THE BAND

I don't think it's a coincidence that I grew up playing team sports. Little League baseball. Youth football. Junior varsity football. The team aspect is a dynamic that, if you've ever experienced it, you know there's something about the harmony of gifted people playing together that's almost impossible to explain. It's the same as being in a great band, performing onstage together. For me, music *is* a team sport.

Being part of a band has meant everything to me. I don't even like being a solo artist. The sensation of singing and playing with bandmates like Leon Russell, Sam Bush, Béla Fleck, and Pat Flynn for so many years, four of the best ever, is to take something organic happening between us—like combustion—and ignite the audience with it. It may sound paradoxical to say this, but the experience is rarely *about* the audience initially. It's about coming together as one, to play our best for the enjoyment of people who paid to see us. In small clubs or giant coliseums, great bands, like NGR, give you their all.

Photo by Carol Cowan

1

IN A PLACE WHERE THERE'S NO SPACE AND TIME

A Memory of Leon Russell

From 1978 through 1980, New Grass Revival was Leon Russell's band. Among my many enduring memories was our recording of Merle Travis's iconic "I Am a Pilgrim" for Leon's album *Hank Wilson's Back Vol. 2*. In the chorus, Leon sings, "I am a pilgrim and a stranger, traveling through this worrisome land. I've got a home in that yonder city, and it's not made by man." Leon Russell was a pilgrim in every sense of the word. At age seventeen, he literally got on a Greyhound bus in Oklahoma and headed to Los Angeles—his own pilgrimage to the Promised Land. Thank goodness Leon stunk at advertising, his original plan, because it led to a sixty-year music career like few have ever known and eventual induction into the Rock & Roll Hall of Fame in 2011. As a boss, friend, and mentor, Leon was kind, encouraging, and very much human. His gigantic lion heart will be what always resonates in my own after all these years of listening and learning with him. This interview was among his last, recorded in the living room of Leon's house, right after lunch.

JOHN COWAN: Leon, you're someone I admired as a fan and actually had the genuine pleasure to work with for almost three years as a member of New Grass Revival. I want to ask you a little bit about Lawton, Oklahoma. Is Lawton a suburb of Tulsa?

LEON RUSSELL: We lived in a town called Maysville, which is south of Oklahoma City. We stayed there for a few years. My dad was a clerk for the Texas Company, and we moved around a little bit. Then we moved to Tulsa. I did the first six grades in Maysville. I skipped the second grade, so I did the five years there. I got to play in the high school band when I was in the fifth grade. I used to go to all the state things and the football things.

COWAN: What instrument were you playing?

RUSSELL: I was playing the baritone horn. Big horn for a little crippled guy.

COWAN: So, what age did you start playing piano? Was it eight?

RUSSELL: No, I started at about three. Somebody gave us a piano, and we had this real creative piano tuner. It was an old upright. He took it upon himself to tune it one step low so it wouldn't come out of tune. Consequently, it made my pitch be off plus or minus one step for my entire life—*to this day!* [*laughs*] I would've had perfect pitch. But, uh, *no*.

COWAN: Wow. So, did you start taking lessons at some point?

RUSSELL: About when I was four.

COWAN: Was it strictly classical?

RUSSELL: Yeah, it was classical music. My problem was that I had a birth injury, and it gave me a slight paralysis on my right side. I was having a hard time. I couldn't play it. I saw that people who had started three or four years after me were playing Carnegie Hall. I just couldn't play that stuff. What it caused me to do was invent stuff that I could play over all those years. I mean, finally, after I had been taking piano lessons for ten years, I just quit. I said, "I can't do it. I'm not gonna do it anymore." But I think if I hadn't had that birth injury, I would've probably been selling insurance.

COWAN: I want to quote a lyric of yours. This is from one of my favorite tunes. What you said in the first line of the verse was, "When I was a young man, I was barely seventeen. I went out to Hollywood, chasing my dream. Dusty Oklahoma was all I'd ever seen, and I was getting older," from "Home Sweet Oklahoma."

RUSSELL: Yeah.

COWAN: Is that kind of how it went?

RUSSELL: Yeah, that's *exactly* how it went. I went out to California to get into advertising.

COWAN: Tell me a little bit about what happened when you first arrived there.

RUSSELL: I went out there with this guitar player. He said, "Come out to California with me. I got a job out there, and we can walk right in and get the job." I graduated from high school on Tuesday, and on Thursday I was on a Greyhound with this guy out to California. We got out there, and we didn't know what we were doing. We played one night and got fired. So, I was out there without a job and without any money. It was rough for six months or so. It was really tough.

COWAN: I'm curious as to how you found yourself all of a sudden playing sessions and eventually becoming part of a group of musicians who are basically making all the hit records coming out of LA? For most of us, I guess, you came into our consciousness with Delaney and Bonnie. Did that precede the first Joe Cocker record?

RUSSELL: Well, yeah. [Producer] Denny Cordell, who turned out to be my partner on *Shelter People*, he'd come over to LA to get distribution from A&M. He heard "Ghetto Song" that I played on Delaney and Bonnie's album. And his deal was, he listened to records all the time. He'd hear people play something that he liked, or sang something, and he'd get somebody to get them to play on the record that he was doing. Then he'd put all those people in a room and basically not say anything after that! [*laughs*]

COWAN: Just let them go at it?

RUSSELL: Yeah! [*laughing*] I met a guy named Stu Phillips when I was playing sessions in LA. He came to one of my sessions that I was playing for somebody. He said, "Oh, right, you're the guy I need! Tomorrow I'm doing 101 strings, Beatles songs, and you're the guy!" And I said, "Wait a minute. It's a trick. It's an *illusion*. I'm the guy they call when they want it to sound like classical music. But I can't read that well." And he said, "Aw, you could play this. This is real simple." And I said, "Well, now, you know, if you're gonna write down a bunch of stuff, I can tell you the guy's name to get, but you don't want *me*!"

COWAN: [*laughs*]

RUSSELL: So, I went to that session, and of course, there were sixty people in Studio A at Capitol. Sixty people!*

COWAN: Is that where they made the Sinatra records?

RUSSELL: Yeah! As a matter of fact, I'm gonna cut my new album—I'm doing a new album with Tommy LaPuma.

COWAN: I love Tommy LaPuma.

RUSSELL: You know who he is?

COWAN: Yeah, I've known about him for forty years. And he just did this McCartney record that's wonderful.

RUSSELL: Yeah, have you heard that? I have a copy of it if you want to hear it.

COWAN: I have it. I love it.

---

* Producer Stu Phillips and the Hollyridge Strings went on to be nominated for a Grammy Award in 1964 for Best Instrumental Performance for the *Beatles Songbook*.

RUSSELL: Well, he did "This Masquerade" with George Benson, which made me a whole lot of money.

COWAN: And won record of the year at the 1976 Grammy Awards.

RUSSELL: That's true.

COWAN: OK, here's a thing that's always struck me about you, as someone who was a fan long before I ever got to know you or play music. I followed your career from the very first record, *Mad Dogs and Englishmen* with Joe Cocker, the Asylum Choir, and then you made *Hank Wilson*. Were you exposed to country music long before rock 'n' roll hit the scene?

RUSSELL: Well, I guess. I mean my main exposure to music was classical music. When we lived in Apache, I have vague memories of my family listening to the Grand Ole Opry. I remember being at my grandma's house one time. I was not really aware of their musical taste, because they were not necessarily *musical*, in my mind. I had some aunts who played the piano. But my grandma had a record player next to her bed, and there was a record on it, so I played it. [*Russell sings an old-time gospel.*]

> Is there blood up on your hands?
> Do you daily take his Holy Name in vain?
> By the very fact you do,
> You will crucify him, too.
> And an evil life,
> You'll never cleanse the stain.

RUSSELL: So, I thought, well, I guess I come from that! [*laughs*]

COWAN: So, when you did *Hank Wilson*, and for little rock 'n' roll kids like me, and a lot of us who were following your career at that time, it might have been *my* first exposure to true country music. Because I was just a Beatle kid who played in garage bands . . .

RUSSELL: Yeah.

COWAN: But on that record, you've got a Flatt & Scruggs song, a Bill Monroe song, *two* George Jones songs, three Hank Williams songs, a Jim Reeves song. Did you *know* those songs?

RUSSELL: I only cut the songs that I knew. What happened was, I was taking my car back from LA to Tulsa, where I lived at the time. When I was out there playing sessions in LA, we used to talk about those Nashville guys all the time.

COWAN: In admiration? Or were you just curious about them?

RUSSELL: Just for information. They would say stuff like, "You know those Nashville guys, they get together, and they talk for five minutes, and they write down a bunch of numbers, and then they're ready to play." I heard that ten or fifteen times. [*laughs*] So, I was driving my car across America, and I went into these truck stops, and they had *hundreds* of hillbilly cassettes. I mean, hell, they was three dollars apiece! So, I bought $100 worth of 'em, and stuck 'em in there, and I started listening to them. I got to thinking about what those guys said about those musicians in Nashville, that they were always ready to play. Well, I myself am *always ready to play*. I mean, if I know what it is, I can play it right then.

COWAN: Right.

RUSSELL: So, I got to thinking about that. I said, I've got to go to Nashville and cut some of those old hillbilly songs that I know. All those songs that you mentioned are the ones that I knew.

COWAN: And that notion didn't strike you as crazy at the time? Because, at that point in your career, that was at the peak of your powers. Some people would look at that as a left turn, artistically.

RUSSELL: Well, most of them can't drive down here anyway. [*laughs*]

COWAN: I'm just saying that you had a lot of responsibility at that point. You had your own record label. You were the biggest act in North America, filling up stadiums. And now, "I'm going to do a country music record called *Hank Wilson's Back*"? You didn't think twice about it? It just seemed like a great idea?

RUSSELL: The thing is, John, I didn't *know* anything about the music business. I mean, if I had known anything about it, I would have probably thought twice. But it was just something that I wanted to do. I wanted to go down and play with those guys, because they were touted to me in LA by all the session guys. The same guys that used to say, "God, why doesn't George Benson have a hit? He's the greatest guitar player in the world." That kind of stuff. They'd talk about these guys down here, how quick they were. So, I just got to thinking about it, and thinking about those songs, and I came down here and cut twenty-seven songs in two and a half days.

COWAN: One of the most important parts of your artistry has been your songwriting. I'm kind of curious when you started attacking that full-time? What was the process where you said, "I want to be an artist. I'm going to start writing. Here are my songs"?

RUSSELL: Well, I had that experience with [producer] Snuff Garrett, and it kind of embittered me because I was writing stuff and not getting money for it, and stuff like that. But when Denny Cordell called me to do the Joe Cocker record, I thought, well, this is a good chance to play some songs. You know, it's

Leon Russell and NGR at the Perkins Palace in Pasadena in 1980. *Author's collection*

weird: in doing those sessions I got different characters that I do. If they call me to play piano, I sit there and play piano and keep my mouth shut. If they call me to do something else, then I'm kind of a different person.

COWAN: I was in the elevator the other day, in a hotel, and I heard the most wonderful version of some young singer doing his take of Donny Hathaway singing "A Song for You."

RUSSELL: Mm hmm.

COWAN: And I thought, this song has just *endured*. I'm guessing that when you wrote it, it was just a thought, right?

RUSSELL: Absolutely not true.

COWAN: Really?

RUSSELL: When I wrote that song, I was trying to write a song, a blues song, that Frank Sinatra and Ray Charles could sing. Almost twenty-five years ago, I checked, and "A Song for You" at that time had been cut 129 times,* and it hadn't ever been a hit. It was all the lounge lizards singing it, you know? "Masquerade" had been cut forty-five times before George Benson cut it. There's a guy, I think his name is Doc [Kupka] who played baritone for the Tower of Power, and he came up to me one day and he said, "Leon, I've played on twelve number one records, and *nobody* else has ever cut those songs. How do you get all those people to cut your songs?" [*both laugh*]

COWAN: That's what I thought when I heard that song yesterday. It's like the Gershwins. It's like Jerome Kern. These kinds of songs are going to exist forever; as long as people want to sing great songs, that song is going to be covered. I'm guessing that that's gratifying on some level?

RUSSELL: Well, yeah, it's gratifying because I set out to do it. I mean, there are so many things that I set out to do that just failed miserably. I wanted to write a song that everybody wanted to sing. I still do it to this day.

---

* "A Song for You" has now been covered more than two hundred times. If you go back and listen to Leon's version again, you'll hear him playing tenor horn on it, too.

I still try to write standards. For all you songwriters out there, there's more money in standards than in hit records.

COWAN: As a collaborator, whether as a producer, a co-songwriter, or appearing on other people's records, the list of people that you've had the opportunity to work with over the years is just stunning.

RUSSELL: Well, and I have to say Elton.

COWAN: Absolutely. I'm not going to leave him out. I want to talk specifically about *The Union* in a little bit. You also made some of the best Freddie King records ever made.

RUSSELL: Well, bless your heart. I like those, too.

COWAN: And your work with J. J. Cale, of course. Eric Clapton. B. B. King. Ringo Starr. Edgar Winter. And George Harrison. I mean, you were a huge star when that happened, when you participated in *All Things Must Pass*. But still, did you pinch yourself a couple of times and think, "I'm working with George Harrison?"

RUSSELL: Yeah. I didn't think I'd ever get to do that kind of stuff. And the Beatles? Lord. They played on my first record. And that organ player . . . Winwood.

COWAN: Steve Winwood.

RUSSELL: Yeah, he played on it. And then part of the Rolling Stones played on it. Charlie played on it. And Bill Wyman. And Eric, of course, played on it. That was all Glyn Johns. I was playing one of those songs, and I said, "Boy, Eric Clapton coulda played this." And he says, "Well, I'll call him up." He got all those English stars to play on my record.

COWAN: When you and Sir Elton John were first coming out with the *Union* album last year, you were playing in London, and I had the opportunity to come see the show and visit with you a little bit. It was an amazing evening for all sorts of reasons. Then of course, in 2011, you were inducted into the Rock & Roll Hall Fame.

RUSSELL: Yeah, that was Elton. Elton's responsible for that. I mean, he really did help me up. He took it upon himself to help me out, and he really did. It was amazing.

COWAN: I saw the show of his, which he produces, and Elvis Costello hosts, called *Spectacle*. I think that was the genesis of that whole thing happening because they ended up spending a great amount of time on that particular interview, as Elvis Costello is interviewing Elton, talking about you and your piano playing and all the nice things you had done for him early in his career. You've seen that, yes?

RUSSELL: Yeah, I have seen that. It was just amazing. I couldn't believe it. I mean he just went on and on. And he did that the whole time I was with him. He basically never stopped talking about how great I was. And I thought, well, OK, you've got good taste!

COWAN: Amen!

RUSSELL: But, uh, I had no idea. Because, you know, I didn't talk to him for over thirty-five years, after we played a couple of shows together.

COWAN: Was it completely shocking to get a call out of the blue?

RUSSELL: It was shocking, yeah. I kept thinking that somebody was going to call me and come get me sometime, but they never did. [*laughs*] Except *he* did! It was great. It *is* great. I mean *he's* great. Olivia Harrison says he's spiritually correct. You know, when you're around somebody like that, who can sell out twenty thousand seats, seven days a week, all over the world, that's amazing. I don't know anybody else like that.

COWAN: It's so openhearted. I appreciate that, as a fan of yours.

RUSSELL: John, I do, too.

2

JAMMING WITH SAM BUSH, GODFATHER OF NEWGRASS

I met Sam Bush in 1973 in Louisville, Kentucky, at a Holiday Inn where our mutual friends The Cumberlands played a couple of nights a week. Truth be told, our meeting was not about music; it was about marijuana. I sold him a quarter pound of it.

In those days, I was working in a car wash on Brownsboro Road, living in an attic with no air-conditioning in a house on Shelbyville Road in St. Matthews. I also was playing in a band called You with two friends from high school and two other friends from college in Evansville. We named the band You because we were heavily influenced by the English progressive rock band Yes. So, when my girlfriend, Liz, later my wife, asked me (dragged me)

Courtesy Rick Gardner

to downtown Louisville to see a bluegrass band called New Grass Revival, I really didn't want to go. I didn't know anything about their kind of music.* But a dear friend, Bill Kennedy, since departed, had bought *Will the Circle Be Unbroken* by the Nitty Gritty Dirt Band, which we'd listened to a lot, and I have to admit I was fascinated by it. Liz had assured me that these guys were really "cool," so I accompanied her to 1800 West Washington Street, a club I had not only played but frequented. The room was crowded, and the stage was on the east side of a rectangle, basically a shotgun bar. We plopped down, and I watched five longhaired guys, including a drummer, jamming and playing their asses off. They were all "plugged-up" with amplifiers and goin' for broke. I thought it was great, but after that show, I never gave the band much thought.

Then, a year later, two months after my father died, out of the blue, I got a call from Sam Bush, the New Grass Revival bandleader, who'd gotten my number from a mutual friend. NGR was looking for a bass player, and Sam asked if I'd be willing to drive down to Barren County, Kentucky, to audition, which I was.

Sam has said that when I was tuning up my bass in Courtney Johnson's front room, he and Curtis (Burch) and Courtney (Johnson) and the drummer Michael Clem were in the kitchen making coffee and smoking a joint. When they heard me warming up, they were pinching each other and saying, "Holy shit, a real bass player!" We played all afternoon, and they offered me the job. Of course, I said yes. I stayed at Courtney's little farmhouse that night. When I awoke the next morning, I went out on the front porch. The drummer Michael was loading his car and literally crying. I asked him what was going on and he replied, "They fired me!" Soon enough, everyone was saying their good-byes, and he sped off. After he left, I asked the guys why

---

* Did I mention that I was in the progressive, Yes-inspired rock band You?

they had canned him, and they said, "We don't need a drummer anymore. We got a real bass player!"

Drummer or not, it was, ultimately the phone call that changed my life. It also kindled a lifelong friendship with my brother Sam Bush, multi-instrumentalist, multi-Grammy winner, member of the International Bluegrass Hall of Fame with New Grass Revival, and the undisputed godfather of progressive bluegrass music. Our conversation is a master class in the birth of progressive bluegrass. It was conducted in Sam's home in the West Meade section of Nashville.

JOHN COWAN: Charles Samuel Bush is here with us. You'd know him as Sam Bush. Sam was born on April 13th, 1952, in Bowling Green, Kentucky, is that correct?

SAM BUSH: The Warren County Hospital, yes.

COWAN: To Charles and Henrietta Bush.

BUSH: Yeah, Mr. Charlie and Miss Henrietta. They were music lovers, and I was one of five.

COWAN: I was gonna ask you about that. What's the earliest memory of hearing music in your home, or on the radio? Or either?

SAM: Well, growing up in Bowling Green and having the advantage of getting great reception on WSM radio, and also watching Channel 4 out of Nashville and seeing country music shows. I think one of my first memories of music would be seeing my dad watching an old show called *Country Style, USA*. So, it would be people like Roy Acuff, Hawkshaw Hawkins, Cowboy Copas, Hank Snow, Ernest Tubb.

COWAN: How old do you think you were at this point?

BUSH: Probably eight or nine. But even at that, those shows were filmed for the armed forces, somewhere either around the time I was born or in there, and they were black-and-white shows. They were on film, and I just remember these shows. They were the kind of thing where, in Grand Ole Opry style, whoever wasn't playing was standing around and cheering on the other performers. So that is one of the first. But my dad loved these fiddle records and back then, it was literally an album, where you had five 78s of fiddle music in like a photo album. So, you'd have five pages with a 78 in each sleeve. Y'know, one of the earliest good memories of music would be, for instance, when our dad would be driving us in to a basketball game at night. He was a fan of Hank Williams, and he would sing the song "I'm So Lonesome I Could Cry" and make my sisters learn harmony with him. I'd just sit in the backseat and watch the lights of town approaching—we lived five miles out of town. He was kind of teaching them to sing harmony, and so I think that Charlie's love of singing and Hank Williams got them going as much as anything.

COWAN: Did you not have a little band with Janet and Claire?

BUSH: I was in their band. It was called The Bush Sisters and Sammy.* It was during the folk boom, and Peter, Paul and Mary were popular artists who did that, and they'd kind of do duet versions of Peter, Paul and Mary songs. And my sister Claire knew enough guitar to play those songs. My sister Janet didn't play anything, although she could have. I just think she never really tried that much because she used to pick up a mandolin and play some stuff, and I think girls just didn't do that as much back then.

COWAN: Did you sing in that band?

BUSH: I did *not* sing in that band.

COWAN: You just played the mandolin while the two of them sang?

BUSH: I "tinked" along, yes! And we played on TV around Bowling Green. Our gigs were playing on an actual television show, and the girls actually got paid. I mean. . . .

---

* Sam, the lone son, had four sisters.

COWAN: Wow!

BUSH: We actually got paid for playing on TV, even though we were only teenagers. Well, they were teenagers.

COWAN: How old were you at this time?

BUSH: I was twelve.

COWAN: Was your playing pretty rudimentary [*Sam starts making mouth sounds*], or was it starting to come along?

BUSH: It's hard to know. I'm sure it was very simplified. I mean, how virtuosic can a twelve-year-old be? OK . . .

COWAN: [*laughs*] Let's ask Mark O'Connor.

BUSH: I was gonna say, OK, go ask Chris Thile. Ask Mike Marshall.

COWAN: Having known your dad for a big part of my life, I know that he was super passionate about music. My parents loved music, and my dad sang music, but there wasn't any communal thing that went on in our family. My knowing him was all based on music, and we always talked about music. He loved it and was so passionate about it.

BUSH: He loved it.

COWAN: I can't help thinking that it must've had a big influence on you.

BUSH: Well, it did. You know, he was the guy who would host the jam sessions at our house. They were basic. Now I look back, and he'd have a couple of fiddle players and a couple of guitar players, and they were like fiddle jams. But my dad never played in those jams. He didn't think he was worthy, you know? He didn't like playing in front of people. Later, I realized that he sometimes would play fiddle tunes and throw an extra beat in somewhere, and I think people had trouble maybe playing with him because, at the time, it would be called breaking meter. He broke meter. It's interesting because once I reached a certain age and realized that if I talked to him about this, we could maybe make these tunes better. And I talked to him about certain fiddle tunes. "Did you know you're adding a beat there?" "No," he'd say. So, I'd show him, and he did correct it.

COWAN: Hmm.

BUSH: He wanted to play violin when he was in high school, in rural Kentucky, and they stuck a clarinet in his hands, and he *hated* it. He just always said that if he could've been taking violin when he was a kid—because that's what he was interested in—that he could've been a good fiddle player. As a young man up in Louisville, when my parents were first married, he got to know the great Clayton McMichen,* and he hung out with them. A great fiddle player named Sleepy Marlin he used to hang with. So, by the time I was about fourteen or so, we'd come down to Nashville and went into what was on Broadway then, the Roy Acuff Museum and Exhibit. And lo and behold, Bashful Brother Oswald was taking the door that day.† And Oswald and my dad, they hit it off. They were friends till Oswald passed away at ninety. But they hit it off, and my dad told Oswald, "My boy plays the fiddle." Now, I'd only been playing a year or two on fiddle and didn't feel very confident about it. [*big breath*] So Oswald goes and gets a fiddle, and I play a tune for him, and Oswald called Mr. Acuff and said [*deepens his voice*], "Roy, you better get down here; we got a boy who can fiddle!" And later that night we found ourselves backstage at the Grand Ole Opry. That was the night I met Peter Rowan. Bill Monroe was playing on the Opry. And there's Pete. It was a pretty magical day. Then, later that night, Mr. Acuff was playing on *The Ernest Tubb Record Shop* that, at that time came on at midnight after the Grand Ole Opry, and he had me come up. I got up and played a tune.

---

  * Clayton McMichen had a long and colorful history in bluegrass, swing country, and jazz. He recorded with The Skillet Lickers, in the late '20s and early '30s. ("Folks, here we are again, the Skillet Lickers, red hot and raring to go! And Maw, don't you let 'em dance on your new carpet. You make 'em roll it up!") He won his first national fiddling championship in 1932 and won it again for fifteen straight years.

  † Bashful Brother Oswald, whose real name was Beecher Ray Kirby, popularized the use of the resonator guitar and Dobro. He was a member of Roy Acuff's Smokey Mountain Boys and member of the Grand Ole Opry. He died in 2002 at age ninety.

COWAN: Do you recall what tune it was?

BUSH: I don't. But through that I met Charlie Collins, the guitar player, and Larry McNeely, who was about to play banjo with Roy.

COWAN: Because you'd gotten some attention and appeared with Roy Acuff, did it change your views about being a fiddler at all? Did it make you seem any more serious?

BUSH: Well, I think I always thought I was a mandolin player. But I got really serious about fiddle. One of my sisters once said, "You used to be such a shy kid. What happened?" [*both laugh*] I said, "I think it was applause." I was just so turned on to the thought of music, but I don't think I ever thought that I would do it for a living till I got out of high school, didn't go to college, and had a chance to move to Louisville and start playing five nights a week.

COWAN: I wanted to ask you: Was it a big thrill for you to see Bill Monroe that night?

BUSH: Oh, goodness! I was already a big fan because of mandolin. I was a fan of all the bands with mandolin. Jesse McReynolds. Bobby Osborne. Bill Monroe. Ronnie Reno with Don Reno's band. And I found this record. My mother worked at Sears, and they had this record for fifty-nine cents by a band called John Duffy and the Country Gentlemen. And there was no pictures of the band or anything, and that was one of the things that really turned me on. Dean Webb of the Dillards: I loved his mandolin playing. I tended to follow the mandolin. I remember one night, we were listening to the Grand Ole Opry, and Bill Monroe played "John Henry," and I just thought it was an incredible mandolin break he took that night. It just knocked me out. I'd been playing the mandolin a little bit, and my dad just went, "That ain't nothin'. You need to hear Jethro Burns play."

COWAN: How did your dad know about Jethro?

BUSH: 'Cause he paid attention to things. My dad was not a Bill Monroe fan. I was. Later, when I met [banjoist] Alan Munde, he had the two Homer and Jethro instrumental albums, which were like jazz mandolin.

COWAN: So, it wasn't until you met Alan that you actually heard Jethro?

BUSH: Right. I had seen Homer and Jethro on the *Joey Bishop Show*. My dad would let me stay up late if he knew that Homer and Jethro were gonna be on television.

COWAN: By 1964, you're playing the fiddle and mandolin, and you've been exposed and pretty much devoted to country music. But you mentioned earlier that your sister had bought Beatles records. So, you came at rock and roll as a country kid.

BUSH: Yeah, totally.

COWAN: I'm kind of curious what piqued your attention about that?

BUSH: About rock and roll?

COWAN: Yeah.

BUSH: Well, now I've got them on DVD, but the Beatles performances on Ed Sullivan were pretty monumental.

COWAN: Did your dad watch that with you?

BUSH: Oh, yeah.

COWAN: My dad did, too. And he said the most horrible things. I can't repeat them.

BUSH: [*laughing*] I can't repeat exactly what Charlie said, either. But I will say he said, "You ain't never puttin' your hair down in bangs!" [*both laugh*] And if anybody ever sees any photos from me as a kid, it's funny that I *easily* had the longest hair in the class, but it just wasn't combed down in Beatles style. That was not allowed, but a Grand Ole Opry style haircut was.

COWAN: You could have big hair, just no bangs?

BUSH: That's right. [*breathlessly preens*] I was the Sonny James of my young generation! [*both laugh*]

COWAN: So, let's go from this point. Because the thing I think is so interesting about you is this mix of traditional music and rock 'n' roll.

BUSH: Well, a buddy had a record, *Between the Buttons*, by the Rolling Stones. That was a great record, and it was always interesting to me, like on the old Stones records especially, and the Beatles, too, how much they used acoustic instruments. We weren't really thinking about that much at the time. Jefferson Airplane got turned on to them. One thing that happened that I got out of going to the Weiser, Idaho, fiddle contest (I got to go to that a few times and had done well), was that when it was over, one of the guys in our car wanted to be dropped off in San Francisco. So we all said, "Let's go down the Haight-Ashbury and see the hippies!"

COWAN: Were there adults with you, or were you all just kids?

BUSH: No, *they* were the adults. I was the only teenager. But it was a big surprise to my parents when I called and said, "We've taken a detour. I'm in San Francisco." [*Bush makes the sound of a trombone splat.*] Yeah, that was kind of a rough time when I got home off that one. I had the hoe in my hand in the tobacco patch a lot after that particular trip. Even at that, though, I had bought a couple of records by Jefferson Airplane, and I bought a record by the Grateful Dead. So, we get to Haight-Ashbury; left Weiser, Idaho, and drove straight there. I guess I was fourteen or fifteen. I just recall that when we got there, it was around 4 a.m., and I had never been to a place that was open at 4 a.m. It was a very cool and safe situation. I didn't really realize all that I was seeing at the time. Or smelling. People were actually sleeping on the street in parking spaces in sleeping bags, and it was safe. It was the first time I ever saw an interracial couple. I couldn't believe the incredible freedom out there. We found a motel, and then the next day there was this giant street concert, and we must've been a quarter mile away from the stage, so you couldn't actually hear the band that was playing. In your mind's eye, you look down, and they're a half-inch tall, they're so far away. And I just remember asking a hippie, "Who is that?" And he says, "It's the Dead, man!" So, years later, when we all got to meet 'em, I said, "Well, I saw you guys in '66. Didn't hear you though." [*both laugh*] But the idea of the freedoms within what was going on, of the hippies and the music and the change and the whole musical climate! Back then, on Ed Sullivan, you'd see the Jefferson Airplane and the Strawberry Alarm Clock, and the Doors, and Cream, and certainly Beatles and Stones, and as much as I liked all that, it wasn't until I heard *Rubber Soul* by the Beatles, and "I've Just Seen a Face" comes on, and that sounds like bluegrass to me.

COWAN: So, you graduated from high school, and was it then and there that you wind up going to Louisville and being in the Bluegrass Alliance?

BUSH: Yes. I was going to go to Western Kentucky University in Bowling Green and play violin. I had taken violin for a year, and my teacher was going to help me get a partial scholarship, and it was just about time to go do it when I got the offer to come up to Louisville and play in the Bluegrass Alliance.*

COWAN: How was it that they were even aware of you, living in Bowling Green?

BUSH: Well, the fiddle player, Lonnie Peerce—we rode out to Weiser, Idaho, together. He knew my parents, and they felt OK about it. Along with another fiddler, Bud Meredith, and a guy named Mac Gibson, who owned the Mammoth Cave Opry, where I wound up playing square dances as a boy, riding out there with them . . . Lonnie Peerce had been helpful to me playing fiddle and turning me on to good fiddle players. Lonnie was the fiddle player in the Bluegrass Alliance, and he and the bass player. . . .

---

* The Bluegrass Alliance, formed in 1967 by fiddler Lonnie Peerce, was a rotating collection of bluegrass giants who had a seismic influence on players for years to come. Besides Sam, some of their members included Dan Crary, Tony Rice, Courtney Johnson, Buddy Spurlock, and Vince Gill. Four of their members, including Sam, went on to form the New Grass Revival.

COWAN: They offered you a job.

BUSH: They came down where I was a busboy at the Holiday Inn and asked me if I wouldn't rather do something besides bus tables. So, yeah, it was the right time. I moved up to Louisville at age eighteen.

COWAN: And your mom and dad were fine with that since they already knew them?

BUSH: Well, I'd already moved out. I graduated from high school and didn't live at home anymore. We were playing down on Washington Street in Louisville in the bars, and there were a few jobs left where the Alliance had already booked these festivals with Dan Crary [flatpicker], and Danny Jones [mandolin and guitar]. So, they were gonna finish out these festivals, which they did, but they would take me along as the sixth wheel, and I'd play the mandolin along with them. I was technically in the band already. We did these festivals, and I remember Gettysburg, Pennsylvania, where we met Del McCoury. It gets to be Labor Day, and we're down in Reidsville, North Carolina, for a festival, and there is the skinniest person I have ever seen sittin' out in the field on somebody's guitar case, one of those Martin uni-pack cases, playing someone's brand new D-45. Like I say, the skinniest man I've ever seen. It was Tony Rice. And I was listening to him play, and he sounded like Clarence White. It was pretty great.

COWAN: You were both eighteen?

BUSH: I was eighteen, and he was nineteen.

COWAN: Did you just walk over and strike up a conversation?

BUSH: I just walked up and said, "Hey, I play guitar in the Bluegrass Alliance, but if you join, I can go back to mandolin."

COWAN: That's great!

BUSH: And he had seen me play mandolin with the band.

COWAN: And what did he say?

BUSH: Well, he said [*Bush lowers his voice to imitate Tony*], "Yeah, let's do it." Well, we went back up to the campsite, and its funny because Courtney Johnson and my dad had gone down to Reidsville in Courtney's school bus because there was this jam session going on with some of the other guys from the Alliance. That's when I learned it ain't cool for one guy in the band to ask somebody else to join the band without talking to your bandmates.

COWAN: Yeah.

BUSH: And I said, "Hey, I just got this guy on guitar. What do you think?" And everybody said, "What?" But we jammed and, yeah, Tony ended up going back to Louisville with us.

COWAN: So, how long was your tenure then in the Bluegrass Alliance?

BUSH: It only lasted like a year and a half, pretty much. I remember in 1971 we played at Monroe's Bean Blossom Festival, and the band just did gangbusters. We were so tight. We'd been playing six nights a week, and we were rough and ready.

COWAN: So, how did you wind up eventually leaving?

BUSH: Well, we'd had disagreements at times with Lonnie Peerce, our fiddler, and it finally came to a parting of the ways, but we wanted him to leave the band. So—*band meeting*—and we said, we want you to leave the band. And he basically said, "I'm not leaving. I own the name." And much to our surprise, we found out he *did* own the name and a Kentucky state trademark and all variations of it that could possibly be done to the Bluegrass Alliance. So, let us put it this way, we all quit, and out of a five-piece band, four of us started New Grass Revival. So, Curtis Burch, who had taken Tony Rice's place on guitar, Courtney Johnson and Ebo Walker and I. So, we started what we later called the New Grass Revival. At first, we didn't have any name.

COWAN: Did Tony, when he left, the Alliance, did he go straight to J. D. Crowe?

BUSH: He did. You can see all this in a movie!

COWAN: Is it the Carton Haney movie?

BUSH: It is.

COWAN: I've seen that. It's so good.

BUSH: It's called *Bluegrass Country Soul*. It was interesting because Tony, that was his last show with the Alliance, playing "One Tin Soldier" with us in that movie. Also, if you see the movie, you'll see Tony playing with J. D. Crowe. There was a big turnaround in bluegrass that weekend. Doyle Lawson had left J. D. Crowe to become the Country Gentlemen's mandolin player.

COWAN: Wow.

BUSH: It was a pretty amazing weekend, because in that movie, you'll see some of Doyle's first performances with the Gentlemen, and Tony was already gone. [*laughs*] Tony was in kind of two bands. The film of us doing the song "One Tin Soldier," which Dan Crary had arranged for the Bluegrass Alliance years before, was the last song Tony played with us. That was it.

COWAN: When you started the New Grass Revival, was there ever a mission statement or an intention on your part to say, OK, we're going to do this now. We're not going to play "Molly and Tenbrooks."* We're going to play our own version of this music. And did it have something to do with your age? I'm just curious.

BUSH: I don't know. I just remember that we had started experimenting with longer jamming things. I think we even started that a little bit when we were still with Bluegrass Alliance, because I remember that we worked up the Leon Russell song "Prince of Peace" in the last month or two we were with the Alliance. I just know that when we had our first practice after we decided that we were going to be a quartet, and that I would need to play some fiddle now, too, Ebo on the bass started playing a little riff, and we wound up

---

* "Molly and Tenbrooks" was a late 1800s Appalachian folk chestnut about a racehorse. It was eventually recorded by Bill Monroe and his Bluegrass Boys in 1947 and again by the Stanley Brothers in 1948.

jamming on this riff, hippie style, until I think Courtney might've been the first guy to . . .

COWAN: Play "Lonesome Fiddle Blues"?

BUSH: . . . went into "Lonesome Fiddle Blues."

COWAN: By Vassar Clements.

BUSH: Written by Vassar. That was the first tune we ever started jamming on. We got to realize that we liked this jamming thing. But, of course, maybe it was new to those kinds of instruments, but certainly we had been listening to bands that had been jamming, from hearing the best of Atlantic jazz to hearing John Coltrane do "My Favorite Things," which is probably the simplest tune he ever played, to the way the Grateful Dead would play longer tunes. Listening to Cream. Like I was just talking about, listening to certain rock bands do these long jams. So, we would just jam.

COWAN: I'm curious if . . .

BUSH: No, there was *no plan*. We had not made a plan like, OK, this is the way we're gonna play. We were literally playing it like we felt it. And they certainly weren't all original ideas, because we also did tunes like, at the time, Norman Blake had given us a tape of this tune he wrote called, "Ginseng Sullivan," and he said you guys should play this. We were also influenced by John Hartford and the Aereo Plain Band. We heard those guys play, and they would do longer jams. Sometimes they would just turn Vassar loose for a while. That even includes seeing John Hartford and Glen Campbell on TV when they used to do it. John and Glen one time—and I happened to tape it that night with an old tape recorder and a jack on the back of my TV—did a version of "Great Balls of Fire," bluegrass style, that later New Grass Revival put on our first album. We made our own arrangements and stuff, but we first thought of doing that because we saw John Hartford and Glen Campbell do it on television.

COWAN: OK, let me back up. You mentioned hearing John Coltrane. How did that happen?

BUSH: Our friend Ken Smith from Bowling Green—we'd become pals because I sold him a guitar. We were so young that we had to get our dads to sign the receipts. So, Kenny and I became friends, and one day he brought over a record called *The Best of Atlantic Jazz*. One cut was from John Coltrane, and it was "My Favorite Things" from *The Sound of Music*, and I could relate to that tune because that melody I'd heard in that movie. I certainly could not relate to "A Love Supreme" by Coltrane at the time. So, that's probably one of the simplest tunes he ever did and one that was made to appeal to people who had no idea what he was doing.

COWAN: But it was him playing, and he surely was improvising.

BUSH: He was totally improvising, and there were little licks I learned off of that cut. How to play in a major 7th key. It made sense to me somehow. Fortunately, I had hip friends who would turn me on to things. Like the time my friend Barry Stevens set me down one day and said, "Today, you're going to learn about the Allman Brothers." And I said, really? And he said, "yup" and played me the two sides of a forty-minute tune, "Mountain Jam." I just didn't know that that could occur, that you could just play a tune for forty minutes and make it interesting. Much less keep other musicians interested while you solo. But that's the deal. So we made a rule in the Revival that whoever is soloing, go ahead, but you're responsible. If you're going to take this plane off, you gotta know how to land it.

COWAN: In the original New Grass Revival, two records that seemed really important to you were John Hartford's *Aereo-Plain* and Leon Russell's *The Shelter People*.

BUSH: Right.

COWAN: So how did you and New Grass Revival wind up, when Leon Russell was at the absolute peak of his stardom, opening his entire North American tour? How the heck did that happen?

BUSH: We had literally walked in the door. It's 4 a.m. in Louisville, and the phone rings, and it's Butch Robbins, who eventually would be our next bass player after Ebo, as it turns out. Butch told us about a filmmaker who was documenting Leon at the time. Les Blank was his name.* And Butch and Les Blank set up all night one night. And Leon, who was going to open the show as Hank Wilson† and come out playing all these country standards that he did, was looking for a band. Then he would do Leon and The Shelter People. Butch said, there are these guys from Louisville, but they're not like a country band, and they love you and do one of your tunes. So, Butch and Les Blank called up and got me on the phone, and then they got Ebo on the phone, and later that day we were in Tulsa sitting in Leon Russell's house.

COWAN: Did he fly you all out there?

BUSH: Oh, yeah, he flew us out, and we got out there and freaked . . . out! I mean I turned twenty-one later on that tour. So, we had gone from being with one hero, John Hartford, to now being with the other one. And we're in Leon Russell's house! You haven't lived until you've seen Leon walk down, straight out of bed. [*both laugh*] So, Leon comes down and has a bite to eat, and we're introduced to him, and I couldn't be more freaked out. He just looked up at us and he says [*does Russell's drawl*], "Well, I hear y'all do 'Prince of Peace.' Let's hear you do it."

COWAN: [*laughs*] GO!

BUSH: So, we're standing around with Leon and the bass player Carl Radle listening to us do "Prince of Peace." [*big exhale*] *Whoooooo!* I mean, I have never been so nervous! My legs were shaking, but somehow, we get

---

* Les Blank was an independent filmmaker who loved to explore the lives of musicians and other folks living passionately on the margins of society. Along with his famous doc into the flower-child subculture (*God Respects Us When We Work, But Loves Us When We Dance*), he also directed the film *A Poem Is a Naked Person* about Leon Russell. It was shot in 1972–1974, but because of creative differences and legal issues with music clearance, it wasn't released until 2015, more than forty years later and after his death.

† Hank Wilson was Leon Russell's country alter ego.

Courtesy of Jimmy Schwartz

through it, and we ended it. Courtney does these great banjo licks at the end that he stole from Bobby Thompson, and Leon, he started applauding.

COWAN: [*laughs*]

BUSH: But it really came back down to Earth the day after the tour ended, and we were in Long Beach, California, and a party on the *Queen Mary*. Leon introduced me to George Harrison, and the whole thing was just . . .

COWAN: Surreal?

BUSH: Totally surreal! I got to stand and listen to his incredible band anywhere I wanted for two and a half months. It was just amazing. I stood behind Carl Radle's bass amp for the most part. Then the tour is over. And the very next day, we flew to Louisville. We get in our '63 Chevy station wagon, drive two hours north to Lafayette, Indiana, and played six nights a week at Arnie's Pizza King, for three weeks, so . . . [*both laugh*]

COWAN: Welcome home!

BUSH: Coffee break's over, boys!

COWAN: So, let's move up to the fall of 1974.

BUSH: Well, right after that, we were not in a good place with the band. Butch Robbins left the band. I think he started playing banjo with Wilma Lee and Stoney Cooper. And then he got back with Bill Monroe.

COWAN: So, you're without a bass player?

BUSH: We knew we were gonna need one. That's when we called our friend Ken Smith in Bowling Green. Once again, Ken, who turned me on to John Coltrane, was a good enough musician, and we thought maybe he can play the bass with us. But Kenny already had a job. But he said, I *do* know this guy up in Louisville who's a great bass player, and I think he'd be really good for you. His name is John Cowan. So, Ken told us about you, and that's how all that started. Now when we asked you to join the band, Michael was still on drums, but . . .

COWAN: He was only there the first day I was there.

BUSH: The first two days or something.

COWAN: No, when I got there to audition, I was tuning up my bass, and you and Courtney and Curtis were in the kitchen. Apparently, you were giggling to yourselves.

BUSH: We got excited.

COWAN: Because I could actually play the bass.

BUSH: Because you could tune one! That was really comforting to us.

COWAN: So, we played all afternoon. Then, when I got up the next morning, Michael Clem was walking around the house in tears because you guys had fired him.

BUSH: Well, yeah.

COWAN: That's my remembrance of what happened. I was like, what's goin' on guys?

BUSH: One of the guys in the band said he didn't want to play with drums anymore. And he said, I'm gonna leave if we keep having a drummer. Of course, then I said, OK, if we didn't have a drummer, would you still be leaving? [*adopts a contrite voice*] Oh, no, no, I would stay.

COWAN: It was Curtis, right?

BUSH: Yeah. But, at any rate, it was the right decision. We didn't need a drummer.

COWAN: Let's talk about the final days of New Grass Revival in 1989.

BUSH: Well, in '88 or '89, we were recording our last record, and I'm proud to say that if there's a best one, that might be it. I'm proud of it, and I thought we all did terrific on that record. But then it was just time for Béla [Fleck] to go, to do all these tunes that he wrote daily. We couldn't accommodate all his ideas. It was obvious that it was time for him to be a bandleader and make his own mark. Which he certainly did. He works hard. And for me, I had been in the band eighteen years, and I think I was in emotional burnout of responsibility. I didn't think about music anymore. I only thought about business.

COWAN: That's something I think a lot of people aren't aware of. I asked Bernie Leadon of the Eagles the same question. Who's the point man? The point man is what you and subsequently your wife, Lynn, became. While the other three of us went off and got home and did whatever we wanted to, you guys stayed on the phone and went to meetings.

BUSH: God, yeah. I remember there was one section where I would literally be on the phone twelve to fourteen hours a day. I just wanted us to succeed. And we did. We played wherever and whatever we wanted.

COWAN: But that was probably part of your decision.

BUSH: Yeah, I just needed a break. I needed a break in responsibilities and decision-making. All I'd ever done is go on the road since I got out of high school. My plan was that I didn't have a plan other than I didn't want to travel. I wanted to stop traveling. So, lo and behold, we were on one of our last trips, The Revival, and we were in Washington, D.C., and I was staying at a friend's house. John Starling from The Seldom Scene had told Emmylou [Harris] that the New Grass was breaking up. She was looking for a more acoustic band. She had sung a long time over the Hot Band, and they had gotten a little loud. It was a loud group. A great group. They defined the way some people still play country music, but she wanted a quieter group to sing over. She called me and asked me if I be interested in starting a band, and I remember saying, "No, but I'll play in yours." [*laughs*]

COWAN: Well, why did you . . .

BUSH: I didn't want any responsibility. I didn't want a partnership.

COWAN: Right.

BUSH: I'd been in a partnership for eighteen years, and I just wanted to be in a partnership with my wife. I just wanted to play music. So, I played with Emmylou and the Nash Ramblers, and after the Ramblers stopped, I played eighty-six shows with Béla and the Flecktones in one year. So, after being in what I thought was the coolest country band ever, the Nash Ramblers, it helped me relax and enjoy music again. Then the Flecktones got me turned back on to improvisational instrumental music. So then, I felt like I was ready to take what I learned to try to be a better singer and better at instrumental jamming. That was some heavy-duty jamming with those guys.

COWAN: As a fan of your songwriting, I'm really happy about the resurgence of you as a songwriter and composer in the last two records.

BUSH: Well [*laughs*], I am sixty-one years old now. I'm old enough to take my own lumps. I'll make my own mistakes. But collaborating on songs with people can be an intimidating process. I'm not sure if it helps or it hurts to be good friends with someone you're writing with, because you kind of have to be a little ruthless with each other. John Pennell, who I think is a wonderful songwriter, he has no problem telling me that an idea I just had just really stinks: [*recalls the voice*] "No, we're not doing that!" And Jeff Black and I, who I met by playing on some of his first demos in Nashville when he was just trying to pitch songs to people. I couldn't believe these songs I was hearing. I thought, God, this guy. And so, to sit down to write with Jeff, sometimes it takes us three or four sessions to get one song because he is just so deep in thought. I trust him so much that when Jeff says it's done, it's done. I love all his records. I love his singing. But I've learned the joy of collaborating because it can be intimidating. Edgar Meyer and I write instrumentals together, and it helps me because I certainly would have never thought of the things that Edgar would think of to put together. Sometimes, some of the things we write are some of the most difficult things I've ever played because he doesn't care what lays out well on a mandolin. How does the melody sound? That's Edgar's thing that's helped me learn the art of collaboration, because I think for a long time, I didn't enjoy it. It wasn't a joyful thing. But now I've learned to have fun with it.

COWAN: I know that you've been great friends with Guy Clark for many, many years. Was that intimidating to finally write a song with him?

BUSH: No. Not at all.

COWAN: Not at all? He's Guy Clark after all.

BUSH: No, I mean Guy doesn't sit around patting himself on the back, even though on the ladder of songwriting, he's just about at the top rung of anyone. One of America's greatest treasures as a writer. And his singing? I mean, nobody does a Guy song better than Guy. Guy and I had written a song together, just the two of us. It's still never come out yet. It might on the next record. It's a pretty dark subject. [*laughing*] I figure, I'm old enough. Who cares? He called me one day and said, "You know Verlon [Thompson] and I are writing a song about Stringbean. I can't believe the story's never been told about Stringbean and Estelle, his wife, and how their lives tragically ended." And he says, "Me and Verlon are over here. Can you come over? I think we need a real hillbilly to help us with this."*

COWAN: [*laughs*]

BUSH: It was crazy how this happened. My father had recently died, and I couldn't be there. I was on the road. And so, my sisters were going through his things, and they found a few boxes of his things that they thought I would want. One of these things in one of these boxes was an old, long-yellowed newspaper from the *Nashville Banner*. On the front page, which was recent after Stringbean's death and Estelle's, there was a picture of an auction at Stringbean's farm and a guy is holding up, on a coat hanger, a pair of overalls. You can see a couple of hundred people out for this auction because the picture was taken from the back, and he's holding up these overalls. That was just a chilling photo to me. Incredibly creepy. My father had kept it all these years, and they didn't get the *Nashville Banner* in Bowling Green, so it was probably given to him by Oswald or Mr. Acuff. String was a good friend of theirs. I just remember reading it and putting it in recycling. I didn't want to keep it.

COWAN: Why? Because it was creepy?

---

* Stringbean, whose given name was David Akeman, was a singer, songwriter, comedian, actor, member of the Grand Ole Opry, and was renowned for his old-fashioned banjo picking style. Everyone who knew him loved him. You may know him best as a main cast member in the hit TV show *Hee Haw*. The song that Sam, Guy, and Verlon wrote about the senseless murder of Stringbean and his wife, "The Ballad of Stringbean and Estelle," eventually was released and nominated by the IBMA for Song of the Year in 2011. The reference to Grandpa in the song is Grandpa Jones, Stringbean's dear friend and neighbor, who discovered their bodies.

BUSH: Because it was sad. It creeped me out. Everybody loved him. And so, just a few days later, Guy calls up. I go over, and we did have a factual sheet of when certain things occurred. And then we took poetic license a little bit, here and there. I just remember telling Guy about that newspaper. I can't say exactly what he said, but it was to the effect of, "Oh, great if you just brought it, we'd have it written by now." [*laughs*] So I said, you're pretty good, Guy. I think you can make it up. Our intent was, melodically speaking and lyrically speaking, to make it like a folk song, like a traditional tale that had been written years ago. We've had a lot of good comments about it.

COWAN: So, let's wrap this puppy up.

BUSH: My job is that when I'm playing, you play better.

COWAN: Amen.

BUSH: I mean, that's what I want people to think. That it was easier to play because, hopefully, I'm giving you good rhythm and a good pad to play on. That's our job, to back each other up.

Photograph courtesy of Alan Messer, Nashville/alanmesser.com

3

BÉLA FLECK THROWS DOWN HIS HEART FOR THE FIVE-STRING BANJO

If you've ever been in a touring band, or perhaps a work situation where you're in daily contact, physically and emotionally, with a group of other folks, then you will have some knowledge of what I mean by "safety in numbers." In a band, you work together, you rehearse together, most days you eat together, and you ride nonstop to your next job together. This produces an intimacy in the workplace that most people don't experience. I spent well over two hundred days a year for eight years with banjoist Béla Fleck. We went through a lot together: miles and miles and days on end in the New Grass "bread truck." Record deals; divorce (mine); drug addiction (mine) and subsequent recovery; Béla's own relationships and family dynamics; and the cultivating, curating, and performing artistic ideas day in and day out. Revisiting all this has revealed to me again my gratitude to Béla, who was, and still is, a great supportive friend, the kind who will tell you stuff that might make you uncomfortable but ultimately lets you know that he cares. I got a good chuckle remembering the times when I wanted to attribute things to serendipity or the ethereal, and he would stop me and say, "Nah, I don't feel that way. That's not how New Yorkers do it." Or, "No, I don't trust that."

Not many folks operate at the level of Mr. Fleck. He is a driven and fearless artist, confident in a way that I cannot summon or reason up for myself. Béla has been nominated in more Grammy categories (bluegrass, jazz, classical pop, rock, and world beat) than any artist in Grammy history, winning fourteen. He once won a Grammy in country and jazz *in the same year* (2000). In 2020, he was inducted into the International Bluegrass Hall of Fame as a member of our band, New Grass Revival. I hope this interview, conducted in his ranch-style home in the Forest Hills neighborhood of Nashville, will give you your own perspective on this wonderful human being.

JOHN COWAN: We have a lot to discuss. I think it nice to have you here to talk about yourself and the banjo.

BÉLA FLECK: This is a banjo-friendly zone. The whole world is not friendly to banjos, so I'm glad to be here.

COWAN: So, as I think about having known you for as long as I have, thirty some years, it's been nice for me to sit and review everything that you've done, which is a staggering amount of music. You grew up in New York City and took up the banjo at what age?

FLECK: Fifteen. I was playing some guitar for a few years before that, and I would characterize it as an interest, as opposed to an all-consuming burning fire, which is what happened the moment I got a banjo. Guitar was something where, OK, I better practice. And I liked it. But it didn't turn me on the same way. It was an interest. You know, you can see it in a kid, where he's interested in a sport, but not *really* interested in it. Or history. But then, when you find the thing that turns them on, it's a whole different story. For me, it was just having that banjo put into my hands, right when I was fifteen, right when I was starting high school. The weekend before high school started, my grandfather got a banjo at a garage sale and gave it to me, and I took it home. I was just a freak from then on. That was it. I had found the thing.

COWAN: Had you already heard Earl Scruggs at that point, or did that come later?

FLECK: No, actually, I had heard Earl Scruggs way before that and didn't know what it was. But I always remember being at my grandparents' house and them letting us watch TV in their room during the day. *The Beverly Hillbillies* came on. Me and my brother, Louie, who you know, were watching it. I can't tell you how old we were. Somewhere between four and six, I'd say. When that sound came on, I said, "Whoa, did you hear that?" And Louie said, "What?" And I said, "That sound. Wait, I think it will come back." Even at that age, we knew that the music comes back at the end of the show. And it did, and I said, "There it is again. Isn't that incredible?" And he said, "I guess it's OK." I guess for some people, that sound is a compelling, life-changing sound. It is for a lot of people when they first hear Earl Scruggs. But for other people, it isn't.

COWAN: Was the first banjo that your grandpa bought you, was that a five-string?

FLECK: Yes.

COWAN: Since you'd already heard Earl, were you already seeking out and assimilating that music?

FLECK: Well, by the time the banjo was actually put into my hands, it was "Dueling Banjos" time. So this was five, six, seven years later, at least, maybe even more. And so, ever since I first heard the banjo, I always had that awareness. We'd be in upstate New York, and there would be some kind of a sale and a little bluegrass band playing on the side, and I would always watch intently. Banjo playing can seem so intimidating that you'd never feel like a real person could actually do it, or, that *you* could do it. I never thought anything else but that I liked it. Then, when "Dueling Banjos" came out, it was consuming. That was a piece of it, too. That song was one of the few number one pop hits of banjo instrumental music. There have actually been a few. So when a banjo got put in my hands, and I had a chance to try to figure out what was going on, I was pretty excited.

COWAN: Well, considering how it struck you at first, have you ever thought it's almost like it chose you?

FLECK: Yeah, well, I'm always cautious about that. I'm from New York, and we don't trust anything, and we're suspicious types. [*both laugh*] We don't like anything that's jive, so if we see that someone is saying that "the banjo chose you, isn't that sweet?," I don't know. Maybe it did. The truth is, that's as good an explanation as any.

COWAN: Well, it's not an instrument that speaks inherently to everybody.

FLECK: Right.

COWAN: I mean, that we could say pretty safely.

FLECK: But I think you could say that a lot of people who choose to play the five-string banjo heard Earl Scruggs, and something happened.

COWAN: Yeah.

FLECK: It was a shock to their system, and the world was never the same after hearing that sound, and I am one of those.

COWAN: When you went to music and art school, were you playing the banjo there?

FLECK: I got the banjo the day before I started high school.

COWAN: So, was it encouraged there?

FLECK: Well, there was no way to incorporate it into the school curriculum. I would play it on the side or bring it to school. Eventually, I couldn't stand to go to school without it. By the time I was a junior, I was carrying the banjo with me everyday at school. I would play it in front of the school and around, and people would do all the caricature stuff that was going around back then. Squeal like a pig, flapping their arms and dancing around, all kinds of insulting sorts of things. As much as I love bluegrass banjo playing, I didn't enjoy being a New Yorker with all those stereotypes. That's not me. I'm not trying to be a Southerner. I just love this instrument. I'm not trying to appropriate another cultural perspective. I just love the sound. Ironically, the more I played it, the more I did fall in love with the southern side of it.

At first, I remember I made a terrible mistake of saying that bluegrass singing sounded like cats being slaughtered. That was a bad move.

COWAN: [*laughs*]

FLECK: But the truth is, as a New Yorker, hearing that music, hearing Bill Monroe sing, and hearing some of that stuff, it was pretty raw. It was not what we were used to. But after my years in the bluegrass scene, I had a very different feeling about that. I always talk about it as being like coffee. You first taste coffee as a kid, and it's bitter, and you think, *how could anybody drink this?* For a Northerner and someone who has no connection to bluegrass in their life, to suddenly first hear that stuff, you could have that same feeling. *Ew, I can't relate.* After the years I spent in it, I fell in love with it, like I love great espresso. I love really raw bluegrass singing.

COWAN: Yeah, I found for myself that my first exposure to the high lonesome tenor vocals, it was kind of the same thing. I just didn't even know what to make of it. I'd grown up with my parents singing at church. My first exposure to vocal singing was just whatever was on the radio, and that went

Four of the most influential and progressive banjoists who ever lived: Tony Trischka, Pete Wernick, Béla Fleck, and Alan Munde. Nacogdoches Bluegrass Festival, Texas—July 4, 1986. *Courtesy Rick Gardner*

all over the place. Certainly, the radio that I was hearing out of Cleveland, Ohio, didn't have Bill Monroe or Ralph Stanley. It just didn't. So my first exposure to it, even being from Kentucky, it was kind of the same. It made me turn my head like a dog when a dog hears an almost inaudible sound.

FLECK: Yeah, but there was something intriguing about it, was it?

COWAN: Oh, yeah!

FLECK: You could dismiss it, and suddenly it would work its magic on you and, after awhile, you'd be like, wow, Bill Monroe's got something that nobody else has.

COWAN: I've had the pleasure of knowing your parents. Your stepfather, Joe, is a cellist, is that correct?

FLECK: Yeah.

COWAN: And your mom is a writer. Were you exposed to classical music at the same time through Joe, perhaps?

FLECK: Right. So, my mother and father divorced when I was about one. Joe came into the picture when I was around seven or eight, and then they got married when I was, I think, fifteen. He was around and played cello in the army orchestra. In fact, he was stationed in Germany for a while, and then he came back and became a teacher. So they were both teachers in the New York school system. But he loved that music, and he still does. He would have people over, it was a social thing for him, to read through string quartets or quintets. I would sit and watch them do that, and sometimes we would go up to Tanglewood and go watch the rehearsals of the orchestra. So, it was in my world, but I didn't feel like I owned it. I didn't have any actual connection to it, but it was working its magic on me as well because, years later when I met Edgar Meyer—I think you were the first person who introduced me to Edgar, by the way—it wasn't an alien thing for me to hear that kind of music. Actually, he's the one who said there's a place for you in this world if you want it. Edgar made me very welcome playing Bach and doing transcriptions with him of different classical pieces. That was the beginning of me thinking that that was a possibility for the banjo. Single-line pieces of Bach fiddle music sounded great on the banjo, but it was hard to do because it wasn't written for the banjo. The jumps were crazy. Just to play a simple thing on the violin was more like a virtuoso piece on the banjo. As I'm struggling with that, I'm thinking that I want music of that type that fits the banjo completely. That's what I'm trying to do now. I want to create music that is not a banjo trying to be a violin or a piano, which it can never be, but itself, and writing new music that's built around the strengths of the banjo and the things that it does that the violin and the piano can't.

COWAN: One of my favorite solo records you made, you made when you were in New Grass Revival, called *Drive*. The reason I want to mention that title is that I was always, and to this day, so amazed by your ability to be so focused and to practice so hard. I am a gifted person, but I was always distracted by what*ever*, relationships, and early in my life, with drugs and alcohol, all that stuff. But you never were. From the first day I met you, you were the guy that spent all day in his room when we were on the road, practicing. Then you'd practice before the sound check. And you'd practice after the gig. I have a feeling that's never changed.

FLECK: Well, the only thing that distracts me from it now is the other things that I'm doing that are musical. Having engineers work on my music when I feel like I know best what I want and having to explain it to them is frustrating. I've eventually evolved to being somebody who mixes his own records and edits his own records and has a lot of hands-on experience with making the music. Sometimes, that can take an incredible amount of time away from playing. Because, you know, first you compose the music, then you record it with some guys, then you edit together a great version of it, or do what ever you do to get it sounding great, then you might spend weeks mixing a record, or longer. Since it's in my own house now, I can spend as long as I want. A lot of that time takes me away from playing, but I'm still involved in music at all of those points. The other thing is composing. Last year I composed a concerto for banjo and orchestra and did it all by myself because I wanted to learn from it. I didn't want somebody to show me how to do it. I wanted to figure it out for myself. Immense hours sitting around in front of a computer, moving notes around on a screen, and very little playing, those are the things that stop me from playing. But they still fit in to type A, bizarre personality traits. [*laughs*]

COWAN: Ultimately, we are who we are. I get that. But you have accomplished so much in thirty-five years. An unbelievable mass of wonderful music. I guess you'd say, that's just who I am. Is it that simple? Is there anything in your family make up that contributed to your drive in life? Because not everybody has it.

FLECK: Yeah, sure, absolutely. One you get the opportunity to make music and make something really good, you get addicted to that feeling. So, what am I going to do, retire after *Drive* in 1988? What am I going to do next? Well, I found the Flecktone guys. But honestly, being in New Grass Revival could have been the end-all for a person's career. That was an amazing band to be in. So, I have been very fortunate, but at a certain point, I was also looking at what I was going to do next, because I did get tired. Eight and a half years in New Grass, and by the end, there was a part of me that was really needing to do other stuff. And that happened with the Flecktones. After a year with the Flecktones, I was so eager to do something that was not that. If we're not going to be super creative, spending all that time creating new stuff, and we're just performing the music we created, I start to drift a little bit.

COWAN: The thing that I thought, and I rarely talk about anything I've done in these interviews, is that as a member of New Grass Revival, once we got a major record label, we got consumed with trying to be on the radio. I think that band was not built for that. I think it was built more for what you were interested in. And we strayed away and, ultimately, it cost us because you left, I think, for that reason.

FLECK: The thing that attracted me to the band was the adventurous nature of it. And, of course, I was a lot younger than everybody else. You guys had already fought the good fight for a long time, and I think that's an interesting aspect of what happened. I hadn't gotten to fight a good fight yet. I wanted to fight a good fight. I wasn't interested in being super successful on country radio, because I wanted to be a better musician. I wanted to learn things. I wanted to break new ground. Now, ironically, we probably could have done that in that world. But it didn't happen. Maybe five years later, it could have.

COWAN: I didn't want to admit it, but I knew pretty early on, when it came to you, Béla Fleck and New Grass Revival, that, man, this guy isn't gonna be here that long. And when Noam Pikelny was in my band, right off the bat, I immediately knew that this guy is not going to be here very long. [*laughs*]

FLECK: But I *was* there a long time. Eight and a half years!

COWAN: No, that was not a criticism.

BELA: That's a long time.

COWAN: No, that was not a criticism. You were meant to do what you turned out doing, which were all these amazing things.

FLECK: Thanks. It was very tough for me because I loved being in that band. That band was the first really incredible band I was in. And it was incredible over and over and over again, and it changed a lot of people's perspectives. I also remember that there were times every once in awhile, after I had been in the band for five or six years, I'd go through a period where I was just thinking about other music that I really wanted to do. I had seen David Grisman go out and have a big success with instrumental music, and I would think, *I have to leave the band*. Then I'd go onstage, and we'd play "Reach" or something, and I'd be up there crying because I couldn't leave this band. It sounded so great. I'd have this whole experience nobody knew I was having, and then, I'd finally go, *OK, I'm not leaving this band. I'm going to stay.* I had actually given up on the idea of leaving the band at a certain point, and I was pretty happy and had come to terms with what it was and my feelings about it. Then all this other stuff sort of happened to me. The Flecktones happened to me. I wasn't looking to leave New Grass Revival when Victor turned up, and Howard turned up,* and I got the chance to make a television show for PBS, *The Lonesome Pines* Special, in 1988. That just happened to me. Then when I put that band together, it was very hard not to give it more time because it was so special, obviously.

COWAN: Well, this is a good segue into talking about the Flecktones, which was a genre-busting, amazing band of musicians, each person phenomenally talented. You know, sometimes you can take things on paper and say, I'm going to have the best guy on each instrument, and it doesn't necessarily mean it's going to be great.

FLECK: Right.

COWAN: I think the alchemy you guys have, to this day, you can talk about that. I'm not going to try to describe that.

FLECK: I remember Grisman† saying to me, "How did you get your thing together?" And me saying, "I don't know, it all just sort of happened to me." I mean, I think I made some pretty inspired choices, but at the time, they seemed like the only possible choices. I had already tried going out on tour with my own jazz-oriented music with Kenny Malone [drummer], and Kirby Shelstad [percussion], and Mark Shatz [bass and mandolin], and it

---

* Victor and Howard are the freakishly talented bassist Victor Wooten and Howard Levy, harmonica virtuoso and pianist with whom Béla founded the Flecktones more than thirty years ago. Among many accolades, the Flecktones won a Grammy Award in 1997 for Best Pop Instrumental for the track "Sinister Minister," which you need to seek out on YouTube as soon as you're done reading this.

† David Grisman, mentioned here a second time, is the "Dawgfather" himself, a mandolin giant who merged bluegrass, folk, and jazz to create an influential, genre-busting style he called "Dawg music."

was heartbreaking trying to get that to happen. It was so much work to try to pull that together. And when we finally got there and went on tour, I really didn't think that the music was such that it was going to achieve the effect. I didn't think that my songs were sounding to the point they would have to be for this to really happen. That was part of me giving up on the whole idea. "Well, it's just not practical, it was a crazy idea, anyway." As much as I loved playing with those guys, it didn't really happen up to the level that it needed to for it to pull me away from New Grass Revival. But, with the Flecktones, it did.

COWAN: How did it feel initially where you go from New Grass Revival to the Flecktones, and you have this amazing cast of characters assembled, and you're completely expressing yourself 100 percent, and writing the songs. It was kind of your dream, was it not?

FLECK: Yeah, it was. And I was very controlling of it, too, because I wanted it to work. I felt like I might know better than anyone else what would make it work for an audience. I felt that it had to have a very common, folksy feel to it, but it couldn't really be as esoteric as everybody actually thought we were. There had to be a thread of warmth and humanity.

COWAN: I think that was accomplished right off the bat, because to see you guys live was equally as thrilling. Besides the music that was blowing past you, visually it's a great band to watch.

FLECK: Ironically, everyone in the band, except for me, are great performers. [*both laugh*] Because, like, Howard, when he finishes a solo, he jumps back, and he throws his hand up in the air, and when he finishes a piano solo, he turns, and he's so excited, it translates. And Victor, and Future Man [Victor's brother, Roy], they worked at Busch Gardens as performers doing the German show and the Country Show and whatever, and the forty-five minute sets and did the same thing every day. So, they're not the kind of jazz guys who are like, "Hey, man, don't tell me to do the same thing I did yesterday, because I'm a free musician, and I don't do that." They're like, whatever is needed. If being loose and open is needed, great. If repeating it just like we did yesterday is needed, great. They just don't have those kinds of things in their heads. We could actually just approach the performance aspects of it in a way that was very satisfying for us and the audience.

COWAN: Let's talk about your documentary, *Throw Down Your Heart*. I found it to be emotionally political. What we learned is that the banjo originated in Africa, and I know that as a banjo player, you decided to pursue this on a much grander scale.

FLECK: Well, the banjo came over from West Africa with the slaves. Whether they had the instruments in their hands, or when they got to the Americas, they built them, is up for discussion. Some people feel that the slave takers actually took musicians because bringing that culture on the ships might actually keep more people alive. That's what I was told over there. But I don't know.

COWAN: To keep other people's spirits up.

FLECK: Exactly. And the slave takers were scared of drums. Drums were always considered part of communicating with each other so, even on the plantations, drumming was not allowed. But something like the banjo was OK. Obviously, it didn't look like our banjos. It was a gourd with a skin over it and a couple of strings, maybe three strings. Maybe four. Ironically, the short string that they always talk about, that Joel Sweeney is credited with inventing in 1836,* the fifth string, I believe was another long string. When you go to Africa, there are lots of instruments with short strings. So this guy didn't invent the short string, and they didn't learn about the short string

---

* Joel Sweeney, born in Appomattox, Virginia, county in 1810, has been credited with popularizing the banjo, a talent he claimed to have learned from local slaves. He frequently performed in blackface throughout Virginia and North Carolina and has been falsely referred to as the inventor of the banjo and other easily refutable claims. Many historians consider this revision an effort to separate the instrument from its African origins. If you need more banjo history (some people do!), check out the exhaustive *Banjo Roots and Branches* by Robert Winans.

from Joel Sweeney and decide to incorporate it in Africa. But I think he might have added the low string.

COWAN: So not only was your documentary a historical journey, but was there some altruism in it as well, like you felt that this was important for people to know?

FLECK: There are several pieces to this. One, is that I feel in love with some music that I heard from over there. This woman named Oumou Sangaré.

COWAN: She's a singer.

FLECK: She's a singer from Mali, and her music is so great. It hits me the same way that Ralph Stanley's music hits me, or B. B. King, or Louis Armstrong. A small group of guys playing really tight, really interesting, really smart, really earthy, that just hits you in the chest. And so when I heard her doing that, it made me think, *Oh, gosh, you know, I always wanted to go to Africa, but I never heard the music that I could see myself being a part of.* I could really hear the banjo in her music. I felt like I could get in there. So, I started thinking about that. This was around the time that we took our first year off from the Flecktones, around 2005. I thought maybe this is the year to go to Africa. It was one of those bucket-list things: "Some day, I'm going to go to Africa." I would get field recordings. You can get field recordings from different parts of Africa and hear people playing cool instrumental music somewhere in the jungle, or in someone's house. It was that whole discovery thing. I was always into pioneers or the old West and *adventuring*, and this seemed like an adventure, to go to Africa and get out there and find people to play with, and film the whole thing.

COWAN: And you financed the whole thing yourself, is what I recall.

FLECK: I did.

COWAN: Which was really a gamble.

FLECK: Well, I didn't intend to. [*both laugh*] I had people at Sony Classical that thought it was a cool idea who were going to pay for it. And then we went ahead and put the whole trip together, and I even advanced the money for the flights, which we had to buy several months ahead of time. Then they got in touch and said we can't do it. They backed out. So, I was left holding the bag. There was no time, at that point, about a month before the trip, to go looking for funding. We just had to do it, you know? I didn't have kids. I didn't have people to pay for college. I had a house and had been working a lot and for a long time and had been basically socking it away, so I actually could do that. Altruistic side? I don't know. I'm hesitant, as a New Yorker, to take any credit for any altruism.

COWAN: [*laughs*]

FLECK: But I think some really great things came out of it.

COWAN: Let me tell you as a viewer, it hit me on a deeper level, emotionally.

FLECK: I wanted to connect with these people. I wanted to get into situations that forced me to go to my deepest self that I could not possibly prepare for as a musician and be forced to dig deep. A lot of things that happened on this trip, I didn't really find out about until I got home. I was working so hard. We were there for about a month and, every single day, we were either traveling or recording, sometimes both, and I was playing music that I'd never heard before. Sometimes I had tapes ahead of time of people, and I was working on it. But every single day was like a calculus exam, musically. Listening back to it now, I can hear it, and it seems like, OK, that seems like a reasonable thing to play. It's not like, holy cow, I reinvented the wheel, but at the time, it was pretty intimidating. The great thing I got to see, because I was involved with the editing of the music scenes, is that I got to experience the African folks in a way that I couldn't when I was there. I was too busy playing the music. I got to watch, not only the scenes in the movie, but the outtakes from different angles, and I could see [*sounding surprised*] that they *actually did like me*. They weren't doing this for the money.

They showed up on time because they were being paid, but they weren't faking it. They were really there, they were really into it, and they were having a great time with it. They were moved. So, that was a really wonderful thing to find out after the fact.

COWAN: What I get from you is that you think the banjo is just full of possibilities. Even when we went to India in 1984, you were always out of the hotel trying to find musicians to play with.

FLECK: Right. That's where I found out a lot of things, on our New Grass Revival trips, because we got to do some State Department tours around different parts of the world. We went to Bangladesh. We went to Nepal.

COWAN: We went to thirty-some countries.

FLECK: Yeah, so what I realized, at some point, is that we were kind of like ambassadors with a little bit of . . . power. I could wire ahead and say, hey, find me some cool musicians to play with when we get to Dakar or wherever. We did go to Morocco, and we did go to Egypt, and so they would find me some guys, and they would show up because the embassy had asked them to show up, and we would sit and play, and everybody would get so happy. All I'd have to do is get out my instrument and start trying to play with them, and their eyes would widen. We didn't speak the same language at all. In most cases, there was no common language. There was something very beautiful that would happen. I would go on these treks to go find people to play with whenever I had any time. A few years later when the Flecktones got to do a Pacific Rim tour of Thailand, China, Mongolia, the Philippines, Indonesia, and Singapore, every single place we played, we had musicians brought to us, and we had them come onstage with us. At the end of every show, we would play their national song, or something that we could understand well enough to play. And people were so moved. It wasn't that hard to do, but the outcome was spectacular. That's how I knew I could go to Africa and play with these people, and something good would happen.

COWAN: If there was an epitaph, let's imagine a gravestone that says, "Béla Fleck . . . possibilities." Mine would probably say, "I forgot."

FLECK: [*both laugh*] Mine will probably say, "I told you I didn't feel well." [*both laugh*]

COWAN: But you're a seeker, so, what now? Whatever shows up?

FLECK: It's a different time for me because, honestly, and I've had to do this a few times in my career, I've achieved a lot of the things that I had hoped to achieve already. This last year, I got to do my banjo concerto, and that was a big deal. I just made this new record with a great jazz musician, a different kind of jazz than the kind of jazz I did with Chick Corea, or the Flecktones, a much more traditional kind of jazz with a musician named Marcus Roberts. That was a dream for me to find a place in a more conventional jazz setting, but a really great one, and this is that. I'm going to be writing a piece for banjo and string quartet. I'm starting to feel like I want to be really compelled by whatever I do. It's actually getting a little harder to find bucket-list things that I would hate to not get to do. There've been a few times in my life where I thought, wow, I've kind of done all the stuff I wanted to do, now what am I going to do? So I keep looking for the next thing that is appealing and interesting. I try to think about two years out, so right now I'm thinking in terms of playing this banjo concerto. I have about ten or twelve orchestras interested that I'm booked to play it with.

COWAN: Excellent.

FLECK: So, I'm going to go out and play banjo with orchestras as a big piece of what I do over the next few years. I've got an agency that handles that kind of work, who thinks that there are a lot of possibilities for me to play this with a lot of orchestras. I'm also creating a piece for banjo and string quartet, and I'll probably do a significant tour with that, where the show is just me with a string quartet onstage doing this piece that I'm writing, probably a thirty-minute piece, and arranging some of my stuff for that. I still want to do traditional stuff. I want to do more with Edgar and [percussionist] Zakir Hussain and learn more about Indian music. But I don't have the big, burning thing right now. I suspect that it will pop up.

Courtesy Rick Gardner

ALL FOR A SONG

I was born to sing. I know this because the moment I could make sounds, there was music going on with me internally. In the same way, I believe there are natural-born songwriters. I'm blessed to know some personally: Rodney Crowell is one. Kris Kristofferson is one. Loretta Lynn was surely one. Darrell Scott, Nanci Griffith, Tim O'Brien, Lyle Lovett, and Wendy Waldman are ones, too. It's a gift that was given to them. They had to learn how to use it, but I think it got implanted into their souls somewhere in the incubation process. I feel bad for songwriters like them in this regard: They have to explain something that's completely heaven sent. "How did you think to write that?" I'm sure I've asked that a dozen times. Nobody knows when it's going to come through the ether. Some of their best songs were written in twenty minutes, sometimes less. It's inexplicable.

For me, sometimes it's the melody. Sometimes it's the words. But as a singer, I've learned that your own experience with a great song can change over the years. Maybe someone you love has just died. Or maybe you've been through a divorce. Or maybe you've fallen in love. Great songs can be so healing. You can sing a song you've loved for many years and in serving that song, still learn something new.

Courtesy Anthony Scarlati

4

"ALWAYS NICE TO GET A LETTER FROM HOME, ISN'T IT, KRIS?"

Me and Bobby and Kris Kristofferson

Part of the legacy of country music is the artist's relationship to words and stories. For fans like me, and people who've covered Kris Kristofferson's songs, rarely have words had a better friend then Kris. He is an American icon. A singer. A songwriter. A poet. An actor. He once flew helicopters as an Army Ranger. He was a Rhodes Scholar at Oxford (where he studied the poetry of William Blake) and a Golden Gloves boxer who played rugby in college. And he was just getting started. Inspired by artists like Willie Nelson and Johnny Cash, he turned down a teaching position at West Point and followed his heart to Nashville, starting as a janitor, to pursue a new chapter in his life as a country music songwriter. For a kid growing up in a conservative military family, that news came as a seismic shock to the people who knew and loved him most.

For this conversation, I met up with Kris at the Opryland Hotel in Nashville. I've done a good number of interviews before, but this one was different for me. I was a lot more nervous than usual. Kris being Kris made it easy to relax. He walked in wearing a long, dark coat and carrying his guitar, along with a distinct air of humility, almost an innocence about him. Not in an "aw shucks" way, but more like "I can't believe I'm here with *you*." You'll feel what I'm talking about as he discusses his encounters with Johnny Cash, Waylon Jennings, Willie Nelson, and others. From cleaning the ashtrays as a janitor at Columbia Studios while Dylan recorded *Blonde on Blonde*, to writing "Me and Bobby McGee" as a favor to the late, legendary producer Fred Foster, Kris generously shared stories I'd never heard before for the benefit of readers like you he knows he may never have the chance to meet. In 2004, he was inducted into the Country Music Hall of Fame and in 2014, earned a Grammy Lifetime Achievement Award. Our conversation opens with us talking about Kris's mother and father, and his life as a boy growing up in Texas and California.

JOHN COWAN: So, were either your mom or your dad musical at all?

KRIS KRISTOFFERSON: Not really. And my mother, in particular, was kind of embarrassed that I was into country music. I guess, back in those days, it had a bad reputation or something, I don't know. But she kind of disowned me when I came here to Nashville.

COWAN: Really?

KRISTOFFERSON: She said, you've done some things to disappoint us in the past, but nothing to compare to this! [*both laugh*]

COWAN: Was guitar the first instrument you picked up?

KRISTOFFERSON: Yes.

COWAN: And what age was that, do you think?

KRISTOFFERSON: I'm embarrassed to say that I was pretty young. It was probably sixth or seventh grade, whatever that age is.

COWAN: Did you just kind of self-teach or did somebody help you?

KRISTOFFERSON: I wasn't very good at lessons. I had taken piano lessons at my parents' insistence for a couple of years, and I hated taking lessons. I think I took two guitar lessons. Most of the stuff I just picked up from the people that I saw and hung out with. But I never got very good. [*laughs*]

COWAN: Do you remember the first couple of songs you were interested in learning to sing or play? Was it maybe Hank Williams?

KRISTOFFERSON: Yeah! Of course, I made people sick when I tried to sing like Hank Williams. If you hear a person yodel who can't, it's pretty scary. [*both laugh*]

COWAN: I know for myself that when you first start playing, you usually start by imitating.

KRISTOFFERSON: Well, I think the first whole song I wrote was called "I Hate Your Ugly Face." [*both laugh*] I was eleven at the time. It was pretty good!

COWAN: That's a pretty appropriate sentiment for eleven, I think.

KRISTOFFERSON: [*laughing*] Yeah.

COWAN: Knowing now that you had been exposed to great country music, you talked a little bit in the past about Bob Dylan. Do you recall how old you were or how far along you were as a songwriter when you first heard Bob?

KRISTOFFERSON: I don't remember when I first heard his songs. I remember the first time I saw him. It was when I was a janitor at Columbia recording studios, and he came in to record *Blonde on Blonde*. I'd never seen anybody like that. I don't know what it's like today, but in those days, if you didn't do three songs in three hours, you were wasting money. And he came in, and all the best musicians in Nashville were in there backing him, and they were playing ping pong all night long while he sat out at the piano, by himself, in the big studio there at Columbia. He sat at the piano, and nobody talked to him.

COWAN: They didn't want to bother him?

KRISTOFFERSON: No. And he had dark glasses on, and he's sitting there at the piano. Around seven in the morning, he called 'em all in, and they'd go in and cut some masterpiece. It was incredible. I'd never seen anything like it.

COWAN: Tell me what kind of impression it made on you, because you were already writing songs at this point.

KRISTOFFERSON: Oh, yeah, well, I'd been writing songs since I was really little. I'd been making them up. I'm sure that his songwriting affected me, just like everybody's who I loved. I mean, Hank Williams was my number one man. And Johnny Cash. I think Dylan's relationship with Johnny Cash did more for Nashville and country music than anything in my lifetime because, in California, people kind of looked down on country music. If you listened to country music, you were a shitkicker. You weren't a rock and roller, or whatever else was popular. His relationship with Bob Dylan really changed all that because Dylan obviously respected John as much as I do.

COWAN: Yeah, I remember the first time hearing "Girl from the North Country." I was just a rock and roll kid living up in Kentucky, and I was like, "Oh, this is cool, Bob Dylan and Johnny Cash." It kind of had the same effect on me.

KRISTOFFERSON: Yeah!

COWAN: Even though Johnny was so iconic, the thing that was so wonderful about him was he was never part of any camp. He was just Johnny Cash.

KRISTOFFERSON: Yes.

COWAN: And he just skirted about wherever he wanted because he was amazing.

KRISTOFFERSON: Absolutely. I've never met anybody like him. Johnny Cash was always Johnny Cash.

COWAN: You came to our consciousness in the mid- to late-'60s, and except for Bob Dylan, I think most of the public thought of singer-songwriters as people like Carole King, people who worked in Tin Pan Alley in New York City, you know? Have you always been comfortable with the title "singer-songwriter"?

KRISTOFFERSON: I think it's very complimentary if they call me singer at all! But a singer-songwriter, those are the people that I looked up to the most growing up, from Hank Williams on.

COWAN: I'm going to tell you something that you might find flattering. My friend Rodney Crowell, when I interviewed him, talked about when he first got here to Nashville, which kinda sounds like the second wave. I want to think the first wave was you and Mickey Newberry, and Roger Miller and people like that. The second wave, in my mind was Rodney, Steve Earle, Townes Van Zandt, and Guy Clark . . .

KRISTOFFERSON: Yeah.

COWAN: And what Rodney said was basically two things: First, when they all first arrived, the songwriting community was so supportive. And second, all of them, Guy, Townes, and Rodney wanted to be Kris Kristofferson.

KRISTOFFERSON: [*laughs*] Well, I would like to be any one of *them*!

COWAN: Amen. But I think that goes along with what we are talking about. People who are in search of the song. I'm not telling you something you don't know, but it's a little different for songwriters than it is for entertainers or singers, because you're bringing something so totally different to the table. You're creating the songs and the words. That is your work. You're not interpreting somebody else's stuff.

KRISTOFFERSON: That's right.

COWAN: Is the process of writing a song much different for you today than it's been most of your life?

KRISTOFFERSON: Well, I have never been able to write as disciplined as a lot of songwriters I respect, like Tom T. Hall. He could get up every day and write songs and *made* himself write them. I can't. Never could. And I haven't made myself. Maybe that's just my laziness. [*laughs*] But I can get away with it. I can only write when it comes to me, when I'm inspired to do it. I've sat down and tried to write songs, and I've worked at songs after I get 'em, after the seed of the song is in there. It'll run over in my head until I finish it. But I can't sit down and say I'm gonna write a song tonight and be ready for tomorrow.

COWAN: Fred Foster [producer] is credited as a cowriter on "Me and Bobby McGee"—is that correct?

KRISTOFFERSON: Yes. Yes.

COWAN: Now, tell me why that is?

KRISTOFFERSON: Well, Fred gave me the title of the song. I had just gone to work for Combine,* which was owned by him. He also had Monument Records.

COWAN: Which is a music publisher on Music Row.

KRISTOFFERSON: It was Bob Beckham [Combine Records producer], who I'd gone to work with because I really admired his work. While I was a janitor at Columbia, I'd seen what he could do with pitching songs. He was really heart and soul into the business. The girl who was a secretary over at Mercury Records told me that he'd like to be my publisher. And so, from then on, we were together. Monument Records came along with that. Boudleaux and Felice Bryant were in the same building that Fred was.† And Fred told me one time, when we were in his office, that he had a song title for me. He said, "Me and Bobby McGee." Well, I *thought* he said McGee. What he *said* was McKee, because that was the secretary.

COWAN: And that was her real name.

KRISTOFFERSON: Her real name, yeah. And he said, "How does that grab you, huh?" And I said, "How does what grab me?" [*both laugh*] He says,

---

  * Combine Records was a publishing house started by the late Fred Foster, who signed not only Kris, but also Dolly Parton, Jerry Reed, Ray Stevens, and Larry Gatlin. On his other label, Monument Records, he signed Roy Orbison, producing hits like "Oh, Pretty Woman," "Crying," and "Only the Lonely." Fred was inducted into the Country Music Hall of Fame in 2016.

  † Boudleaux and Felice Bryant, husband and wife, were one of the greatest songwriting duos in music history. Their songs included classics like "Rocky Top," "Love Hurts," "Bye Bye Love," "Wake Up Little Susie," and "All I Have to Do Is Dream." It's estimated that their records sold half a billion copies worldwide.

"Here's the hook: Bobby McKee . . . is a *she*!" And I'm looking at him, and I thought, *there's no way in hell I can write this song!* So, I hid from him for about a month!

COWAN: [*laughs*]

KRISTOFFERSON: I was working down in the Gulf of Mexico at the time, flying to offshore oil rigs in a helicopter. I'd go down there for a week and then come back and try to pitch my songs for a week. I hid from him for about a month. And then it came to me when I was coming home. I remember that I wrote it by the end of that day. I know that Billy Swan and I went into the studio—there used to be a little studio at Combine—and it was actually the place where I'd first worked with Marijohn Wilkins for Buckhorn Publishing. Billy and I went in there and overdubbed and overdubbed and sang harmonies with it and everything. Billy, I remember, said, "This is a monumental song! This is like 'Hey Jude.'" [*laughing*] And I said, "Oh, sure. This could be like 'Hey Jude.'"

COWAN: And he was right, wasn't he?

KRISTOFFERSON: He was right.

COWAN: Was Roger Miller the first person who cut it? I love his version of it.

KRISTOFFERSON: Yeah. Yeah. Mickey Newbury pitched it to him. Roger flew us out to LA. He was going to be on the *Johnny Cash Show*, the new TV show, which was the biggest thing that happened in my time as a songwriter here. Johnny Cash brought in all these people that might not have come to Nashville, like Joni Mitchell and James Taylor. All these people were coming in here. I had just gotten fired from my job down in the Gulf because I was spending too much time in Nashville. [*both laugh*] And Mickey said, "Great, because they got this new TV show going on in Nashville. Two acts a week come in to do the *Johnny Cash Show*, and we can pitch 'em songs. Every one of 'em." And we did. We were like their mascots. Mickey had a room at the motel where their headquarters was. The whole TV show was there, all the crew and everything, and we would pitch songs. Then he said, Roger Miller wants to fly us to LA, and he said we can pitch him songs there. So, we went out there to see him, and I was just thrilled. We were in first class. But he would go off in the morning and do a TV thing, and he'd come back at night and go to bed. And so, we didn't get a chance to see him.

COWAN: You never actually saw him?

KRISTOFFERSON: I never saw him at all! I thought, well, it was still nice to go out there and hang around and watch some of the TV stuff and everything. But I didn't pitch him any songs. Then we were flying *back* to Nashville together where he was gonna be recording, and he says, "Mickey tells me you got a song that I should hear." That was it. He cut "Bobby McGee" and another song or two of mine, I think "Darby's Castle" maybe, and "Best of All Possible Worlds."

COWAN: Fred Foster eventually said, "I want to make a record on you." Were you excited at the time or was it kind of daunting?

KRISTOFFERSON: Well, I was pretty amazed at everything that was happening at the time. I really didn't think that I was up to it. The only reason I was singing my own demos at the time was because my publishing company couldn't afford to hire a singer!

COWAN: *You* sing it! [*laughs*]

KRISTOFFERSON: Yeah, they just had me do 'em. I wasn't at all impressed with my own singing at the time. But Fred thought it was possible and got me in there and did it. I really owe him a lot of gratitude. He and Bob Beckham believed in me a lot more than I did at the time. Not that I didn't believe in myself, but I never thought of being a performer, because the voices that moved me are the same as the ones today. Like George Jones and Hank Williams, Lefty Frizzell and people who could really sing. And there was a difference to everything.

COWAN: But you obviously came to accept that.

KRISTOFFERSON: Oh, yeah. I'm amazed looking back from now that I wasn't more amazed. When I think of being there, being Dylan's janitor, and Jack Clement introducing me to Johnny Cash? Jack took the letter that my mother had written to me disowning me. I had read it first in Jack's office, and he said, "I've gotta have that letter! I have to show it to Johnny Cash."

COWAN: Was it basically saying that they disowned you because you've chosen that way of life?

KRISTOFFERSON: Yeah, and said, "You've always been a disappointment to us, but nothing is going to measure up to this. We always thought that it was kind of cute that you liked Hank Williams. But to find out that at your age, after years at Oxford, that you'd still idolize somebody like Johnny Cash? Nobody over the age of fifteen listens to that kind of music, and if they did, it wouldn't be anybody *we'd* want to know."

COWAN: [*laughs*]

KRISTOFFERSON: Well, Jack Clement had to show that to Johnny Cash. So, the first time I actually met Johnny was when I was working there at the studio at Columbia. He said that he had already read the letter, then he said, "It's always nice to get a letter from home, isn't it, Kris?" [*both laugh*] That's the first thing he ever said to me. I was the janitor. You could've scraped me off the ceiling.

COWAN: It's important to note here for our readers that you'd gone to college in Oxford. You were a Rhodes Scholar. You'd been offered a teaching position at West Point. I can see your mom's thinking. "After all this, he wants to be a hillbilly?"

KRISTOFFERSON: Yeah, well, y'know, eventually I can remember her being hugged by Johnny Cash, and she was just thrilled. [*laughs*] So we got past all of that.

COWAN: That's nice.

KRISTOFFERSON: . . . *Eventually.*

COWAN: And your dad? Did he live to see your success as well?

KRISTOFFERSON: No, not really the big success, but he told me that he understood what I was doin'. He said nobody could've told him not to be a pilot, although a lot of people did. He was in the Army Air Corps, and the Air Force, in two wars, and he had done just what he wanted to do. And he understood me. We had a good relationship.

COWAN: I went through the same issues with my parents. "What are you doing?" But, at the same time, I always hear my dad saying, somewhere in the background, you got to do what you want to do. Be true to yourself.

KRISTOFFERSON: Yes. Yes.

COWAN: Well, that's what I ended up doing. My dad, unfortunately, died when I was twenty-one. He didn't get to see that. It's so funny that you fight with them so much about the very thing they've told you to do all those years.

KRISTOFFERSON: Yeah, they finally realized that it was where my heart was. And that was all that mattered.

COWAN: I kind of get this feeling that you're the kind of person that once you make friends with somebody, it lasts a long time.

KRISTOFFERSON: It's true. One of the blessings of my life is that I've gotten to be close to people I idolized from afar. Like Johnny Cash. Roger Miller. Muhammad Ali. And these people I got really close to. Willie. Waylon. The fact that the janitor was up there singing right next to Johnny Cash. I remember one time I sang with him, I used to harmonize with him on one of his standards, and one time he finally said, "You know, nobody has ever sung harmony with me. Ever." I suddenly realized he didn't like it . . . *at all!*

COWAN: [*laughs*]

KRISTOFFERSON: I just felt horrible! So, I didn't the next show. And he felt so bad about it! [*laughs*]

COWAN: He asked you to sing again, didn't he?

KRISTOFFERSON: [*laughing*] Yeah, he asked me to sing again! Oh, God. But that's the way my whole life has been. It's just like a dream, y'know? You wake up, and all of a sudden, you're standing there with Johnny Cash, and Waylon, and Willie, and performing with them as if you're part of it. And you are! Nobody called us The Highwaymen and *That Guy*.

COWAN: Yeah, you always think that someone's gonna come in and say, "Ah, I caught you! I knew you were a fake!"

KRISTOFFERSON: [*laughs*] Yeah, get your ass back in there and empty the ashtrays!

COWAN: I want to ask you about your last record, *Feeling Mortal*. What a wonderful record. I love the production on it. I love what [producer] Don Was has done, and I love the musicians on it. Besides the songwriting, I just love that I get to hear you. I can hear your voice. Is that you singing with yourself on all these songs?

KRISTOFFERSON: Yeah. A couple of people sang with me on a couple of things, but I always sang the harmony. Don has been on my side. He's probably been the best thing that's ever happened to me as far as recording my songs goes. Way back in, shoot, '80, '79, right at a point when nobody wanted me for anything. This is right after *Heaven's Gate*, and Rita Coolidge and I had split up in an ugly divorce, and I was at the bottom of my life. And Don came in. Now he produces everybody, but at the time, he was more a musician than producer. But he really was into my music, really into my songs. Every record I made with him was probably the best stuff I've ever recorded because like you said, the important thing was the songs.

COWAN: I love hearing you sing with yourself and hearing your guitar. I know that Sara Watkins sang and played fiddle on one tune. But the first thing I was taken with was the atmosphere of the sound.

KRISTOFFERSON: That's great.

COWAN: Is "Mama Stewart" a fictional song?

KRISTOFFERSON: No, that was real. Mama Stewart was Rita's grandmother, and it's just what happened. From the time I met her, she amazed me. She couldn't see when I met her. I remember I was sitting in a room with her, and I had just been quiet and hadn't said anything, and when I did, she just looked over and said [*mimics the voice of an elderly woman*], "Well, Crisp . . ." She called me Crisp. She said, "Well, Crisp, you was just sittin' there rattin' on me!"

COWAN: [*both laugh*]

KRISTOFFERSON: Well, they took her out to California. I think she was ninety-four when she got her sight back. She just took it for granted that it was going to happen. She believed it. She said when she got on the plane that she was going all the way to heaven. She'd never been on a plane.

COWAN: That's amazing.

KRISTOFFERSON: It was incredible.

COWAN: The line in there that caught me is "another shining reason to believe."

KRISTOFFERSON: Yeah.

COWAN: Kris, I want to thank you so much. It's really been an honor and a pleasure to talk to you.

KRISTOFFERSON: Well, thank you, John, for asking questions I could answer.

5

"YOU CAN'T TELL NOTHIN' IN A MOVIE"

High on the Mountaintop with Miss Loretta Lynn

In 1985, New Grass Revival was offered an opening slot for Loretta Lynn at the Kennedy Center in Washington, D.C. To this day, that's a humbling sentence for a kid from Ohio to write. Of course, we jumped at the opportunity, and it led to a lifelong friendship. I still have a black-and-white photograph

Miss Loretta at the Grand Ole Opry, 1974. *Photofest*

of Loretta standing between guitarist Pat Flynn and me that I will try to grab if the house is on fire. A generation later, it was Loretta's daughter Patsy who graciously suggested that we conduct this interview at their home in Hurricane Mills. We stepped into Loretta's large, open kitchen, and she greeted us dressed in a lovely, business kind of way for company. She'd also covered almost all available table and countertop space with every kind of chip, cookie, candy, spread, and dip you could imagine. It was like winning the game of Candy Land for real.

We lost Loretta while this memoir was in production on October 4, 2022. I will forever be grateful for her staggering musical gifts, her sense of humor, and for her tireless inspiration to "stay true to yourself and never take your talent for granted."

JOHN COWAN: It seems like everybody seems to think they know a lot about you because of . . .

LORETTA LYNN: The movie.

COWAN: The movie. But you can't tell a whole life story in a movie.

LORETTA: You can't tell nothin' in a movie!

COWAN: So, were your mom and dad musically inclined at all?

LORETTA: Mommy and Daddy could pick up any instrument and play a tune on it. It didn't make any difference what it was. I thought everybody could do that. When I got married and moved away, nobody could sing. Everybody couldn't sing, y'know? Or play an instrument. I thought somethin' was wrong with them. I really did!

COWAN: Did you have guitars or autoharps in your house? What kind of instruments were in your house when you were little?

LORETTA: Well, there was somebody in the holler who would have a banjo or a fiddle or whatever, at all times, and it would go from one house to the other. They were just circulating all the time, one house to the other.

COWAN: Did you all sit around and sing songs with your mom and dad?

LORETTA: Me and my first cousin sang together. Mommy taught me the songs to sing when I was little. But outside of that, no.

COWAN: Did you guys sing in church and stuff like that?

LORETTA: Me and my first cousin would sing "If I Could Hear My Mother Pray Again." That's the one we sang in church. It was a little one-room schoolhouse. That's where we had church. My great-grandfather built that little schoolhouse. And grandpa went to school there. And my daddy went to school there. And we went to school there.

COWAN: Unbelievable. So, where did you meet your husband? Did he live in Butcher Holler, too?

LORETTA: Yup. He lived up one holler, and I lived up another. You know how a holler does?

COWAN: Yeah, sure.

LORETTA: It branches out into different . . . well, he was up one holler, and I lived up another. And he was bidding off the pies the night that I made my pie with salt [*laughs*], thinkin' that I had sugar, cause they was in the same brown paper sacks, y'know?

COWAN: So, you guys got married. You were pretty young. You were sixteen?

LORETTA: Oh, I wasn't that old. But that was old to me. Sixteen years old.

COWAN: Well, you were younger than I guessed.

LORETTA: Oh, yeah, I was younger than sixteen. I had four kids in school by the time I was twenty-one.

COWAN: Wow. Is it true that you didn't really start playing the guitar until he bought you the guitar for your anniversary?

LORETTA: I had learned to play, but I never had one. And this one was $19. You couldn't keep it in tune. He got it from Sears, I think. But it was a mess, the guitar was.

COWAN: When you started playing, how did you know what to do? How to tune it or where to put your fingers?

LORETTA: I learned to play a little bit as I was growing up 'cause, like I say, everybody in the holler, one family or the other, owned a fiddle or a guitar. Every family owned one instrument or the other. And they just kind of circulated through the holler. Everybody knew how to play.

COWAN: Did you guys have a radio when you were a little girl?

LORETTA: No. Mommy and Daddy got a radio when I probably was thirteen or fourteen years old.

COWAN: Was that when you first heard the Opry?

LORETTA: The Grand Ole Opry. We went to the neighbor's house to hear the Grand Ole Opry when I first heard it.

COWAN: Was there any particular song that you heard when that switch goes off? Was there a voice that you heard?

LORETTA: I *loved* Ernest Tubb! I loved Ernest Tubb. I liked to hear him sing "It's Been So Long Darlin'." Remember that song? [*sings*] "It's been so long, darlin', since I had a kiss from you . . ." That was my favorite song.

COWAN: So, Ernest Tubb was *it*.

LORETTA: Well, he was the big star. Him and Little Jimmy Dickens. Little Jimmy Dickens *was* little. "A-Sleeping at the Foot of the Bed." "Take an Old Cold Tater and Wait." Remember? That's what I heard when I first started listenin' to the Grand Ole Opry.

COWAN: Any women that you paid attention to, even way back then? Long before you heard Patsy?

LORETTA: I never heard a woman on the Grand Ole Opry.

COWAN: I guess there weren't too many back then.

LORETTA: If there were, they didn't stick out in my mind.

COWAN: Mm hmm.

LORETTA: Now, I got married, and we lived in the state of Washington for thirteen, fifteen years.

COWAN: Why did you guys go to Washington?

LORETTA: That's where Doo's daddy took *his* family. They lived out there for about five years. Then when me and Doo got married, me and him went to Washington.

COWAN: What was he doing for work at that time?

LORETTA: Farming. At the end, when we moved back here, he was a heavy-duty mechanic.

COWAN: Wow.

LORETTA: That's what he did.

COWAN: So, was it up there that you started writing songs?

LORETTA: Yeah, it was up there. I wrote my first song probably when I was twenty-three or twenty-four.

COWAN: Do you remember what it was?

LORETTA: Yeah, "Honky Tonk Girl."

COWAN: That was the first song you *ever wrote*?

LORETTA: That's the first song I ever wrote.

COWAN: Well, you're a gifted person, aren't you, if that was the first song you ever wrote?

LORETTA: Well, not really! [*laughs*] I mean, what else was I gonna record? [*laughs*] Nobody up there liked country music. There wasn't no country music out there.

COWAN: I was gonna ask you if you heard any out there?

LORETTA: There was no country music out there.

COWAN: So, you were just bringing with you what you knew.

LORETTA: What I knew. And right at the end, Buck Owens started doin' a little half-hour show on television from Tacoma, Washington. So, where did we go? We went to Tacoma to get on Buck Owens's TV show. And I won the show that night. It was on a Saturday night, and there was about seven or eight people that did the show, and I won. I got a watch. The next day, it fell apart!

COWAN: [*laughs*]

LORETTA: So, I call Buck Owens up, and say, "Hey Buck! My watch just fell all apart." And he says, "Well, Loretta, what do you expect for three dollars?" [*both laugh*] I couldn't believe he only give three dollars for that watch! I figured it was a hundred-dollar watch! Knowin' me, I didn't know how much stuff was. I figured he'd get a hundred dollars for that watch. And it just fell apart. [*imitates Buck*] "What do you expect for three dollars?" Tore me up!

COWAN: I think one thing that's always been different, to this day, for women in country music is that it wasn't that common for women who were stars to be writing their own songs. And you started off by writing your own songs.

LORETTA: You know, when I come to Nashville, Kitty Wells was the only one that I'd ever heard of, besides Patsy Cline. Patsy was on the *Arthur Godfrey Show*. That's where I seen her, and she wasn't country. She was singing a different kind of a song. It was pop music really. "I Fall to Pieces" and "I Go Out Walkin'." That wasn't country. But that's what I heard.

COWAN: So, you're up in Washington. You're playing the guitar. What made you decide, I'm going to write a song?

LORETTA: Well, Doolittle pushed me out on the stage one night. He took me to this dance. And he never took me anywhere, so I shoulda' known somethin' was up, 'cause I never got to go nowhere. Never! He took me to this dance, and he pushed me out on the stage and told the band, "She's the greatest singer. Next to Kitty Wells, she cain't be beat!" Well, the band looked at me like he's crazy, and you are, too! [*both laugh*] I said the only song I knew was "There He Goes" by Webb Pierce. Remember that old one? [*sings*] "There he goes. He's walkin' away . . ." That was the only song I knew. And I sang that song, and they give me a job.

COWAN: Wow.

LORETTA: For Saturday night, yeah. They said, next Saturday night, we'll give you five dollars. Man, I was there with bells on, you know. [*laughs*]

COWAN: Was it through Buck that you wound up making a record for Zero?*

LORETTA: No, it was a guy who had seen me. He was a logger. Or, he owned the logging outfit. He didn't do the loggin', but other people did for him. He owned this big outfit in Vancouver, Canada, and he seen me on the *Buck Owens Show*. First time on his show.

COWAN: The night you won the watch?

LORETTA: Yeah. The night I won the watch. He recorded me. He sent me to LA to record in some little tiny studio. The reason I remember the guy's name that recorded me is *my* daddy was Ted Webb. And his name was Ted. So I remember the guy that recorded the song.

COWAN: Was that the session that you did "Honky Tonk Girl"?

LORETTA: "Honky Tonk Girl," yeah.

COWAN: So, did you do four songs? Six songs?

LORETTA: I done a whole album.

COWAN: You did?

LORETTA: I done a whole album in one day. We didn't sing 'em over one time.

---

* Zero Records was Loretta's first record label, founded in Vancouver, British Columbia, in 1959. Her first single and the first song she ever wrote, "Honky Tonk Girl," went to number fourteen on the U.S. Country charts. She would eventually record more than fifty Top 10 hits.

COWAN: So, at that point you made a record, and now he has you. Was there some decision made about it? Like, "OK, *now* what are we gonna do? We gotta get out of there and . . ."

LORETTA: They didn't know what to do, and neither did I. We just made the record. It was a little studio, like I said. We put the record out, and I went out working with the record, y'know? Meeting all the disc jockeys. And they put it number fourteen across the nation.

COWAN: Did you drive all the way back?

LORETTA: We drove all the way to Nashville. All the way back, a different way. We hit every station we could hit. A lot of the disc jockeys would say, hey, we don't play your country records in here. Or they'd make me feel real bad, you know? It was hard, but I did it.

COWAN: What'd you do with the kids when you guys were out there? Did they go with you?

LORETTA: My brother and his wife.

COWAN: They watched after them for you?

LORETTA: Mm hmm. For a month. A whole month.

COWAN: So you guys just loaded up and went everywhere? And anyone who'd open the door, you'd go in there?

LORETTA: We'd go in there.

COWAN: Did you have to play music, too? Or just play the record?

LORETTA: Oh, sometimes I'd sing before they'd even play my record. I'd say, "Well, I can sing. Do you want me to sing?" It was terrible. It was a bad thing, but I didn't know any better. And it was a good thing I didn't know any better.

COWAN: 'Cause you probably wouldn't have done it.

LORETTA: That's right.

COWAN: So, your record had gone to fourteen. Is that when MCA came to you?

LORETTA: No. I had come back to Nashville.

COWAN: Did you move back?

LORETTA: We moved back. When the record hit number fourteen across the nation, I had left three thousand quarts of stuff canned. That's the only thing I hated was leaving my canned stuff, you know? That's what happened.

COWAN: Well, back then, that's what we had to live on.

LORETTA: If you didn't can it, you didn't have it! They'd let me pick potatoes in the fall when everything was over, and they'd quit selling potatoes. I could go in and pick up potatoes. And I would do that and have 'em all winter long. Put 'em in the cellar!

COWAN: So, where'd you settle in Nashville when you came? What part of town did y'all move to?

LORETTA: Madison.

COWAN: Did you rent a house? Buy a house?

LORETTA: We rented the house. Why, heck, we didn't have money enough to rent it, let alone buy it. [*laughs*] But that's what we did.

COWAN: What's the next thing that happened in terms of getting a recording contract?

LORETTA: Well, I was in Nashville, and I was at a radio station every day and every night. I mean, I didn't stop. It wasn't easy for me. It was hard. It was something that no women did. Like I said, there was no women singing country music. Kitty Wells had a record out, "Honky Tonk Angel." But as far as country music singers, Jean Shepard had one out with Ferlin Husky called "Dear John," remember that? [*sings*] "Dear John. Oh, how I hate to write."

COWAN: So back in Nashville, how did you wind up getting the record deal?

LORETTA: I went in and met Doyle and Teddy, the Wilburn Brothers. Their names were on the door, so, naturally, I had their record with Ernest

Tubb. [*Loretta sings*] "Hey, little bluebird . . ." Remember that? Well, I had never heard it, but that was the name of the song on the record. I picked it up because Ernest Tubb was on it, and I was an Ernest Tubb fan. I seen the Wilburn Brothers on the door, so I went in and told them who I was and the record I had out, and they played my record, and Teddy looked over at Doyle and said, "Well, the only thing I can say is, she sounds too much like Kitty Wells." That broke my heart. I thought, well, that sounds pretty good if you can sound like Kitty Wells!

COWAN: Yeah.

LORETTA: You're a pretty good singer! [*laughs*]

COWAN: Absolutely.

LORETTA: But, they kinda dropped it there. I kept on going down to see them every day. Every day I was in their office. They either had to do something with me or run me off! [*both laugh*] So they started pushing my record to Decca Records and Owen Bradley, who they recorded for. So, he took me.

COWAN: And then, those records, almost forever, were done by Owen.

LORETTA: Oh, yeah. Owen was my producer forever. One of the greatest producers in Nashville. I don't care what you were recordin'. Pop, rock, country, whatever, Owen Bradley was the best. And we sure lost a good one when we lost him.

COWAN: I know you loved Ernest Tubb. Had you met him before you guys did "Mr. and Mrs. Used to Be"?

LORETTA: No. Ernest was a different person than most people. He was just such a great guy.

COWAN: Just genuinely sweet.

LORETTA: Yeah, he'd do anything for anybody. And I heard about that he would drink when he was younger. I heard that he was the meanest thing that ever was when he got drunk. So, I said to Ernest, not thinking anything about it, I said, "Ernest, I hear when you get drunk, you're quite a character." And he said, "Oh, hon, I hope you never see me drunk." I never did. He completely quit by the time him and I recorded.

COWAN: So when did you finally meet?

LORETTA: Doyle and Teddy had me at a meeting. I did the Grand Ole Opry, and naturally I was wantin' to see Ernest Tubb, and Ernest wasn't there that night. But I kept on until I seen Ernest Tubb, and Ernest put me on the *Ernest Tubb Record Shop*. That night, Doyle was drinkin'. And when Doyle got drunk, y'know, Doyle could make some bad mistakes. [*both laugh*] Him and Teddy, they'd fight like cats and dogs, and I'd usually have to be the one to . . .

COWAN: Step in between them?

LORETTA: Step in between them! But I loved them boys. Doyle got really upset with Teddy and told Teddy, "If you're gonna work with Loretta, you better start working with her instead of letting her do all the work, and you sitting by and watchin' her!" Well, that didn't go over real good. So him and Doyle had a big fight about that. And of course, Doyle loved to drink, and Teddy didn't like that. Teddy moved to LA. And that didn't work either. If they woulda' stayed together, y'know, them boys coulda' really been a lot bigger than they were.

COWAN: When I was a kid growing up in Louisville, they had a TV show that I watched on Saturdays.*

LORETTA: Yeah, I was on that.

COWAN: I was a rock 'n' roll kid growing up. But that was the first time that I saw country music. Every Saturday, the *Wilburn Brothers* TV show would come on.

---

* The *Wilburn Brothers* was a syndicated TV show of classic country singing and playing that lasted for eleven years. It featured a who's who of country artists who many fans like me were introduced to for the first time, including Loretta, Dolly Parton, Patty Loveless, Waylon Jennings, Willie Nelson, George Jones, Tammy Wynette, Tom T. Hall, and Hank Snow. Doyle and Teddy Wilburn were the original managers of Loretta's Sure-Fire Music Co. label.

LORETTA: I had that part on that show, no matter who the guy was, whether it would be Bill Anderson, whoever . . .

COWAN: You were the duet singer?

LORETTA: No. I was the girl singer. Whoever got the TV show, I was already hired for the girl singer. But I never told Doyle and Teddy that.

COWAN: They didn't know?

LORETTA: No, and I never did tell 'em!

COWAN: [*laughs*]

LORETTA: Never did tell 'em.

COWAN: I wanted to ask you about your songwriting. You got started writing your own songs early. You got your foot in the door. Had big hits. You've been on the Opry. Have you continued to write songs all the way up to now?

LORETTA: Oh, yes.

COWAN: Do you just love to write music? Or is it a pain in the butt? [*laughs*]

LORETTA: I'd rather write than sing. I like to write. It's kinda like, "Here, this is how I feel." That the whole time that Doo was alive, if I got upset with him, I'd write about it. Since he's been gone, I've kinda let down on my writing, and that's bad for me to do, 'cause I *love* to write.

COWAN: And you're so gifted at it.

LORETTA: I love to do it.

COWAN: So let's talk a little more about what you said a minute ago. If you and your husband were having problems, you might go off and write a song about him. Think about all the songs we know because of that.

LORETTA: You got it. [*laughs*]

COWAN: "You Ain't Woman Enough to Take My Man." "Don't Come Home A-Drinkin' . . ."

LORETTA: "Fist City."

COWAN: And it goes on and on.

LORETTA: It goes on and on.

COWAN: What did he think about that?

LORETTA: He'd just grin. He knew where I got 'em from. You couldn't fool Doolittle. I mean, that'd be like fooling God almost! [*laughs*] Here I am comparing him to God—*no I am not!* But trying to fool him would be bad.

COWAN: I know that you're uncomfortable with people using the term "feminist" because that's not what this was about for you. But, at least to my way of thinking, you were one of the first female voices in country music, just talking about what life was really like.

LORETTA: Well, I wrote it like it was. I didn't realize that nobody did that.

COWAN: Nobody'd done it.

LORETTA: I know! I don't understand that. I never could understand that. Why?

COWAN: You'd probably agree that the best songwriting are songs that are just purely honest.

LORETTA: Or true.

COWAN: And then there were some songs that radio wouldn't play, right? Like, "The Pill" and "Dear Uncle Sam."

LORETTA: "The Pill"? You'd a thought I shot somebody.

COWAN: Right.

LORETTA: I couldn't figure out why. Why are they making such a big deal out of this? Every woman I knew at the time was taking the pill. Every woman except me. And I had the kids to prove it! [*both laugh*] I had a whole house full of kids!

COWAN: I was listening to "Dear Uncle Sam" today. Did that come out right at the peak of the Vietnam War?

LORETTA: It did. The war was all you could hear on the radio. My husband was in the car, and I said, "Honey, I hate this war. I can't stand it. That's all you hear on the radio." And he said, "Well, write about it." And that's where "Dear Uncle Sam" comes from. Who better to write to than dear Uncle Sam?

COWAN: What is nice to me about that song is that not only were you singing that war is a terrible thing. You're also saying, "I love my country."

LORETTA: But I also love my man.

COWAN: Exactly. That was beautiful. I guess you took a lot of what they say in England, "shite," for that song.

LORETTA: Oh, yeah, I did. And "One's on the Way"? I mean to tell you, you'd a thought I'd a killed somebody for recording that. I didn't understand that either. Why? Because maybe it was good to be dumb. [laughs] It was good to be not smart about everything.* I think it was.

COWAN: That wouldn't be my take on that song.

LORETTA: Well, it was a lot of people's take.

COWAN: Once again, you're just expressing an honest woman's viewpoint.

LORETTA: Yeah, but no other woman had done it, and no other man would dare put his name on a song like that. It was weird how people felt about writing. I never could understand it.

COWAN: At the time, whenever you would run into that kind of controversy in your life, did it hurt your feelings? Did you get angry? Or, did you just say, well, whatever. I did what I did.

LORETTA: There wasn't no use gettin' mad about it because I knew there was people out there that were stupider than me! But I figured, well

---

* "One's on the Way" was written by the hugely talented Chicago-born writer, poet, and cartoonist Shel Silverstein. Shel also wrote "Hey, Loretta" for Loretta, "A Boy Named Sue" for Johnny Cash, and "Cover of the Rolling Stone" for Dr. Hook as well as the books *The Giving Tree* and *Where the Sidewalk Ends*. He was inducted into the Nashville Songwriters Hall of Fame in 2002.

here they all are having kids, but they don't want to talk about it. Everything I wrote about was life. A lot of people didn't want to talk about that. It didn't bother me to.

COWAN: Did you ever have those moments, at different parts of your life, knowing where you came from, a little mining town near Paintsville, Kentucky, and you're at the White House,* or had those moments where you . . .

LORETTA: You know, a lot of people have brought that up and even brought it up when I *was* at the White House. "Did you ever think you'd be here? Blah, blah . . ." It hadn't fazed me. I figure, why not? You don't have to be a college-educated idiot. [*laughs*] A lot of people didn't think I should be singin' some of the stuff I sing, but I sung it, and I'm glad I did.

COWAN: Yeah, 'cause that's opening doors for a lot of other people to go through.

LORETTA: It really is.

COWAN: That's the hardest thing.

LORETTA: Yeah, and I couldn't understand why somebody else hadn't thought about it. I imagine Owen Bradley did because Owen probably said [*snaps her fingers*], "There's another hit." [*laughs*]

COWAN: Did you ever come to him with songs, and he would say, "Boy, Loretta, I don't know."

LORETTA: No, he never said that to me. Only thing he said to me, after Conway Twitty died, and I'll never forget it because we were all having a tough time with Conway passing away so young, he told me, "You're gonna have to get back into writin'. Writin' your own songs! Do you hear me?" Oh, he was scolding me like I was a little kid. To him, I guess I was because I had been with him so long.

---

* Loretta was a Kennedy Center Honoree in 2003, along with James Brown, Itzhak Perlman, Carol Burnett, and director Mike Nichols.

COWAN: It's almost like having another dad.

LORETTA: At first, I had to sit down and sing at least twenty-five songs for him to pick one. And I had to be singing my own stuff. He wanted to hear more of me and nobody else. He didn't want nobody else writin' for me, and I couldn't figure that out because when I got so busy on the road, I needed somebody to help, y'know? He didn't like it. He wanted me to write. He said, "Ain't nobody can write like you can for yourself. Write! I don't wanna hear you bringin' stuff in here that don't belong to you." And he would really get . . . The only one he never jumped me about was Shel Silverstein. He wrote, "Hey, Loretta!," and I didn't want to sing it because I felt like people would think I was braggin' on myself. So I really raised holy heck. Well, Owen got a little uptight about it. He said, "I'm telling you right now, you need to sing that song." Well, I didn't want to sing it, and I really just had it as, more or less, a throwaway thing. Then, when it come out, everybody was hollerin', "Hey, Loretta!" It was like something that nobody would ever expect me to do.

COWAN: Now, I want to ask you, when you're in the thick of it making the records with Owen, did you come back in after the fact or would you sing along while they're cutting the tracks?

LORETTA: I would sing with the band there.

COWAN: Like a scratch vocal?

LORETTA: Yeah. While the band was there, we would make the record.

COWAN: But then would you go back in and resing it?

LORETTA: No.

COWAN: Wow, those are live vocals?

LORETTA: Those are all live vocals. Oh, yeah. Everything I ever recorded with Owen Bradley are.

COWAN: Did you ever think you were a great singer?

LORETTA: No. I know to carry a tune. You don't really know how good you are.

COWAN: I'm just saying that one of the reasons we all love you, besides your words, is your voice.

LORETTA: Well, thank you! [*laughs*]

COWAN: I'd like to talk to you a little bit about your recording relationship with Conway Twitty, which was so unbelievable. You guys had so many hits together.

LORETTA: He was such a great guy. You know, he was the only person in the music business that my husband really loved. My husband really loved Conway Twitty.

COWAN: Was Owen the person who said let's get Conway and Loretta to sing?

LORETTA: No! That was me and Conway. We went to England together on tour, and me and Conway got together on the way back and said, "Hey, wonder how it would be if we recorded together?" We were on the same label.

COWAN: Right.

LORETTA: So, when we come in, we talked to Owen. Owen said, well, Ernest is not gonna be happy about that.

COWAN: Right, because you had two singles with Ernest.

LORETTA: Yeah, but Ernest was OK with it. He didn't care.

COWAN: That was a long and wonderful recording relationship.

LORETTA: Twelve years. We had twelve albums.

COWAN: [*laughs*]

LORETTA: We had twelve albums together. We were like sister and brother. I'd know what Conway wouldn't like and what he would like. And he knew that I'd sing about anything as long as it was a hit. He said he didn't worry about me, because he knew I'd sing anything with him. He said, as long as it's a good song, Loretta will sing it.

COWAN: Most of us first heard him do "It's Only Make Believe." That's such an amazing song.

LORETTA: That was his first song, too.

COWAN: I know. But if you look at the chords of that song, it's very sophisticated.

LORETTA: Oh, I know it. And he tried to be sophisticated with it. Because you know he preached till he was seventeen years old. Did you know that?

COWAN: I did not know that.

LORETTA: I didn't know it either. When I heard about it, I couldn't believe it. But he did.

COWAN: And talk about a hard song to sing. You know that song keeps going up and up and up?

LORETTA: Yeah, I know, I've sung it!

COWAN: [*both laugh*] I'm sure you have. It's like jumping over hurdles, isn't it?

LORETTA: Yeah, I did it the first time in the *Ernest Tubb Record Shop*, without Conway. I did "Only Make Believe." He was in the hospital, and he couldn't believe that I sang that song for him.

COWAN: He probably loved it, didn't he?

LORETTA: Oh, yeah. He loved it. He was such a good guy.

COWAN: I'd like for you to talk for a minute about how you met Patsy Cline.

LORETTA: Well, when we come to Nashville, I think I met her backstage at the Opry. She tore her skirt getting to the stage, and she was madder than a hornet. I asked her what was wrong, and she said she tore her skirt gettin' on the stage. From there on, we were just friends. We talked every time we seen each other, and we just got closer and closer. She had me and Doo come over and have dinner with her. So we got close that way, y'know? We were just close. I've often wondered what it would've been like if she'd have lived. [*quiet pause*] She died within a year after I come to Nashville. She died in one of them little old Cherokee planes, is that the name of 'em?

COWAN: Yup.

LORETTA: And I hated that worse than anything because I always bragged to her about being Cherokee and Irish. After that plane went down, I didn't care if anybody ever heard of Cherokee after that, you know, I was upset so bad. That night I remember listening. The wind was blowing so bad that night that that plane went down. And that was in March, wasn't it? The wind was blowin' real bad that night, 'cause I remember listenin' to it.

COWAN: Did your life change when the movie came out?

LORETTA: When we did the movie, I think more people knew about us. But you had to be known pretty good to get a movie made about you in the first place. So, it just kinda added on.

COWAN: Think about the millions of people who saw that who didn't know country music from Adam. Suddenly they get exposed to you, and the history. You must've made millions of new fans you never had before that.

LORETTA: Well, you're right. I worked by myself most of the time. I miss working with other people. For the last five to ten years, I've just worked by myself. I like to work with other people.

COWAN: I do, too. I like teamwork.

LORETTA: Yeah.

COWAN: Plus, it's not so much responsibility for yourself! [*laughs*]

LORETTA: Yeah, except for me. If nobody's there, it's my problem. If the place is full, it's my problem. But I miss working with somebody.

COWAN: Were you pretty hands-on for the movie since it came from your book?

LORETTA: Yes, I had Sissy on the road with me for a year! She had me wore completely out. She did. It was rough. It'd be four o'clock in the morning before I'd get to sleep, because she'd be asking me all kinds of questions about how it was when I was this old or that old, cause she was fixin' to do the movie. And she had me wore out. Then, when the movie come out, it was tiresome because I was trying to keep up with her goin' from here to there promoting the movie. That liked to kill me, too. [*laughs*] So I was doin' my job, and that one, too! It was rough.

COWAN: Care to talk about your *Van Lear Rose* record?

LORETTA: [*smiling*] With Jack. Jack White.

COWAN: Was Nancy Russell, your manager, the one whose idea it was for you and Jack to make a record?

LORETTA: She brought it up one day. Wouldn't it be great if y'all made a record? Well, I'd never heard Jack sing, and I thought that's what she meant. Me singing with Jack White. I said, "Well, what does he sing?" I thought maybe he was country, and I just didn't know it. She said, "Well, he's rock and roll." It kinda shocked me to think that she thought that I would work with him. I said, "Well, maybe you'll have to introduce me to him." And he come down for dinner, and I made chicken and dumplin's.

COWAN: Ooh.

LORETTA: And that's the first chicken and dumplin's I guess he ever ate. Because he's laughing . . .

COWAN: He's from Detroit.

LORETTA: From Detroit, yeah. But you know he'd been married, and his wife played drums for him. His ex-wife. I said, "Jack, tell me what's wrong with your ex-wife?" And he said, "What do you mean?" I said, "Something's wrong with her." He said, "I don't know what you're talking about." And I said, "She just acts like she ain't in this world. She acts like she's from another world. You know? She just hits the drums and looks straight ahead. Never speaks to nobody." It's true. I never did find out. He said there wasn't nothin' wrong with her. But I say there is! [*laughs*]

COWAN: Had those songs for *Van Lear Rose* been sitting around, or did you just say, I'm making a record, so I better write twelve or thirteen songs?*

LORETTA: Oh, no, I've got songs you wouldn't believe. I've got a lot of songs wrote that nobody's ever heard. I'm liable to take a notion and do another album with nothing but myself.

COWAN: Well, you should.

LORETTA: Yeah, I will. I'll do it.

COWAN: So, you're working on what they're calling an Appalachian record?

LORETTA: Yeah, we've got that finished, I think.

COWAN: Is it traditional songs? Your songs?

LORETTA: Yeah, some of them are mine, and some of them are hill songs.

COWAN: So you're using banjos and fiddles?

LORETTA: Banjos and fiddles, yeah. It's bluegrass. Old hill stuff. Stuff like I've listened to when I was little, growing up.

COWAN: So it's like full circle, isn't it?

LORETTA: It is. Yeah, it really is. That's what I started listening to.

COWAN: And here you are.

LORETTA: Going back down and doin' what I heard from the start.

COWAN: That's sweet.

LORETTA: Well, I think Jack wants to sing on one of the albums, and I think it will probably be the bluegrass album. That's my opinion. I think he'd want to sing one of them bluegrass songs.

---

* Loretta and Jack White recorded this entire album in two weeks, including eight songs in one day, on old eight-track studio equipment.

COWAN: He'd be perfect because you know, even though he's a rock singer, he has a high, lonesome voice.

LORETTA: I know. He loves bluegrass country music. He does.

COWAN: I can see that. And the tone of his voice, it's not that different from Del McCoury's or Bill Monroe's.

LORETTA: [*laughs hard*] You're right! Bill Monroe. I've never thought of that, but you're right. Yeah.

COWAN: You ought to get him to sing "Uncle Pen" or something.

LORETTA: [*sings*] "Late in the evenin', about sundown . . ." I bet he could do it, too!

COWAN: I bet he could. Well, OK, Miss Loretta, I think I've got what I need.

LORETTA: Well, if you haven't, John, you just holler. [*laughs*]

6

RODNEY CROWELL AND A BLESSING FOR THE UNFINISHED SONG

I followed Emmylou Harris right out of the chute from "Pieces of the Sky" to the present day. Like a musician-geek-detective, I scoured the back of her albums with my musicologist's magnifying glass searching for clues that could explain the otherworldly nature of the music I was hearing. That was the first time I ever read the name Rodney Crowell, but it surely would not be the last.

Courtesy Brian Smith

Songwriter, guitarist, vocalist. Hmm. Who is this guy? This guy, it turns out, is considered by many to be the godfather of Americana music.

Rodney's story-songs and studies of the heart, including classics like "Ain't Livin' Long Like This" and "Shame on the Moon" have been recorded by the likes of Waylon Jennings, Bob Seger, Etta James, Keith Urban, the Grateful Dead, Willie Nelson, Johnny Cash, and of course, Emmylou. He's a two-time Grammy Award winner and in 2006, received the Lifetime Achievement Award in Songwriting from the American Music Association. His 1988 album *Diamonds & Dirt* was the first country album ever to have five consecutive number one singles on the country chart.

While producing Rosanne Cash's album *Hits 1979–1989* (yes, he's a producer, too), Rodney invited me to come sing on it, which ignited a musical and personal friendship that has lasted for more than three decades. For this interview, we met in the home he shares with his wife Claudia in Thompson Station, Tennessee. We started our visit by talking about his earliest influences, his mom and dad back in Texas.

RODNEY CROWELL: My mother and father were dirt-poor sharecropper farm kids. My dad took me to see Hank Williams when I was two years old. Two years and four months to be exact, in December of 1952. I had just enough of a memory of it, and my dad told me the story over and over and over enough, that I was able to create a kind of impressionistic memory of that. That was the music that was going nonstop around our house on a little record player on the floor. You know, none of those records were in their dust sleeves. They were just lying on the floor. All scratched. That to me is how music sounds best. Just scratchy. Scratchy old 78s.

JOHN COWAN: You've been characterized as a singer-songwriter. I'm not sure when this term came along, perhaps with James Taylor and Jackson Browne and people like that.

CROWELL: Probably it was somebody in management or a press officer in promotion one day said, "We got this Joni Mitchell. She's a singer *and* a songwriter. Boy, you know, that's like ringing the big one." It's like, that'll stick. It became a buzzword.

COWAN: I'm sure you don't think it's unflattering.

CROWELL: No, I'll pretty much accept 'em all now. It's like, boy, if I could just get somebody to call me a poet, I think that's the one I would lie in the weeds for. I'd give 'em a puppy dog look and say, aw, please tell me I'm a poet!

COWAN: [*laughs*] There you go.

CROWELL: I want to be a poet! Then I'll be good and poor.

COWAN: Well, maybe not. [*both laugh*] When I talked to Leon Russell, I asked him about a particular song he's known for, "A Song for You."

CROWELL: Mm hmm.

COWAN: While it's become a standard, it's never really been a hit. But it's been covered by a lot of different people. A beautiful song. I asked him, were you just writing a song that day? And he said, absolutely not. He said, my intention was to write a song that Ray Charles or Frank Sinatra could sing.

CROWELL: Wow.

COWAN: He said, for all you songwriters out there, hits are great, but standards live forever.

CROWELL: I know what he means. Timelessness is pretty good.

COWAN: Right now, your song "Please Remember Me" is a hit for a second time.

CROWELL: Is it?

COWAN: Scotty McCreary, and earlier Tim McGraw had a hit on it.

CROWELL: I know it was on *American Idol*. I know it's being played on there, and I'm grateful.

COWAN: When I first heard the Scotty McCreary version, I started looking around on the internet and noticed that that and "Song for a Life" had been covered by a ton of people from Emmylou to Alan Jackson, as well as "Shame on the Moon." I think it would be safe to say that you've written some songs that people are probably going to cover for a long, long time. If there are natural-born singers, is it fair to say there are natural-born songwriters? Do you believe that?

CROWELL: I do.

COWAN: I do, too. I am not one, but I have the pleasure of knowing some, like yourself.

CROWELL: Well, I was lucky to stumble on to some natural-born songwriters at exactly the right moment, meaning Guy Clark and Mickey Newbury and Townes Van Zant. You know, when I first came to Nashville in '72, Kris Kristofferson's glory was everywhere. They call Hank Williams the "Hillbilly Shakespeare." But it was Kris Kristofferson who came along and was acknowledged as a poet. A Rhodes Scholar, genius, poet. And so, on the street, at the street level, we all wanted to be Kristofferson, man. We'd gone from wanting to be the Beatles, to wanting to be Bob Dylan, to wanting to be Kristofferson. But when I got to Nashville, I bumped into Guy Clark, who was Guy Clark. He didn't want to be Kris Kristofferson. He was already Guy Clark and writing "L.A. Freeway" and "Desperados Waiting for a Train." And Townes Van Zandt was Townes Van Zandt, writing "Pancho and Lefty" and "Mr. Mud and Mr. Gold." And Mickey Newbury was perhaps the genius of that whole crew. Mickey Newbury was the biggest influence on my songwriting, of anybody, still to this day. Without Mickey Newbury, I would not have written "Till I Gain Control Again."*

---

* Kris Kristofferson has said the same thing about Newberry, one of America's greatest songwriters. "I'm sure that I never would've written 'Bobby McGee' or 'Sunday Morning Coming Down' if I had never known Mickey." Newberry's songs, which include "American Trilogy," "Heaven Help the Child," and "It Doesn't Matter Anymore" have been covered more than a thousand times. His songs defy easy categorization, which is why he has been compared to other songwriters like Randy Newman and Tom Waits.

COWAN: Were those guys open to a kid who just came up here?

CROWELL: Guy Clark was definitely open. Guy Clark was the most generous songwriter that I was around. Townes was truly a genius. I recognized that as a young man. But Townes was also very competitive. Townes wanted to fight you, and you had to earn his respect, and he gave respect grudgingly. Whereas Guy was like, "Come here, man. What are you up to? What do you want to know?" And Newbury was in his world. He heard some music somewhere, and he was following it. Turns out he followed it all the way to Oregon. But it was just great for me to be around, to stumble into that scene, because it could've gone another way for me. Maybe I am a natural-born songwriter. Or maybe I'm just a quick study, and I got around these guys and went, "Oh." These guys don't want to be Dylan. They don't want to be this star image. They are already working artists, and they are already realizing themselves.

COWAN: That's where I think the notion of singer-songwriter was really a healthy thing. What I make of that period of time was that you were a thriving community of poets who were sponges to the craziness that was going on in the early '70s. We were all out driving around in vans, taking copious amounts of drugs, and having a great time creating with other people. I'm guessing that the same thing was happening to you in its own little greenhouse.

CROWELL: Yes. It just happened to be that the one that I fell into was very much about language and music. It's where language and music meet. If I take the liberty of imagining you, John, coming up, vocal gift that you have, playing in bands, then you guys were trying to figure out how to express music, how to get your voice to work with that group and everything. You had to have songs, but it was a performance-based ideology. Whereas where *I* came in, it was a writing-based ideology, and the musicianship came back later.

COWAN: Was there a natural amount of discipline that went along with that—an idea that this is my job, and I'm really going to be disciplined about it—or did it just come organically?

CROWELL: It did happen organically. Let's take Picasso, one of the iconic artists of all time. The man got up and worked every day. [*laughs*] He went to work being Picasso. Without sort of noticing over the years, I realize that I get up and I work every day. I work every day. I goof off a few days, but chances are that if I'm goofing off really good, and I'm in a place where I'm not thinking about anything but "relax," that might be when I write the best song. When I'm *not* trying. But I work at it every day.

COWAN: I read a piece about a guy I have great respect for, John Mayer. He did a conference recently in Boston, and he talked about changing his way of thinking, which was, don't throw stuff away. Don't start something and throw it away. Finish it. Is that what you do?

CROWELL: Absolutely. God bless the unfinished song, because sometimes the unfinished song is what get's me back to work. I go, man, I really got to unlock this one, and then something else creeps out, and I'll write a whole song while I'm trying to figure out why I can't unlock the mystery of this one song. And then again, it's like, *finish* them. They're not all going to be good. I've written hundreds and hundreds of songs. I've probably recorded 115, 120 songs myself, and let's say half of them are really good songs and could last, and I could sing for anybody. Well that's fifty or sixty songs. Well, fifty or sixty songs, out of a thousand? You know? Those other 950 songs all went into the fifty that were good.

COWAN: I've always been a fan of your music. You've been really consistent. Do you have that feeling as well?

CROWELL: Well, thank you, John. I always strive to be consistent, and I still maintain that I'm trying to paint my masterpiece every time I do one of those things. Otherwise, why bother? I wanna make "Moondance" or "Sgt.

Pepper's," the Rodney version of it. The most honest thing I can say is, for the past ten years, really, when you started helping me out on my records, the records that I started around 2000, with *The Houston Kid*, from then on, I feel are very consistent. I think the ones that led up to it were sometimes inspired and sometimes for me, flat. I think back then, I was still more interested in claiming my acreage in the stardom pantheon when I was making those records. It was somewhere around 2000 that I became more dedicated to the art.*

COWAN: I want to work my way up to the record, "Ain't Living Long Like This," which, for most of us, is how you reached our consciousness, so to speak. I guess that's a result of your association with Emmylou Harris.

CROWELL: Mm hmm.

COWAN: What I was curious about is, did you get songs to her before you were a member of The Hot Band?

CROWELL: That's how I *became* a member of The Hot Band. Emmylou heard them and started recording them.

COWAN: Is "Leaving Louisiana" on her first record?

CROWELL: No, it's "Bluebird Wine."

COWAN: So, you had a song on her very first record?

CROWELL: Yes, I did. Opening track. And then, "A Song for the Life," "Till I Gain Control Again," and "American Dream," that the Dirt Band did. They were all on that tape.

COWAN: Oh, wow. How long was that period of time that it took to create that little canon of songs?

CROWELL: To write them?

COWAN: Yeah.

---

* In his wonderful 1997 autobiography, Johnny Cash said, "I don't listen to music on the farm unless I'm going into songwriting mode and looking for inspiration. Then I'll put on something by the writers I've admired and used for years—Rodney Crowell, John Prine, Guy Clark, and the late Steve Goodman are my Big Four."

CROWELL: Oh, a couple years.

COWAN: So, you were knocking around and . . .

CROWELL: I was knocking around for about six months, and then it *bloomed*. It took me the first six months I was here. Maybe nine months. But being around songwriters like I'm telling you, it sort of bloomed. And then I wrote, "A Song for the Life" and "Till I Gain Control Again" and "Bluebird Wine," and the next thing I know, I'm a professional songwriter.

COWAN: You were young and probably good to go joining The Hot Band. What were you, twenty-three or twenty-four?

CROWELL: Twenty-four.

COWAN: That must've been a pretty heady experience. When we look back now at the musicians in that band, yourself included, it's pretty ridiculous.

CROWELL: Well, it was ridiculous for me. My musicianship wasn't up to any of those guys' level by any stretch of the imagination.* The only reason that I was in that band was because, in me, Emmy had a confidant and a songwriter. I think that gave Emmylou more of a reason to have me because she could've had Herb Pedersen playing guitars and mandolins and fiddles and singing far better and more in tune than me. But I don't think Herb was writing songs like I was. I think that's why I stuck around. Eventually, I put out my first solo record, and I couldn't get a gig! [*laughs*] I had gone from Dodgers Stadium with Emmy to "I can't get a gig!" But the good thing about it was, I guess I *am* a natural-born songwriter, because all of those songs got recorded and caught on. All of those songs were covered. Several of them were number ones, you know, so suddenly I'm able to put a roof over my head. So, there's always been the songs for me.

---

* The Hot Band was an all-world group of musicians assembled by producer Brian Ahern to back Emmylou Harris on her first studio album. It consisted of several members of Elvis Presley's band (guitarist James Burton, pianist Glen Hardin, steel guitarist Hank DeVito, bassist Emory Gordy, and drummer John Ware) and eventually, Rodney. When James Burton couldn't tour with Emmy for contractual reasons with Elvis, Albert Lee joined the band.

COWAN: I remember this story you told me one time that was funny and sweet about when your dad said to you, "The sun doesn't make a sound going down." Tell that story.

CROWELL: Oh, yeah, well he heard the album *Ain't Living Long Like This*, and he said, [*imitates his dad's old voice*], "Well, I like your record pretty good, but that one song, you didn't get it right." And I said [*annoyed*], "Well, what song is that, Dad?"

COWAN: [*laughs*]

CROWELL: He said, "That sun goin' down song." He didn't know "A Song for the Life." That didn't mean anything to him. "Gimme 'Your Cheatin' Heart,' son!" He said, "You can't hear the sun going down." And I said, "I can!" And I huffed off and was kinda mad for a couple of *years* about that. Then he had a heart attack. So, with the money I made off of that record, I took him to Hawaii. And I made sure that he knew that the tickets to Hawaii came from that record. [*both laugh*] And he was standing out at a sunset on Maui, and he kinda waves at me and says, "Come down here." So, I walk down to the water's edge and he says, "I can hear it!" And I said, "What?" And he said, "I can hear the sun going down."

BIRDS OF SONG

The Beatles were like a gateway drug, especially their first records. It's a lot of Motown and Chuck Berry. They were reflecting back to us things that were uniquely American that white kids like me didn't know much about. So, we can thank the British Invasion for helping us discover African American music. Isn't that strange?

Many of the singers who've influenced my own vocal style have been women, with some notable exceptions like Stevie Wonder, Donny Hathaway, Gregg Allman, Sam Moore, Lowell George, and Gordon Stoker and the Jordanaires. But really, it was Aretha, Mavis, Gladys, Mahalia, Dionne, and Bonnie Bramlett who did it for me.

I don't know if we as a species can know for certain what about them rings a truth bell within us. But I know that I got really obsessed with many of them. I listened to their records over and over and never tired of them, to this day. Often, I just laid on my back on the living room floor, like a sponge, trying to absorb everything. I'd have the record cover, and I'd just be staring at it overhead, fixated. I'd read who wrote the songs, who produced the record, who sang and played what. In time, singers who could take the delicate imprint of a song in its original structure and make it their own in a way that was equally over-the-top beautiful (Donny Hathaway's spellbinding version of Leon's "Song for You" leaps to mind) came to occupy a special place in my heart.

Courtesy Brian Smith

7

"WE KNEW HOW TO BE GREAT. FAMOUS WILL KILL YA."

The Unsinkable Bonnie Bramlett

Bonnie Bramlett and I met many years ago while rehearsing vocals together for an award show that no longer even exists. The arts and music community here in Nashville sometimes seems small in that if you live here long enough (since 1980 for me), you eventually work with everybody. The main thing I remember about that day was that Bonnie didn't hold anything back vocally. She wasn't protecting her voice by easing up on the gas pedal. She was singing in rehearsal like it was a show with ten thousand fans in attendance, or a network television special. Here she was, one of the greatest rock, soul, and gospel singers of all time, no entourage, no managers, singing like her next breath depended on it, in a way that only Bonnie Bramlett can. What was revealing to me was to watch the musicians accompanying her. These were cream of the crop, A-list players who had done this very thing a million times. I could see in their eyes and demeanor that they were thrilled and not about to phone it in with Bonnie up there bringing it.

In my opinion, Bonnie has taught a lot of singers how to sing, including me, and for many years I tried to emulate her vibrato and phrasing. In NGR, Sam Bush and I were fixated on Delaney & Bonnie. We played "Lonesome and a Long Way from Home," which Delaney cowrote with Leon Russell, and we were so obsessed with them vocally that we rehearsed it this way: "I'm going to do Bonnie. You're going to be Delaney." I had assumed that she was from Alabama or Mississippi or Texas, not Illinois. It was just the Pentecostal phrasing, the gospel vibrato, the *Tina Turner* of it. Embarrassingly, despite her work with the likes of Tina, Eric Clapton, Leon Russell, Albert King, Duane Allman, and George Harrison, Bonnie is not a household name. I don't know if that matters to her. It might. But it doesn't to me or the millions of people for whom her voice, melodies, and words have touched and inspired. You will see here what a sweet, intelligent, hilarious woman she is and how she let her voice guide her through a world that, at the time, was both burgeoning with creativity and weighed down by violence, racism, misogyny, and war. I believe Bonnie was one of the voices calling us to follow the spirit and helped us heal the things we could not explain nor even understand.

This interview was conducted in the production office of WSM AM radio out near Opryland in Nashville. That sounds like a tourist plug, but it's not. It just happened to be the city that Bonnie and I shared as a residence for a while. Bonnie has since moved back to the Tri-Cities area in southern Illinois where she was raised, across the Mississippi from St. Louis.

JOHN COWAN: You just celebrated a birthday, November 8th.

BONNIE BRAMLETT: I did! November 8th. Me and a whole bunch of other people here in Nashville. To name a couple, Delbert McClinton, Gary Nicholson, Bonnie Raitt, Rickie Lee Jones. That sounds like an HBO special to me.

COWAN: It should be.

BONNIE: That's a lot of November 8ths.

COWAN: So you were born Bonnie Lynn O'Farrell.

BONNIE: That was me.

COWAN: A lot of us seem to think we know a lot about you, but tell me about your nuclear family, the family you grew up with, and tell me a little bit about growing up in Illinois.

BONNIE: I grew up in Granite City, Madison, and Venice, Illinois. They call it the Tri-Cities because when you cross the bridge from St. Louis, you're in Venice, Madison, and Granite. There's not a split. You don't know that you've left three towns. They're all three little towns: The Tri-Cities. Locally, we had what was called "teen town." Little Milton, Albert King, Ike and Tina Turner were all the local bands at our teen town. And that's how I got to sing with Little Milton. Me and Fontella Bass, and Bobby McClure. We went the first year of integrated school. That's how I met them.

COWAN: Wow.

BONNIE: And Mary and Molly and Robert Mosely were gospel singers. So, I come from a long line of gospel singers.

COWAN: How many siblings did you have?

BONNIE: I have two brothers and two sisters.

COWAN: Were either one of your parents musical at all?

BONNIE: On my mother's side of the family were seven generations of gospel singers.

COWAN: So, you started singing at three or four in the church?

BONNIE: Absolutely. We started singing at the revivals. Vacation Bible schools. And my aunt played piano in our church, so we went to church every night! You know, it was young people's meeting. It was choir. Sunday morning church. Sunday night church. Saturday night church. We did church! A lot of it!

COWAN: Any of your siblings musical as well?

BONNIE: Judy, my mother says, can't carry a tune in a bucket with a lid on it. But she's an artist. She can draw beautifully. We all have pearls. Everybody's talented I guess, but I'm the only one that went for it. Me and my first cousin Lucien. He made it to lounge lizard because he left the church. I kind of followed him, but nobody else. Everybody else is still in the church and singing.

COWAN: So, you have this wonderful heritage in that you grew up listening to gospel music, and you grew up singing in the church, living in the St. Louis area. When did you get bit by the rock and roll bug?

BONNIE: It was not so much the rock and roll bug as it was demonstrative expression. I wanted to sing louder than everyone. I wanted to shout louder than everyone. My feelings were bigger than everybody else's feelings. And I was lucky to find a safe place to put 'em. I got a lot of punishment. Too loud! Shut up! I talk too much. But that's the side effects of our gift! [*laughs*]

COWAN: Right.

BONNIE: When you're a little kid, and you're one of those, it's hard being a little kid. Because your feelings are too big, and you don't mind.

COWAN: You would've been the perfect age, maybe ten or eleven, when Elvis hit. Or when Bill Haley came out. Do you remember hearing that stuff and it having an effect on you at all?

BONNIE: No, because my dad used to take me—my *real* dad—Harold O'Farrell, was a drunk and a hardworking steelworker, and he went to bars at night. And so, when he picked me up on the weekends, we did bars. I had a really schizophrenic life. I went from the church to the pits of hell every weekend! [*laughs*] But all of those old drunks were my fans. And I was listening to Laverne Baker and Etta James. So, I didn't listen to Elvis right away. But, when I saw him, and I was like eleven or twelve, my little hormones kicked in. What can I say? I *loooved* him.

COWAN: I don't know if you have an understanding of this, but for me, you were one of the people who helped me discover my own voice. It was through listening to your voice. I'm pretty confident in saying that there's a generation of singers, my generation, that learned how they wanted to sing from listening to you. Do you have an understanding of that?

BONNIE: No. I'm overwhelmed by that. It's kind of like, I hope so. Y'know, I love to hear that. You're about to make me cry. But I don't think about it like that. I hope so. Because I know that I have been blessed. In my days, the artists who were my heroes would groom us. They brought us on their stage, and they groomed us, and they made sure that we didn't get hurt. You know, I never had anyone be inappropriate with me. And I was only a fifteen-year-old little girl, way developed. I didn't look anything like I was fifteen. I was protected. I felt that way towards Tina. I felt that way towards a lot of other singers who were around at that time. Rosetta Culberson, you might not have heard of her. And Robbie Montgomery, who was Sweetie Pie, remember, "Welcome to Sweetie Pie's?" She was the other Ikette with me.

COWAN: How did you get the gig being part of the Ike and Tina Turner Review as one of the Ikettes, at age fifteen? How did that happen?

BONNIE: Well, I was singing with Albert King and Billy Peek, and I was singing around. I was good! I was very good. It just came natural. But the gospel expression, when I heard Tina live and I heard her *growling*? I had to growl, too! I mean I just growled until I threw up. [*laughing*] But I got it down. I got it. All I knew is that I was looking at her, I knew what I was feeling, and I'd look around and could see that other people were feeling the same. I mean she just blew . . . my . . . mind. She turned into the most beautiful color of burgundy. Her veins were sticking out of her neck, pulsating, and I just went, "I want to do that! I can do that!" I knew that I could do that, not just that I wanted to. I knew I could. And I wanted to make people feel like I'm feeling right now. I wanted to do that to people. That is what I want to do.*

COWAN: Then what happened after that?

---

* Bonnie was hired by Ike Turner after one of the original Ikettes, Jessie Mae Smith, quit. Bonnie's mom said that she could help them out but she couldn't stay. So, wearing a black wig, Bonnie sang for three shows, undercover, as the first white Ikette.

BONNIE: Then I started singing around St. Louis with mostly Albert King and Billy Peek and then Duane Allman. They weren't the Allman Brothers at that time. I think they were Hourglass. I worked at Pepe's A-Go-Go, and Duane worked across the street. So, Duane would come over and play with Albert and us. What they'd do, intentionally, was that one side of the street would take a break, and the other side would be playing. So, we could go across the street and jam with each other. Duane would just walk in with his plug in his hand, up to Albert and plug in. Yay! Sometimes our horns might go over and play with them. I pretty well sang Gaslight Square out. That's when I started doing some jazz. Because when the Beatles came out, me and my background singers and my horn sections were out of work. Everybody went to four-piece boy bands. Needless to say, the Beatles were not my favorite band at that time.

COWAN: Yeah, you weren't enamored with them?

BONNIE: I wasn't enamored with the Stones or the Beatles. I thought the Stones needed to tune up. You have to remember that I'm playing with Albert King and Ike and Tina Turner, the kings of rhythm. And I was a purist. A blues artist. I was sure I was black! I didn't realize that I was white again till I was about twenty-three. [*laughs*] Then a band came in to see me, this band, they looked like the Beatles. A four-piece band. And I guess I just blew their mind. The manager came over and said, "Oh, if you ever make it to California, you can come and sing with our band." They were the enemies.

COWAN: And?

BONNIE: And I said, OK. Bam! Quit my job! One of my girlfriends was crazy enough to drive out with me. [*does a voice*] "We're going to California to be a star!"

COWAN: Who were they? Do you remember?

BONNIE: Yes, I do, as a matter of fact. They were Three Dog Night.

COWAN: [*laughs*]

BONNIE: It was Corey Wells and Danny Hutton. [*laughs*]

COWAN: How about that? So, you arrive there, and what happens?

BONNIE: Well, I arrived there, and we went to their manager, Gene Jacobs, the enemy's manager, and we stayed at their place. This is all taking place in one year, because Delaney and I met each other. We got married in 1967. The minute Delaney heard me sing, he said, "We'll back you." And I said, "No you won't. You'll follow me for three weeks." They were so good, the Shindogs.* So good. So, I wanted to give up. But I'm Irish, y'know. I couldn't help it. I was holding my ground. And he was gorgeous. Just drop-dead handsome. All that three weeks he was bringing Leon Russell and [producer] Snuff Garrett. He was bringing everybody in, saying, "Wait until you hear this girl sing," right? I didn't know he was doing that.

COWAN: Who was with the Shindogs at that time?

BONNIE: It was Delaney, Joey Cooper [bass], Don Preston, and Chuck Blackwell. All very good-looking men. Really lovely to look at. Delaney was just so gorgeous. I swallowed my tongue every night. Gulp. At the end of the three weeks, when the gig was done, I went back to the Magnolia Inn where I was staying. Delaney said could he have my number? And I said, "I'm staying at the Magnolia Inn. "Well, I didn't know there were a trillion Magnolia Inns! It's like the Best Western in LA. He called every one of them until he found me. He came over and never left. We got married seven days later.

COWAN: '67?

BONNIE: July 12th, 1967. Bekka was born in '68.

COWAN: Not only falling in love and being romantic, but . . .

BONNIE: Oh, we fell SO in love! It was ridiculous!

COWAN: Was the immediate thought of both of you, "Let's do music together"?

---

* The Shindogs were the house band for the ABC television music show *Shindig!*

BONNIE: No. No. But when we sang, we could burp in harmony. It was ridiculous, the magic. We phrased exactly alike. I didn't hear the harmonies that well because I was singing lead, and I didn't do a lot of background vocals, so Delaney would tell me, "Think harmony, Bonnie. I mean, with everything. If you hear a horn honk, hit the harmony note to it." And I did that. I gotta tell you something, man, I harmonized with a popcorn fart! [*laughs*] I couldn't help it. We did that. Delaney and I are magic. Bekka and I are the same way. There's just a little something extra there.

COWAN: So, Delaney and Bonnie as an ensemble is born somewhere right about then?

BONNIE: Right then. Immediately! We stopped what he was doing. And the seven days before we got married, we agreed: [*lowers her voice*] "What did you come here for?" "I came here to be a big star." "So did I!" "We're really good, ain't we?" "Yeah." "Well, let's do it then." "OK, you stop everything you're doing." See ya, Shindogs! I was the Yoko Ono of the Shindogs. I came along and broke them up. Took him with me and did duets that made history.

COWAN: Why did you name yourselves Delaney & Bonnie and *Friends*?

BONNIE: The reason we named it "and Friends" is because we didn't know who was gonna be playing that night. Now, we knew we were gonna have a drummer. It'd be either Jim Keltner, Jim Gordon, or Jim Karstein. And the keyboard player would be either Leon Russell or John Galley. You know what I'm saying? So, we never knew. But we knew that *somebody* would always show up for the gig. We were playing bars when everybody was a four-piece band. Nobody was hiring ten-piece bands.

COWAN: For guys and girls in my generation, you know, we're right in the middle of psychedelia. Hendrix is big. Cream is big. The Beatles have made *Sgt. Pepper*. I have a friend who's a sophomore in high school, and I've already played in a couple of bands, and this guy goes, "Have you heard of Delaney & Bonnie?" And I'm like, no. And he says, "Well, you need to hear

"We Knew How to Be Great. Famous Will *Kill Ya*."

Bonnie and Delaney Bramlett, New York City, June 1970. *The Estate of David Gahr/Getty Images*

it because Eric Clapton's on this record. And Dave Mason. And George Harrison." And I was like, "Well, what IS it?" And he says, "Well, I can't really describe it. I'm gonna give you the record to listen to." How did you guys wind up, all of a sudden, touring Europe, and every rock star in the world wants to be part of this? In fact, Eric quits his band so that he can be a part of your band? What happened?

BONNIE: It was our spirituality. I've got to keep going back to that because that's what it was. It was attractive. I think it was how it *appeared* that we didn't know. Delaney was a lot more learned about the business than me. I was very sheltered. Naive is being gentle. But he was naive, too, in the big picture, although he had a wealth of wisdom beyond me. He was naive as well.

COWAN: The only other people I can think of at the time who were doing that was your friend Levon and Robbie and the Band.

BONNIE: Yes.

COWAN: In other words, as popular culture is caught up in psychedelia, suddenly you guys come along, and the Band comes along. And it's not about fashion, and it's not about . . .

BONNIE: Politics.

COWAN: Yeah. There were no protest songs. It was kind of a really unhip place to come from at that point. But it was authentic.

BONNIE: Yeah.

COWAN: And so, you guys come along, and the Band comes along, and it kind of changes the whole game. All these guys start wanting to play like Robbie Robertson. And they want to be in your band. So, there was some authenticity that you guys brought to the music culture at that time that didn't exist.

BONNIE: It was prayer. I don't want to sound corny or anything like that, but we prayed, man. And it blew their minds. I mean we had Joe Cocker talking about Jesus on *Motel Shot*! And he's not Christian! He didn't know about Jesus, but he felt it. So, when Delaney and I started improvising, which we did, it came from a real honest place. And they liked that.

COWAN: So, you guys go to Europe. You're traveling with superstars. And back here in the States, it's being promoted as such. Delaney & Bonnie and Friends with special guests Dave Mason, George Harrison, Eric Clapton, Leon Russell. You made five records altogether?

BONNIE: Four maybe. It was a shame, because it was too much too soon. And we were like boot camp for everybody. Everybody came and played with us. But they had more money than we had. So, they paid our guys more and got our band; what can I say? And we couldn't recover from that. We couldn't recover from Mad Dogs. Because the Mad Dogs and Englishmen tour, they took our band right out from underneath us. What can we say? But bless Buddy Miles. Buddy Miles offered his band, because we're all musician's musicians. But what happened was Leon and Denny Cordell approached Joe Cocker and promised him a band. It just happened to be ours. They paid them more money, and they went. Bobby Whitlock stayed with us right at first. And we tried to recover the best we could. Elvis offered his band. And Delaney took Ron Tutt [drummer] and Jerry Scheff [bass] for a while. We had to make the gigs.*

COWAN: Were there open hard feeling when everyone left?

BONNIE: [*agitated*] With me? Ooooh, I was madder than a wet hen! I was protecting Delaney. Delaney was crushed. Cause those were his friends. I mean, when I met Delaney, I met all those people. I didn't know them either. If that's what your friends do to you, dude? I didn't say that, but that's what he was hearing. So, he was crushed. And I was defending him. We were coming down an airport when that was going on, and somebody flipped me a Mad Dogs and Englishmen button, and I went berserk. I was hurtin', man. Delaney was hurtin', no doubt about it. We were not happy campers. And it destroyed us, too. We did it, too. It was our stuff. We didn't know how to be famous. We knew how to be great. Famous will kill ya.

COWAN: It's a funny position to be a bandleader. I've had this happen to me as well, on a much smaller scale. When you've had people that you play with, that are your band, you get completely invested in them. And you think, when they leave, that nothing is ever gonna be the same. If you can hang in there long enough, what you'll realize is that when somebody else comes in, it's just gonna be different. It's not going to be worse or better.

BONNIE: Yeah, but those were the days. I mean we were the Little Rascal bunch. We were a gang. I don't mean gang in the bad way. We did that blood-brother friendship. Bands and friends, you didn't break up. No, we're gonna stay together. All for one and one for all. Aerosmith, same way. Allman Brothers. Come on! We stayed together no matter what.

---

* Denny Cordell, producer of Mad Dogs with Leon and Joe Cocker, also produced artists like Chet Baker, the Moody Blues, Procol Harum's "Whiter Shade of Pale," Bob Marley, and in the '70s, signed and produced a young band out of Florida called Mudcrutch, who grew to become Tom Petty and the Heartbreakers.

COWAN: Yup.

BONNIE: So that killed us.

COWAN: Do you think that was kind of the end?

BONNIE: That *was* the end! We couldn't recover. The only people we had to take it out on was each other. And we couldn't recover from *that*, man. We didn't make it.

COWAN: That must've hurt.

BONNIE: It still hurts. But, you know, you're still standing. I'm still standing.

COWAN: Some of the fruits of your labor paid off way down the road, some of your songwriting that you did. Tell me about "Superstar." This is a song that was a huge hit for the Carpenters. Huge. Tell me about writing that song. It was you and Leon?

BONNIE: No.

COWAN: Who are the composers?

BONNIE: It was me and Rita Coolidge. When we finished it, we took it to Delaney, and Delaney brought it in and put in a beautiful chart. And we sang three-part harmony. Rita brought that song to the table, and I finished it.*

COWAN: Are you performing much, Bonnie?

BONNIE: I don't. Not now. Nashville's doing its own thing, and I'm, I do mine. I am, I like to say, "retired," but I haven't quit. I'm just not chasing no golden ring no more, that's for sure. I have been thinking about doing a class. Not necessarily a singing class, but an acting class. Because when I started acting, it took my singing ability from here to here. I can't tell you the giant step I took when I learned to transpose lyric to dialogue, and I learned

---

* The original title of the song was "Groupie," based on Rita's insight of the groupie culture at the time. There are not many who dispute Rita's claim that she cowrote this song with Bonnie, but the omission of her songwriting credit for what turned out to be a very lucrative song tells you something about the lack of power women had in the music industry in 1969.

to embrace that song even stronger. I went from singing a lyric to telling a story. To take a natural beat. When you're talking to people sometimes, take a beat. That's a breath in singing, but there are specific places to breath during a song, they say. Well, I challenge that. I think you should breathe the same way you breathe when you talk.

COWAN: I've been thinking for years that when you look at the sidelines of basketball, hockey, and football or baseball, they're filled with older people trying to impart their knowledge, through their experience, to young players.

BONNIE: Yes.

COWAN: We don't have that in the music business.

BONNIE: Well, we need to! We need to.

COWAN: Yeah.

BONNIE: First of all, I'm not going to dress somebody up. I'm not going to create you. Come to me, and I'll help guide and direct. Like my wonderful acting coach, Bobbie Chance, told me, "If you come here because you want to be famous, turn your little butt around and walk right back out the door. If you want to be great, you're in the right place. Famous will kill ya."

COWAN: There's no denying that most of us who got into the music business wanted to be rich and famous.

BONNIE: Well, sure.

COWAN: We're kids.

BONNIE: You want that when you're a kid.

COWAN: However, I think, personally that pedigree is everything in an artist. If your only goal is to be rich and famous, and you have some raw talent, substance is built upon those ten thousand hours you spend before you hit the stage. Pedigree is everything in an artist and I think that's what you're talking about.

BONNIE: That's exactly what I'm talking about. And I've never heard it put better. Pedigree.

COWAN: Well, the artist is only going to be a deep as his own roots are.

BONNIE: There you are. I'm a part of this. I'm in for the long haul. In my turn, I think we did really well, but that part of my life is over, and I think we did well and left a whole lot behind. There's a lot more to do, and what can I do to help the younger ones right now.

COWAN: There you go.

BONNIE: That's what I'd like to do. I think I have something to offer. A different point of view, that's for sure.

8

"YOU KNOW WE CAN'T COPY THEM JORDANAIRES!"

A Closer Walk with the Legendary Gordon Stoker

I have a bass guitar that I have been playing consistently since 1975. It is an original Fender Jazz Bass made in 1962. Over the years I've had various people sign it whom I admire: Gregg Allman, Elvis Costello, Billy Gibbons and Dusty Hill of ZZ Top, Chris Squire from Yes, Gary Tallent from the E Street Band, and the peerless Gordon Stoker, founding member of the Jordanaires, right on the front. Gordon was like my singing-angel grandpa whenever our paths crossed, always happy to see me, always kind and generous. He was not only familiar with our band, NGR, but talked enthusiastically about singing and told me that he loved my voice.

Although Gordon and the Jordanaires appear on records that have sold more than eight *billion* copies, one thing that they did not experience much was notoriety on a personal level. To many, they were just the guys singing behind stars like Elvis, Patsy Cline, Ricky Nelson, George Jones, and Johnny Cash. As a kid who sang in church and barbershop, just as my dad did, I know exactly how much work it takes to do the things that the Jordanaires made seem effortless. Even less well known is that they also wrote and arranged so many of the amazing parts that elevate these songs. Record producers had so much faith in them that they'd often ask, "Gordon, what do *you* guys think

Elvis with Gordon Stoker of the Jordanaires (right) at RCA's McGavock Street Studio, Nashville, April 14, 1956. *Photo by Don Cravens/Getty Images*

would be good on this song?" He'd go sit down at the piano, gather everyone around, and write the arrangement on the spot.

Gordon passed away about a year after we did this interview, at the age of eighty-eight. We recorded our conversation in the production studio at WSM AM Radio 650. He was accompanied by his sons, Brent and Alan, who, to this day, make his dad proud by keeping the Jordanaires legacy alive.

JOHN COWAN: I am just pinching myself. This is one of the happiest days of my life. I want to tell you all who don't know this that the Jordanaires appear on records that have now sold eight billion *plus* copies. That's eight *billion*, plus. How's that feel, Gordon?

GORDON STOKER: It feels good. Especially when they use them for jingles!

COWAN: There you go. [*both laugh*] I'm going to run down a list of some of the songs that we know and love that you and the Jordanaires have appeared on. "Big, Bad John" by Jimmy Dean. Loretta Lynn's "Coal Miner's Daughter." Ricky Nelson's "Traveling Man." Patsy Cline's "Crazy." Elvis Presley's "Are You Lonesome Tonight?" "Don't Be Cruel," and countless other Elvis recordings. Jim Reeves's "Four Walls." George Jones's "He Stopped Loving Her Today." Conway Twitty's "Hello Darlin'." Don Gibson's "Oh, Lonesome Me." Tammy Wynette's "Stand by Your Man." Kenny Rogers's "Lucille," and on and on and on. Gordon, I want to talk a little bit about the history of the Jordanaires, who in the '40s were first called the Foggy River Boys by the Matthews Brothers. That was Bill, Monty, Jack, and Matt, correct?

STOKER: Right. Four brothers.

COWAN: And they were all ordained ministers.

STOKER: Yep.

COWAN: Tell me a little bit about that part, before they became the Jordanaires.

STOKER: Well, there was two brothers who didn't want to move out of the Springfield, Missouri, area. So Bill and Monty Matthews came to Nashville with two other guys. Bob Hubbard, also a minister, and Culley Holt. They worked here in Nashville on [radio station] WSM for quite some time. And one thing led to another, and before we knew it, a lot of requests for shows were coming in, and what have you. Then the piano player, Bob

Money, was drafted. When he was drafted, I auditioned for the position, and how I got it, I'll never know. [*laughs*] But I got it.

COWAN: At that time in your life, were you also a singer as well as a pianist?

STOKER: Yessir.

COWAN: Which came first for you? And which did you do best, do you think?

STOKER: I came to WSM in 1942 as a piano player for the John Daniel Quartet. We used to come on early in the morning, every morning, and I did that until I was drafted. It was funny that once you're drafted into the service, before you know it, it stops everything. And that's what it did for me, because I was really enjoying my work with WSM. I was really very fortunate to have that position.

COWAN: Once you joined the Jordanaires, did you continue to play piano, or did you just sing only at that point?

STOKER: I played piano for about two years, then I started singing. The first tune was because the singer had a nervous breakdown. Bill Matthews had a nervous breakdown, and I took his place singing the tenor part, and I've been singing it ever since. [*laughs*] It don't sound like it too much today, but that's the way it is.

COWAN: Well, you know, it's early in the day for us tenor singers. We start sounding a little higher as the day goes on.

STOKER: What was it that the guy used to say, "You don't throw up till ten o'clock at night?"

COWAN: Exactly. [*both laugh*] So you have been the de facto leader of the Jordanaires for a very long time.

STOKER: A long time. I joined the group in 1950 and started being the manager of the group in 1954, maybe it was. So, that's how long I've been hanging on.

COWAN: One thing I wanted to talk about a little bit was how the music world, and of course, the world in general, was very segregated at that time. The black gospel groups were known as spiritual groups.

STOKER: Yeah.

COWAN: Besides your own unique sound, what I get when I hear you guys is the black spiritual influence. As I listened to "Don't Be Cruel" for probably the ten thousandth time, that spiritual influence really comes to mind.

STOKER: Yeah, that's what we loved. We loved those spirituals. We bought album after album. Anything we could find by a black group, we would buy it. We loved the beat they had and, actually, that's the beat that Elvis loved so much, and Bill Gaither loved, too. Bill Gaither has taken a lot of our numbers and tried to sing them, well, they *do* sing them. They've sung a lot of our songs, but he doesn't have that black beat in there that I think makes it.

COWAN: That's one thing that I've always loved about Bill and the Gaither Family and the Homecoming events, is that they've been very inclusive about all sorts of gospel music. They have bluegrass and gospel artists. They have African American gospel artists. I've always thought that was really wonderful.

STOKER: Yes. Yes.

COWAN: I want to tell a story on you about how we met. I don't think you'll remember this, but I remember it because, as I'm going to say over and over again, I'm just a lunatic fan of your singing and everything that you've done in your life. This must've been about 1988, and the band I was in at the time, New Grass Revival, we were enjoying some notoriety, particularly here in Nashville. We met at a music event, some kind of music business industry event. You just came up to me, and you said the nicest things to me, and you could have knocked me over with a feather.

STOKER: I'm a fan of yours.

COWAN: Well, thank you, Gordon. I'll always remember that. I've loved you for so long.

STOKER: Thank you, I appreciate that.

COWAN: I believe your first hit record that you guys sang on as the Jordanaires was "A Closer Walk with Thee"?

STOKER: With Red Foley.

COWAN: So, let's go forward in time from Red Foley and get to Mr. Jimmy Dean. I remember this record so well from my childhood, called "Big Bad John." When you listen to the recording, I think you can hear a female singing in there somewhere.

STOKER: Yes, Anita Kerr walked in at the last minute and started singing with us. She was down in Studio B, downstairs at the Quonset Hut. We had a studio downstairs where we did lots of things, like "Young Love" with Sonny James and "Gone" with Ferlin Husky. Many things. Anita had been working down there, and she came through the studio, and Don Law said, "Hey, Anita, sing with the guys. Everybody join in." So, that's what we did.*

COWAN: I want to ask you a technical question about singing in a quartet and how difficult that can be sometimes. If you're singing in a church choir, you get to rehearse all the time, and hopefully on Sunday, when you get together to sing, it goes pretty well. But imagine yourself under the pressure of making records. When people made records at this time, they didn't get to go back and fix things very often. So you guys had to be perfect right then and there.

STOKER: Well, you had to be good or they'd say, "Next." [*both laugh*]

---

* Anita Kerr and later, the Anita Kerr Singers, became hugely popular background singers for country music stars in the '50s and '60s, recording in both Nashville and LA. You can hear Anita and her distinctive vocal arrangements on recordings by folks like Eddy Arnold, Chet Atkins, Brenda Lee, Roy Orbison, and Willie Nelson.

COWAN: Did it depend on the artist and the producer of the artist as to how much creative input you guys had? So, you go into the studio, and here's the artist, and here's the producer, and we have this song? Would they say to you, "Gordon, we want you to sing this in this section," or would they say, "What do you guys think?"

STOKER: Most of the time, they would say, "What do you guys think?" But a lot of times they would just say, "Sing what you feel." Neil Matthews, he took the numbers down, so we would ooh and ahh with them. The old thing we used to say was, "We've been oohing and ahh-ing all day over a hot microphone." The best thing that we did was when they let us have what we wanted to do.

COWAN: Right.

STOKER: Then it kind of falls in line. Elvis would always listen to us, and if he didn't like what we were doing, he'd stutter and say [*imitating Elvis*], "Uh, uh, uh, would you sing something else here?" [*both laugh*]

COWAN: We're gonna get into Mr. Elvis Presley in a minute, but I want to play one of my favorite records from this period as well. One of the reasons I always loved this record is because of what you guys did on this. Ricky Nelson's "Travelin' Man."

STOKER: Oh, yeah.

COWAN: You told me a story a minute ago about how you met Ricky Nelson. Tell that story again about how y'all met Ricky Nelson.

STOKER: Well, we always stayed at the Knickerbocker Hotel in Hollywood when we'd go out there. He would hear by word of mouth about us being there because the Nelson family lived very close to that hotel, so they knew pretty much what was happening. He heard that Elvis was going to bring us out a certain week, at a certain time, on a certain day. And so, he came up to the hotel and rang the doorbell. I went to the door, and he said, "Hi, I'm Ricky Nelson." [*Cowan laughs*] And I said, "Yeah, I know who you are!" And he said, "You know who I am?"* And I said, "You ain't kiddin' I know who you are. I see you on TV all the time in Nashville." He said, "You know we went up back east last year, and we ran into a lot of people who've seen us on TV." They lived in such a small world in Hollywood. You don't realize how big you are. He was the nicest guy. There could be no one who we'd ever worked with who was as nice a guy as Ricky Nelson. We just recently finished an album with his baby boy, Sam Nelson.

COWAN: Oh, my goodness.

STOKER: There are the twins.

COWAN: I know Matthew and Gunnar.

STOKER: Yeah, he's got three of 'em,† but Sam had never been to Nashville, so he was really glad to come. Rick died when he [Sam] was eleven years old.

COWAN: Oh.

STOKER: So, he did really get to know him. Sam was so interested in everything we had, pictures and everything. He said, "Everything you've got, I want to see."

COWAN: So, was "Travelin' Man" done in California or Nashville?

STOKER: All of Rick's stuff was done in California.

COWAN: When you sang on "Travelin' Man," did you guys come in after the fact, or were you there when James Burton‡ and all of those guys were recording the track at the same time?

STOKER: No, we came in after.

COWAN: You did.

STOKER: Yeah.

---

* In a five-year period between '57 and '62, teen idol Ricky Nelson had thirty Top 40 hits, surpassed only by Elvis and Pat Boone.

† He and his wife, Kris, also had a daughter, Tracy.

‡ James Burton, who we also mentioned in the Jim Messina interview, was a self-taught guitar kid from Louisiana who's now considered one of the finest guitar players who ever lived. He played on most of the songs in Ricky Nelson's career, was a member of Elvis's TCB Band, and Emmylou Harris's Hot Band, among so many others. In 2001, he was justifiably elected to the Rock & Roll Hall of Fame.

COWAN: Well, let's listen to this because it's just so hip and I love everything about this. [*both listen to the record* "Travelin' Man"]

COWAN: Now, I'm going to tell a story on you. I'm going to tell the beginning, and I would like you to fill in the blanks for me. In 1955, the Jordanaires traveled to Memphis with Eddy Arnold to promote a TV show.

STOKER: Yep. We done a TV show in Chicago with Eddy Arnold. *Eddy Arnold Time.*

COWAN: And you met some young gentleman. I don't know what his name was . . .

STOKER: This young kid came back behind the stage, and the way he was dressed was the only reason I paid any attention to him. He had on black pants with a white stripe down the side of 'em. And he had on a pink shirt! Now, in '55, a boy didn't wear a pink shirt. [*both laugh*]

COWAN: Did he have his pompadour going already?

STOKER: Yeah, very much so.

COWAN: And what was this gentleman's name again?

STOKER: This gentleman's name was Elvis Presley.

COWAN: Oh, yes, Elvis. I've heard of him. Tell me about what happened upon meeting him.

STOKER: He said, "I'm gonna do some records. Some real records. I've been doing some records on a small label here in Memphis. But I'm gonna be signed by a big company, and when I do, I want you guys to work with me." And we never thought a thing about it. We never thought we'd hear anymore from him.

COWAN: You'd probably heard that a couple of times before, hadn't you?

STOKER: [*laughs*] Every day!

COWAN: So, he called you back, didn't he?

STOKER: Yeah, well the thing was, for the first sessions, Chet Atkins called me and said, "We just signed this long sideburned kid from Memphis.

I think he's just a passing fad, and I don't think he's going to be around long. Would you guys just come along and work with Ben and Brock Speer?"* I said, "Chet, I know those guys, but I've never worked with them." He said, "Oh, it don't make no difference. He's just a passing fad. He won't be around long." The first thing Elvis said to me when he got there was, "Where are the rest of the guys?" And you know, he didn't like Chet till the day he died.

COWAN: Because he wanted all the Jordanaires.

STOKER: He wanted all the Jordanaires.

COWAN: The Speer Family who were on RCA, too, were a wonderful gospel group.

STOKER: Oh, yeah, they are still my good, good, good friends.

COWAN: So, what was the first track you appeared on with them?

STOKER: "I Want You, Need You, Love You." "I Was the One" was the second one.

COWAN: And what was the first Elvis Presley track that all the Jordanaires, the whole quartet, was involved in?

STOKER: "Don't Be Cruel."

COWAN: One of the things that strikes me about "Are You Lonesome Tonight?" is Elvis's vocal performance on that. It's almost operatic.

STOKER: Yeah.

COWAN: He sings in full voice. He sings in what we call technically a head voice. He almost goes up into falsetto. And I wondered, not knowing as much as you do about him, was it all just intuitive with him?

STOKER: Yeah, it's just whatever he felt. He had a lot of feeling for different songs, and he really felt your song if you had written it and he was doing it for you. He'd put a different feeling in it.

---

* Ben and Brock Speer, lead singers of the Speer Family, were considered Nashville's first family of gospel, with more than seventy-five albums in a career that spanned decades. Ben and Brock worked with both Hank Williams and Elvis Presley, and in 1956 they sang with Gordon Stoker on these first recordings for RCA's up-and-coming new star, Elvis.

COWAN: Do you think he had sung that song a lot prior to recording it?

STOKER: No, he hadn't.

COWAN: That kind of singing, I can tell you as a singer, and you know this, too, really takes some thought about how you're going to present it, what you're going to do with your voice, how you're going to flip through these different parts. His singing on that is just so unbelievably beautiful. I'll say once again, it sounds operatic to me in some sections.

STOKER: It does. On "Fool Such as I" and several of the others, he's got operatic tones and sounds. It was always funny. Like, we did, "Crying in the Chapel" at three o'clock in the morning. We had been working on sessions all day. We'd go to RCA Studio B at night around seven o'clock, and he comes in around eight, nine, ten, and then he plays around and cuts up on the piano for hours, and we sing it around with him. About three o'clock in the morning he says, "Uh, let's do 'Cryin' in the Chapel.'" And of course, "Crying in the Chapel," if you listen to it, I hum and ooh all the way from the beginning to the end. [*both laugh*]

COWAN: Was that a little taxing on the vocal cords?

STOKER: Yeah, a little taxing. But Elvis was always in such a good mood and left you in such a good mood, you just couldn't be mad at him.

COWAN: I want to talk about Ray and the other members at the time who were making these records with you. Can you tell us a little bit about them? Wonderful singers in their own right.

STOKER: Ray Walker sang the bass. He passed in 2013. Hoyt Hawkins sang the baritone. He passed away in '82. Then Neil Matthews, who sang the second tenor, he passed away in 2000.

COWAN: One of my favorite Elvis records is "Don't Be Cruel." One thing I was thinking about as I was listening to this repeatedly the last few days is that if you took the Jordanaires' part out of that song, I don't know if it flies. I know it's Elvis. But what the Jordanaires are doing with their voices is so percussive, it sounds like a rhythm instrument, like a guitar or a drum even.

STOKER: Yeah. Yeah. It does.

COWAN: To me, that brings up that old, gospel, spiritual thing that we talked about earlier. Let me ask you about that. Who decided to do what on "Don't Be Cruel"?

STOKER: Well, Neil wrote the arrangement. He took the numbers down, and then it kind of all falls together.

COWAN: Did it start out as [*sings high and staccato*] Buh, buh, buh, buh? Is that what you came up with first?

STOKER: Something like that.

COWAN: Really?

STOKER: Yeah, Elvis didn't tell us what to do, and we didn't tell each other what to do. It was always just kind of what we felt.

COWAN: Now, was that recorded with the band at the same time?

STOKER: Yeah, mm hmm.

COWAN: Whoa! Can you imagine that?

STOKER: Yeah, we didn't do any extra tracks with Elvis. All the duets I did with him, everything was done on the same mic. He liked it that way, and we liked it that way, too.

COWAN: It's almost a perfect record, if you think about it. That you did it live, that what you're hearing on the record was everything done at the same time is just so amazing.

STOKER: Yes, it was actually recorded in New York City.

COWAN: Really?

STOKER: We did three numbers in New York City. That was one of 'em.

COWAN: Do you recall the other two?

STOKER: Oh, yeah. "Hound Dog," which I had to play piano on. [*laughs*]

COWAN: [*laughs*] I didn't know that.

STOKER: Well, the piano player said, "I've got another session, and I've got to go to it." So, [producer] Steve Sholes said, "Gordon, get over there on the piano." So we did that in New York, and we did, "Anyway You Want Me." It was on that number where I punched a guy and said, "Hey, this kid can sing!"

COWAN: Yeah.

STOKER: Listen to him on "Anyway You Want Me." It's a little bit spiritual, and at times he would step into something like that.

COWAN: So, you spent fifteen years making records with Elvis.

STOKER: That was from 1956 to 1970. That's almost fifteen years. Anyway, he went into Vegas doing two shows a night, and I would always regret that we had to quit. But we had so many sessions booked here in Nashville. We only worked with Elvis when we didn't have sessions booked here in Nashville.

COWAN: I was at your induction into the Country Music Hall of Fame, and I remember that there was talk about that. About how many sessions the Jordanaires did a day for how many years in Nashville. Let's talk about that.

STOKER: We did, for twenty years, two to four sessions a day, if we were able. If you were not able, there was substitute number one and substitute number two to sing for you.

COWAN: Did you enjoy most of it?

STOKER: Oh, yeah, when I think back about it, how much I enjoyed it. Of course, we don't do nearly that much now. It's good that we don't because, first off, we aren't able. [*laughs*] But we've got eight numbers to do on Monday.

COWAN: When you were performing with Elvis, this was during the crazy, screaming, teenage girl days, right?

STOKER: Yeah.

COWAN: Could you hear anything?

STOKER: No, we really couldn't. Elvis just made signs to us. He thought it was funny.

COWAN: What did you think?

STOKER: It just happened so fast, and it just happened so quick. One time he threw his coat out in the audience, and they grabbed that coat and tore it into fifty pieces.

COWAN: That must've been quite something to experience.

STOKER: It was. There's no feeling that I could tell you that I experienced like when we walked out on that stage, and Elvis walked out with us and heard all of those people screaming and hollering.

COWAN: Now, when you got off the road in 1970 and were just consumed with making records all the time and being in the studio, was there ever a part of you that missed performing live?

STOKER: Oh, yeah. Oh, *yeah*.

COWAN: There's kind of nothing like that either, is there?

STOKER: No, and especially to be onstage with him. Of course, we did a lot of shows with Ricky Nelson, and the kids loved him, too. But there's been no one on a stage like Elvis Presley.

COWAN: One thing that's always occurred to me about making records, and I don't think that most people understand this, and maybe you can verify this, but it's hard on your *brain*. You get really brain-tired making records all day long.

STOKER: Yeah, you do!

COWAN: It's fatiguing in a different way than someone who is polishing windows or cooking all day long. It's just as fatiguing to stand there and have to be right all the time and not make mistakes.

STOKER: You have to be. If you make mistakes, as I said a while ago, they'll say, "Next group!"

COWAN: Exactly. [*both laugh*]

STOKER: You just don't make mistakes. There are a lot of groups that have been in here from time to time and said, "We're gonna move in on the big money." I'd always say, "If you can cut it, we'll welcome you." But before long, little by little, they disappear out.

COWAN: I know that two of your current members, Curtis Young and Michael Black, are both real in-demand session singers and have been. Curtis has been for thirty years here in Nashville.

STOKER: Yeah, Curtis has been around a long time, and he's a great singer.

COWAN: Oh, my goodness, yes, he is. Gordon, I just found out you played on a song, and I don't know why I didn't put those two together, but it may well be my favorite Johnny Cash song. "I Still Miss Someone." Why don't you tell that story you told me earlier about this song?

STOKER: Should I?

COWAN: Why not?

STOKER: Johnny was so pleased with this record that he called June and said, "I just want you to come over and listen to this. It's so good, you just got to hear it!" So, she came over and set down, and he started playing it for her. She said [*imitates June's irritation*], "Why, you know that we can't copy them Jordanaires on nothin' you're doin'!" [*Cowan laughs*] She really didn't like it. It really knocked the feathers out of him!

COWAN: Did you continue to record with him after that, or was that it?

STOKER: [*big laugh*] Oh, I'm sure we did, because he liked us as a group.

COWAN: Tell me a little bit about Millie Kirkham.*

STOKER: Millie was one of the finest singers. She just sang beautifully.

COWAN: What numbers would people know?

STOKER: "Gone" was the first single she did here in Nashville, with Ferlin Husky. Ken Nelson called and said, "We're doin' 'Gone' next week with

---

* Millie Kirkham was known with great affection around Nashville as the "Fifth Jordanaire." You've heard her beautiful soprano on Elvis's "Blue Christmas," "He Stopped Loving Her Today," by George Jones, and a host of hits by stars like Sonny James, Roy Orbison, Brenda Lee, and more.

Gordon Stoker seated (right) in studio with me and Gordon's son Brent (center). *Courtesy Stoker Family*

Ferlin, and we need a girl singer. Do you have a girl singer?" This was in '55, and I said, "No, we haven't been working with one, but I'll check around." So, I checked around, and I found out that Millie had been singing around quite a bit, so I asked her, and she said, "Me, sing with four men? Are you kidding me?" But she came in and sang it, and that thing hit five million right off the bat. Isn't that funny?

COWAN: Wow. That's amazing. I also want to ask you about a couple of other songs before you go. I want to ask you about one by Conway Twitty. Is there anything you want to say about, "Hello, Darlin'"?

STOKER: Conway was just one of the nicest guys you've ever seen. First of all, he had fifty number one records! What person do you know like that would be at the airport getting his own bags? Standing in line with everybody else? I've always respected that in him because I really thought that was wonderful. He didn't think he was a big star, which he was, and I'll just always treasure that in him.

COWAN: Gordon, I can't thank you enough. This has been one of the best days of my life. Thank you so much for your time. I love you to death.

STOKER: Well, I'm honored, John. Really, I'm a fan of yours.

Sam Moore performing at the Ryman Auditorium, Nashville, June 4, 2014. *Photo by Erika Goldring/Stringer/Getty Images*

9

TOUCHING THE SOUL OF THE GREAT SAM MOORE

In the summer of 1966, I was thirteen years old living in Louisville, Kentucky. Our local AM radio station was WAKY. I was lucky enough to unknowingly be living in the "golden age" of popular music. That little speaker on top of the radio in my mom's white Chevrolet station wagon was pumping out magic nonstop, 24-7. Stevie Wonder, the Beatles, Buck Owens, Ray Charles, the Rolling Stones, all Motown, and Stax. You know the label, at least I did, by heart. Light aqua blue with records stacked like pancakes at the top, or the yellow-gold ones with a picture of a hand snapping fingers in time. Jeez. Then one unforgettable day, out of the radio jumps the horn intro to "Hold On, I'm Comin'." Then Sam Moore sings, "In a river of trouble and about to drown, just hold on, I'm comin'," and I was a goner, lost to "Double Dynamite" and the "Sultans of Sweat," just two of the nicknames for Sam Moore and Dave Prater.

Sam Moore is and will always be one of the greatest tenor singers in popular music, alongside Sam Cooke, Jackie Wilson, Stevie Wonder, Eddie Kendricks, and David Ruffin. He's a member of the Rock & Roll Hall of Fame and the Grammy Hall of Fame and has been called the greatest living soul singer. I first met Sam in Los Angeles for an MCA Records event celebrating "Rhythm, Country & Blues" in 1993 where everyone who participated in the recording of the record performed live. I was there singing "The Weight" with Marty Stuart and Mavis Staples. As a tenor myself and a lifelong fan, I jumped at the chance to meet Sam, shake his hand, and "gherm" him.* Our conversation took place at WSM AM studios in Nashville, where Sam was accompanied by his lovely wife, Joyce.

JOHN COWAN: It's Samuel David Moore, isn't it?

SAM MOORE: It's really Sammy. Sammy David.

COWAN: What I don't know is where you were born. And where did you grow up?

MOORE: I grew up in Florida.

COWAN: Florida? What part?

MOORE: In Miami.

COWAN: It seems like we know a lot of stuff about your life from Sam & Dave on, but I'm real curious about things like how many kids were in your family and your homelife growing up?

MOORE: Well, my mother and father only had one child, which turned out to be me. [*laughs*]

COWAN: So, you were an only child?

MOORE: Yes, so I don't know if that was good or bad, but I'm here!

COWAN: Seems like it worked out pretty good.

MOORE: [*laughs*] I hope so!

COWAN: Were your mom or dad musically inclined?

MOORE: My dad. My poor mother, bless her heart, she tried. I used to just sit in church and watch her, and when they gave her a little solo to sing, a little piece of the song, I just cried for her because she tried so hard. But my dad was the one. He never got involved with it because in those days that was not to be. He didn't go out to be an entertainer or a gospel singer or anything like that. But he was a very good singer.

---

* Gherm, pronounced with a hard "g," is a slang expression unique to the Nashville music community. Among other things, it means praising someone effusively and without any sense of restraint. Gherm can be a noun or a verb. With Sam, I was the verb. ("I totally ghermed him.") Unless he recounted this story later. Then I was a noun. ("What a gherm John was!")

COWAN: Was he a tenor as well?

MOORE: Yes. Better than I.

COWAN: Did they both live to see your success?

MOORE: No.

COWAN: Neither one?

MOORE: No.

COWAN: My goodness.

MOORE: My mother died in 1960. And my grandmother almost did. That's when I met Dave, in '61. Dave and I were working in a club, not too far from the house, called the King of Hearts. A lot of times I would leave home, and I would say I was going to sing at some church, that I had a group concert to do, but instead I would go to the club. I soon got busted with that. I had a friend who was a gospel singer who started working at the same club. The Soul Stirrers with Sam Cooke came to town. Back in those days, blacks could not stand on the beaches or the avenues or whatnot in Miami. They'd stay with some of the members of the congregation who came to see the concert. And my mother and my grandmother were members at the time and saw the gospel stuff. My mother loved Sam, so she would let him come and stay at the house, and Sam started telling on me! [*imitates Sam Cooke's voice*] "Oh, wow, wow! I enjoyed that song you sang, Sam." And my mother said, "Did he really turn the church out?" And Sam said, "*Church?*"

COWAN: Wait, so Sam Cooke is staying at your house and ratting you out for singing in a nightclub, is that what you're telling me?

MOORE: [*laughs*] Yeah! Sam was about twenty-one at the time, and he was young, and she believed everything. She'd say things like this: "Now, don't you go out there with this God-fearing man and get him in no trouble." And I'm just looking at her.

COWAN: And you're thinking, me get *him* in trouble?

MOORE: Me get *him* in trouble! [*laughs hard*]

COWAN: I think he was seventeen or eighteen when "Jesus Gave Me Water" became a big hit.

MOORE: Yes, yes, yes.

COWAN: Was church music the first music that you heard? Or did you hear other stuff on the radio?

MOORE: Let's understand, my mother and my grandmother, they didn't like that rock and roll in the house, and I honored that. I respected that. Even as naughty as I could be, I respected that they didn't want that kind of music in the house. Believe it or not, my first was the Fairfield Four. And I liked that. But I would put my head under the covers at night, and I would turn it up and listen to the Ink Spots. You know, Bill Kenny?* And my mother would yell, "Turn that down! Who is that you're listening to?" And I'd say, "The Fairfield Four!"

COWAN: As you started becoming a young man, is there someone who touched your heart and reached into your soul, who maybe wasn't gospel music? A popular artist who just spoke to you in a way you can't explain?

MOORE: Well, I can share this much with you. Dave and I were working at the King of Hearts. And Sam [Cooke] was getting ready to leave the Soul Stirrers. I don't think Sam would have left as soon as he did—I think he might have stayed another six months to a year—but he put out this song, "Lovable." And how, in those days, could you put it out as *Dale* Cooke, which was his middle name, and how do you sing, "Lovable" when the song was "Wonderful"—he just changed the name—and you don't recognize that voice? So, when they put it out, it got to be an attention-getter. *That's not no Dale Cooke. That's Sam!* And it forced him out into the open.

COWAN: So, when did you come into the picture?

---

* The Ink Spots, led by Bill Kenny, were much beloved balladeers in the '30s and '40s. With songs like "If I Didn't Care" and "I Don't Want to Set the World on Fire," they laid the foundation for the rock, R&B, and doo-wop eras to come. They were inducted into the Rock & Roll Hall of Fame in 1989.

MOORE: Sam and the Soul Stirrers were looking for a lead singer. Sam told J. J. Farley, their manager, "There's a guy down there in Miami, maybe you would like to listen to him." If Sam didn't like you, he wouldn't never said that because Sam was all for Sam. So, they came down and did a program without Sam. Mr. Paul Foster was the lead singer at the time, with the rough voice and everything, the second lead to Sam, and they spoke to me. The manager got me to try out, and I went over. Now, I had done a show and was real hoarse. And I went in and every song they brought in, I'd say, "Can I try this, or could I try that?" Well, they had a certain style with Sam and with Johnny Taylor and everybody else. So, I didn't meet that criteria, but it was close enough because they had that smooth, smooth gospel. That worked because Sam was such a presence. Not because he was so strong and could turn a house out. Sam could turn a church out because of his body language and the way he carried himself and how he sang and how he did things. Mine was not that, but it was close enough that they said, yeah, we can go with this and nurture this into what we want. So, I rehearsed, and they said, "Yeah, can you be ready to leave after Sunday, because we're going back Monday morning to Chicago? We've got to get you fitted for outfits." And I said, "Yeah, yeah!"

COWAN: And you were a Soul Stirrer?

MOORE: Well, on Sundays we didn't work at the King of Hearts. On Sundays we were off. And I went over to sit with the guys, you know, and I saw this sign outside of the Night Beat Club. It was a predominantly black section of Miami. And I saw this guy standing, and I'd heard "Rags to Riches" and all that stuff, and I said, "That's Jackie Wilson!" I want to see the show! I'd never seen him. And I went in—you know, I could go in free—and I sat, and everybody sat, and they said, "And now, ladies and gentlemen, Jackie Wilson!" And he came out, and the lights went down, and the next thing I knew, here's a guy coming between the chairs and the tables, spinning, with a pretty white suit on. And right away, the man started singing, and I'm going like the women! "Whoaah! I want to be with him!" And I look around and said [*laughs hard*], *Oh, Lord, wait a minute! What are you doing? You want to be with him?* And I meant, I wanted to be doing what he was doing! He fell onto the floor, and women jumped on top of him. Oh, jeez, would I have liked to do that! I wanted to do that! Well, I didn't even get a chance to meet him. I was so excited, man, to see this guy, his hair dripping wet. [*takes a big breath*] *Whooooo!* So, I went back to the club the next week, and I started stuffing papers down in my pants! [*laughs*]

COWAN: So, does this mean you passed on being part of the Soul Stirrers?

MOORE: Yeah!

COWAN: Because you'd seen Jackie Wilson?

MOORE: Yeah! [*laughing hard*]

COWAN: And you thought, now that's what I really want to do?

MOORE: Yeah, I did! [*laughs*]

COWAN: I want the women! [*laughs*]

MOORE: Oh, gosh, it was really something else. But such a coward I turned out to be. Because instead of calling back and letting Farley and Paul Foster and Thomas Breuster know that I wouldn't be joining them, I ducked. And my grandmother found the card releasing me, because I was still young, you know, and I ducked. And they called and they called and they called. And my grandmother said [*adopting his grandmother's high, thin voice*], "I'm not gonna go lying for you. You know what? You call 'em and tell 'em. I'm not gonna do this." So, I just got one of my girlfriends to say that I wasn't there.

COWAN: So, did they just finally quit calling?

MOORE: Yeah, they left.

COWAN: How old were you at that time?

MOORE: Oh, I was young, about nineteen or twenty.

COWAN: So, how old were you when you and Dave Prater met? Did you meet and immediately start working at the King of Hearts? Is that how it worked?

MOORE: No. Dave had been an amateur at a club where I was supposedly an MC, comedian, and singer for this club. An MC for future entertainment at the club. That's what the manager wanted. He wanted to start bringing in top acts, which, after a while, he started doing. That's why a lot of those entertainers who came to the King of Hearts knew about Sam & Dave because that's where we were. We had a following that you wouldn't believe. Two guys with no formal education, singing and whatnot. They came to this club to see Sam & Dave. Then, in 1961, my mother passed. She saw Dave. She knew Dave. But I got to tell you, we never, as I said in this conversation before, never disrespected her by singing rock and roll in the house. And I didn't lie. I just didn't fess up that I was doing that *outside* the house. Eventually, when she passed, I opened up then. In the last years of her life, she saw me leaving the house with suits that didn't look like suits for church.*

COWAN: Right.

MOORE: But I guess, being so sick then, it didn't really matter. I think mostly she really loved the fact that I didn't disrespect the home by singing that ungodly music in the house, which they called it at the time.

COWAN: Sure. When you guys arrived and started making the records that became gigantic hit records, there's no doubt that the planets aligned and that you guys were finally presented in a form that the world could enjoy.

---

* A word about the late, great Dave Prater, the other half of the most successful soul music duo in history. Dave was born in Ocilla, Georgia, in 1937 and grew up singing gospel in the church, and later with his brother J. T., in the Sensational Hummingbirds. He met Sam in the King of Hearts Club in Miami in 1961. They first signed as a duo to Roulette records and then, as you're about to see, to Atlantic in 1964. Together, Sam & Dave recorded ten straight Top 20 *Billboard* R&B hits. Tragically, Dave died in a car crash on April 9, 1988, in Sycamore, Georgia, while driving to his mother's house.

MOORE: Yes and no. Because when we were assigned to Atlantic, I didn't know anything about Tom Dowd* or Ahmet Ertegun. I just knew that we were signed to the label. Now, you must understand, at that time, Atlantic had some of the biggest stars on that label. I grew up listening to that stuff, y'know. Oh, Clyde McPhatter, Ruth Brown . . .

COWAN: Ray Charles.

MOORE: Ray Charles, and on and on and on. So, when they sent us down, they had no inkling. It wasn't like they said, well, you're gonna go down to Memphis, and they'll have this hit for you. Jerry Wexler so much believed in us, he really did. Ahmet and I had a love hate, cause when he first met me, he said right away, "You've got a big mouth! [*both laugh*] I hope you can back it up. I hope you can sing as well as you run your mouth." You know, I was always saying stuff when Ahmet was around, and I didn't care nothing about it. But I think Ahmet was trying to teach us a lesson. Cut 'em so we can put 'em up on the shelf.

COWAN: When you say that, you're saying when Jerry Wexler sent you to Memphis?

MOORE: Yeah, yeah.

COWAN: So, here we are. Sam & Dave finally get signed to Atlantic Records.

MOORE: Yes. I was on Stax, yeah.

COWAN: Jerry Wexler signs you. Then what happens?

MOORE: Well, let's drop it back a little bit. They came to the club where we were performing. They signed us, and they tried us on a couple of things. It just didn't work. The next thing you know, we were signed to go down to Memphis. And I saw Duck Dunn, and I said, oh boy. That wasn't so bad. And

---

* Tom Dowd was one of the most influential producers and engineers in jazz, soul, and rock history. If you own any records from the twentieth century, like Aretha Franklin, Ray Charles, Otis Redding, John Coltrane, Dusty Springfield, Charlie Mingus, Diana Ross, Willie Nelson, Eric Clapton, Bee Gees, Lynyrd Skynyrd, or the Allman Brothers, you have his production work in your house and probably didn't know it.

then, out came the man himself, Jim Stewart. That went pretty good. "Hi, Sam, how's everybody doin'?"* I'm standing near the street, and Jim is talking to us. "We have big plans, and we've heard of you guys locally," and blah, blah, blah, when, around the corner, coming up the street, here comes this guy with a pair of *chartreuse pants*. White belt. Pink shirt. *See-through!* White shoes. Pink socks! Something wasn't right with this picture. And hair. And a beard. And he walked up and he said, "Hi, Jim." And coming around the corner *next* was a guy with a beanie hat on his head. Hot as it is, he's got on this sweater, a pair of pants that look like pedal pushers, and shoes that went high up. And Jim says, "Sam, Dave. This is Isaac Hayes and David Porter, and they are going to be your producers." And I thought, *Oh, Jesus. Oh, Jesus. What is this?* But they took us inside, not knowing that Isaac was doing just what they should have been doing at other record companies: Try until you find a niche. Find a key. Well, he tried us on "Jody Rider," which is a country song. Big tears came up in my eyes as I'm standing there. Like water out your nose and stuff. Hot summer. Then he came up with another song, and another song, and said, "We're gonna start off cutting these." Well, I was really looking for rags to riches and to be loved, all that kind of stuff, man! But I just wanted to go back home. I really did. I said to Dave, "Man, I don't want to do this." But we didn't have that kind of clout. Nor were we strong enough to reject it. So, we stayed. And it worked out well, because each time we recorded a song, it got much attention. Much attention. Then all of a sudden, we hit a stride. "I Take What I Want." "You Don't Know Like I Know." "Wrap It Up." And they were just going, boom, boom, boom. Not right behind one another, but they were *going*. Then there was "Hold On, I'm Coming," which I didn't like. I didn't like any of their songs.

---

* Jim Stewart was a producer and cofounder of Stax Records. The name is a combination of ST in Stewart and the AX of his sister Estelle Axton, who mortgaged her home to help invest in her brother's studio. Stax went on to rival Motown as a great discoverer of Black music talent, including Otis Redding, Booker T. and the M.G.'s, the Staples Singers, Isaac Hayes, and Johnny Taylor. Jim passed during the writing of this book, in Memphis, at age ninety-two.

COWAN: What didn't you like about "Hold On, I'm Comin'"?

MOORE: None of it!

COWAN: What do you mean?

MOORE: It didn't do nothin' for me. It just didn't come out right, for me, you know? And you got a guy standing in front of you, spitting and yelling at you. My God, you got to yell at me? God! And spitting? Come on, boy, your mouthwash is not doing well here.

COWAN: [*laughing*]

MOORE: But anyway, I sang. And I *liked* "I Take What I Want." [*Sings "I take what I want . . ."*] Now we're bouncing a little bit. Then, "You Don't Know Like I Know." OK! Then we kept on and *now*, here comes "Hold On, I'm Coming." But it was done at first in like a blues, like Ray Charles.

COWAN: Like a slow shuffle?

MOORE: Like a slow shuffle, yeah. And that wasn't working. So, Isaac—Isaac Hayes—started piddling around with it while David Porter had to go to the loo. And Isaac just kept piddling around with it. And when he got the beat and the hook, he hollered from the piano, "Porter! Porter, I got it! I got it, Porter!" And from the back you hear Porter saying, "Hold on, I'm coming!" And Isaac says, "Yeah, yeah. We gon' use that!" Then there was "Soul Man," which I *hated*.

COWAN: You didn't like "Soul Man" either?! [*laughs*]

MOORE: No!

COWAN: I'm so surprised to hear this.

MOORE: I didn't like no "Soul Man." Didn't like no "Soul Man." And that went over and over and over and over. I was deliberately not doing it, not staying in the pocket with it 'cause I didn't like it. Isaac got me to the side and said [*lowers his voice*], "C'mon, blood. C'mon, man. I know what you're doing. Don't do this. I got it. We got it." So, you know, I believed in him. If he believed in me, you got to be together. You got to trust in your producer, and your producer has got to trust you.

COWAN: Well, then you just exploded. I was a little kid growing up in Kentucky, a little white kid, and I bought those records. It didn't matter. You guys became part of our culture and our consciousness. I'm sure what happened is that you guys just stayed on the road all the time, right? Did you get to experience it? What did it feel like when all of a sudden you went from being a kid, singing gospel, to having the biggest radio hits in the world? Did you get to feel it? Did it feel good to you?

MOORE: Speaking about it today, I think I did a good fake act. I was never satisfied or pleased with that stage work. My mind was always still on the country. And, if I could, on the gospel side. Any chance I got, I would go back. There were times I would run into Ray [Charles], and there were times on the road where we would see George Jones. And stuff like that. We were big stars. And we'd see Kenny [Rogers], before he got into the country thing.

COWAN: With the First Edition.

MOORE: Yeah. Then I heard what Pickett was doing, and what Aretha was doing. I knew where Aretha was coming from because of her dad.* But I think I did a good *fake* stage act. So, what I did was, I put a big band that would throw horns, and jump and dress flashy, not overly, in suits and whatnot, and preach and make the songs sound like a gospel caravan. That I could live with. I could sing a song so far and then break it down and go to preaching. If you listen back to all that stuff, you'll hear [*sings as if in a choir*], "Ahhhh." I wasn't satisfied with singing a song as written, or as is. I would take "If Something Is Wrong" and make something out of it. "Blame Me," and all that stuff. All the fast stuff, I would let Dave go as much as he wanted.

---

* Aretha's dad, C. L. Franklin, was a Baptist preacher of national renown. He broadcast on Sundays from the pulpit of the New Bethel Baptist Church in Detroit. Many of his electrifying sermons in the '50s were recorded and sold in record stores.

But when it came to the ballads, and the churchy things, you'd hear all that stuff in me. Ad-libbing and all that stuff. I didn't know at the time that I was writing the song. I didn't know. I think I did a pretty good church act.

COWAN: Are you cognizant of the fact that by now you've influenced two or three generations of vocalists? Do you get that about you?

MOORE: No. You know, I've been told that, and I'm honored. It's an honor to be put in the same class vocally as a George Jones.* It's an honor to be put in that class.

COWAN: Well, it's deserved.

MOORE: I hope so.

COWAN: I understand that it's hard to look at ourselves from the perspective that everyone else sees us.

MOORE: It is, yeah.

COWAN: I just hope in some part of your heart it's gotten through to you over the years, from the millions of people who've bought your records and heard you sing, how much you've done for us, for our souls and our being.

MOORE: I would hope so.

---

* I did not see that one coming.

PACIFIC STANDARD TIME

Anyone who's made his living playing music knows that we're all on the same river. We're just in different boats. It's likely that my first conversation with each of these Californians, Chris Hillman, Bernie Leadon, and Jimmy Messina, started exactly the same way, with me saying something like, "I need you to know how much your artistry has affected me in the course of my life." I was never blowing smoke their way. It was just the reality of the situation. As I've often said, I came into this business as a fan.

There's no doubt that geography affects how people think and how they act. All three benefited greatly from the LA music scene, from the Troubadour and the Whiskey, to the folk clubs like the Ash Grove and McCabe's. And while I was never in a band with Chris, Bernie, or Jim for any length of time or tried to emulate how they sang, it was our music that connected us. Their body of work and my appreciation of it is where our friendships started.

I wrote Chris Hillman a note when his own memoir came out a few years ago and told him how much I liked it. He sent me a note back that was really flattering, saying, "You're one of my heroes." All I could think was, *What are you talking about?* But he was a bluegrass guy at heart, and the very first time I met him, decades ago, he knew who I was, and I've enjoyed our friendship and mutual respect since then. If you're really, really lucky, you get to keep that friendship for years.

Photo by Jordi Vidal/Redferns/Getty Images

10

A BYRD, A BURRITO, AND A SQUIRREL BARKER WALK INTO A BAR

The Cosmic Life of Chris Hillman

A little over five years ago, I made a solo record with my dear friend John McFee from the Doobie Brothers. He not only produced my record but also added his prodigious talents as a guitarist, Dobro player, violinist, banjoist, and singer. We made the whole record at his Lizard Rock Studio in Solvang, California. It was called *Sixty* to celebrate the occasion of me leaping headlong into my "golden years" but also to acknowledge all the wonderful music and artists who I not only enjoyed friendships with but who also had influenced me so deeply as an artist. Near the very top of that list is Chris Hillman.

As a founding member of the Byrds, the Flying Burrito Brothers, Manassas, and later, the Desert Rose Band, Chris touched every signpost and mile marker on the road to melding the heart and sensibilities of country music with rock 'n' roll. In knowing and observing him for almost fifty years, I believe that he deserves every bit as much recognition as Gram Parsons in pioneering what we used to call country rock, or as we say these days, Americana. Because he lived about an hour away from the studio, we called and invited him over to sing and play, which he thankfully agreed to do. That is Chris. When you're done reading this, check out his vocals on "Why Are You

Crying?" with Bernie Leadon on banjo and the soulful "Fate Full of Shadow," recorded that same afternoon at Lizard Rock. It was a result of this happy session that I also asked Chris to hang around for this interview. Over the next three hours, we mined deep into his early bluegrass life, his curious affection for the mandolin—which tortures him to this day—and other events that made him an icon of American contemporary music and ultimately, a member of the Rock & Roll Hall of Fame. Chris Hillman is a brother.

JOHN COWAN: It's so great to have you here, Chris.
CHRIS HILLMAN: Thank you, John.
COWAN: You grew up in rural San Diego County?
HILLMAN: Well, my dad moved us down to a place called Rancho Santa Fe. That's about seven hundred people, in San Diego County. That was 1946. I was two years old. And I stayed there till I was seventeen.
COWAN: Were your mom and dad musical at all?
HILLMAN: I think my mother played piano at one time in her life, but they loved music. I grew up listening to the music they had in the house. Big band, and Sinatra. Peggy Lee and Lena Horne. And they had great taste. They'd go out and dance on the weekends. They'd been married since the '30s, and that's what they did. So, they were very encouraging, but no, they couldn't sing or hold a note.
COWAN: What perhaps was your first musical experience of significance? In other words, what was the first musical experience or first thing you ever heard that perked your ears up and piqued your curiosity? Can you remember?
HILLMAN: You know, John, I *can*. [*sings*] "If your baby don't treat you right, come up and see old, Dan." That was "Sixty-Minute Man," and that was probably 1954 maybe? My dad even had a copy of that because it was really a risqué record. I remember that record for some reason. What was I,

in the fourth grade? Then, of course, in the fifth and sixth grade Elvis came out and all the rock and roll started up in '56 and '57. But what happened where I lived, I would tune in every Saturday night on our old TV with the rabbit ears, and I'd get Spade Cooley live from LA and the *Johnny Otis Show*.

COWAN: Wow.

HILLMAN: So, there was two different ends of the spectrum. Here's Spade Cooley, who was really our Bob Wills in California. And Johnny Otis was a full R&B band. Etta James was on it. She was fifteen or something. Great stuff. All live. And that's what it was. I really loved it. And I really like the country stuff. My dad actually said, when I'd be listening to bluegrass records later in high school, "Are you sure this is our son? He wasn't left on our doorstep by some family in Oklahoma?" [*laughs*] So that was it. I think "60-Minute Man." I don't know why. That sort of just resonated.

COWAN: What was your first instrument?

HILLMAN: I had a guitar at about fifteen. Now, granted, when rock and roll came out, I didn't really have an inclination to play guitar. But when folk music started to get into my head, then country music and traditional folk, that's when I wanted to learn the guitar. That's when my mom bought me a $10—seriously a $10 guitar—in Tijuana. We were about sixty miles from Tijuana.

COWAN: Did you teach yourself?

HILLMAN: Yeah, I taught myself chords out of a chord book. And of course, I got into the mandolin. There wasn't *anybody* around where I lived who could play the mandolin. I was just learning. I had a passion. I had to learn. So, we'd slow records down.

COWAN: Why the mandolin?

HILLMAN: I don't know. It has been torturing me for fifty years now, that little . . . I call it Satan's instrument. [*both laugh*] It tortures, but I loved it. I think I watched the New Lost City Ramblers. Mike Seeger was playing an F5. Just the scroll and the mandolin, it was so beautiful, and the way he played. It was old-timey music. And, of course, I'd watch. I saw these bands in *per*son—Flatt and Scruggs, and Bill Monroe and the Stanley Brothers. They'd come up to LA, and I'd drive 140 miles up there with my friends, and we'd watch them at the Ash Grove, this really great club. Man, we were ten feet away from the stage, and we're watching them, and you're looking at their instruments. It was really nice.

COWAN: I find it really curious that you guys leaned so heavily into traditional country and bluegrass music as teenagers, because I think most teenagers, when Elvis, and later on as the Beatles came along, just gravitated toward rock and roll. It's so cool to me that you gravitated toward folk music, bluegrass and country, and decided that's what you wanted to play.

HILLMAN: There was a period between '58 and '63 or '64, when the Beatles came out, that rock was asleep. We had Fabian and Frankie Avalon and stuff like that. Then folk and bluegrass came on. I was one of two or three guys in a high school of six hundred people who liked bluegrass. Bernie Leadon was the same way. I met Bernie when he was still in high school. We, of course, worked in a band together, the Squirrel Barkers, and he was just a fantastic banjo player back then.

COWAN: Geographically speaking, there was a burgeoning folk music scene that included people like Elizabeth Cotten, Doc Watson, Mississippi John Hurt, Bill Monroe, Flatt and Scruggs, that, I'm gonna guess here, was born partly out of where you lived. Los Angeles, California, or New York City. If you lived in the middle of the country, I'm not sure that these people were going there to play those places. I think you were probably fortunate that you could go to the Ash Grove and hear a lot of these folks.

HILLMAN: Yeah, it was fantastic, because I would go and see Bill Monroe, and I remember that's when I met Del McCoury. He was the guitar player. He was a young guy. And Kenny Baker. It was just really good. The bands I saw, like the Stanley Brothers? Fantastic. Then I'd come up and see Lightnin' Hopkins. I loved all of that coming up from that roots area. The other thing that's interesting about bluegrass in the LA County area, you had the White Brothers, the Kentucky Colonels, Clarence and Roland White, and you had The Golden State Boys. Basically, there were so many people who had immigrated out to California during the Depression, the Dust Bowl, and right after World War II, to work. They were from the Southeast and the Midwest, Arkansas, Texas, and they brought that music. So, when I was eighteen, I had a fake ID and worked all the hillbilly bars with Vern Gosdin and Rex Gosdin and Don Parmley and the Golden State Boys. What an education.

COWAN: Well, let's talk about how that evolved into the Byrds.

HILLMAN: Well, that's interesting, too. Eventually the Golden State Boys [the Hillmen[, broke up. We were all starving, really. Vern and Rex had kids. Don had his son, David, who is a wonderful bluegrass singer . . .

COWAN: To this day.

HILLMAN: Yeah, and his nickname was Butch back then, the little guy. And I went to work. If anybody out there went to see *A Mighty Wind*, that mockumentary on folk music, I was in one of those bands for a little while! After playing with Vern Gosdin and Don Parmley, I'm in this fake bluegrass group called the Greengrass Group for a couple of months because I needed some money to eat. It was like *A Mighty Wind*. Awful music. Just awful. So along come the Beatles, 1964. I'm still in that silly group, the Greengrass Group, when Jim Dickson, who worked at this studio says, "Come down to the studio and listen to these guys. You know 'em. David Crosby and Jim [Roger] McGuinn. And Gene Clark." I said, I don't know Gene Clark. He says, "Come down and listen to 'em. They've really got something goin'." So, I go down there one night, and I listen to them. They were *good*. And I was spoiled from listening to the Gosdin brothers sing and I thought, *Gee, they are great! David Crosby, man*. A couple weeks later, Jim said, "They're putting a band together. Do you know how to play bass?" And I said, "Oh, yeah." I did *not* know how to play bass.

COWAN: [*laughs*]

HILLMAN: I did not get ahold of it till maybe the second album. But I went down. I knew it was going to be something. Here we are, we call us, the Byrds. There's five of us. David Crosby was going to play bass, but he went to guitar, which was a good thing because he's a great rhythm guitar player. We worked at it for about six months. We got hold of a song, and on we went.

COWAN: Is it true that the first single released was "Mr. Tambourine Man"?

HILLMAN: It was the first single that came out on a big label, yeah.

COWAN: And it exploded.

HILLMAN: It took off and all kinds of stuff. It started going and going and going. All of a sudden, we were working a lot on the Sunset Strip and developing as a band. We were good players, but we were coming out of folk music. So, plugging in amplifiers and learning how to perform is a different deal than never smiling in a bluegrass band. And you're sitting there, like really serious, because you've got a lot to think about. When you play in a rock band, you're supposed to be dancing around and moving to all that stuff.

COWAN: I'm almost sure of the answer to this. Now that you're in a rock and roll band, were you also a Beatles fan at that point?

HILLMAN: Huge. Loved them. Absolutely loved them.

COWAN: So, it wasn't a big leap for you artistically.

HILLMAN: No, not at all. I mean, initially the Byrds would emulate the Beatles. Of course, how we looked in our clothing. But I mean, Gene Clark was writing Beatles-type songs in the beginning. Then, once again, Jim Dickson is back in the scene as our manager helping us.* Here's the great advice

---

* Jim Dickson was a self-taught producer who was a historic influence in bridging folk, bluegrass, and rock in the California music scene in the '60s. His impact on Chris's career, and '60s music in general, is worth learning more about.

that I got from him, that we all got. He said, "Don't go for the quick hit. Go for substance and depth in your music, and you will record something that you're going to be proud of in forty years." And, so, he brings in "Mr. Tambourine Man," which had four verses, I believe, of the most beautiful poetry.

COWAN: And almost six minutes long.

HILLMAN: It's beautiful.

COWAN: Was Jim the one who decided to compress it and get it down to two minutes?

HILLMAN: No, *we* had to do that because in those days, 1965, a two-minute thirty-second single, very rarely three minute*s—that* was AM radio.

COWAN: So, you as a band . . .

HILLMAN: . . . took one verse. I didn't play on that record. The only guy who actually played on that session was Roger McGuinn. Then they sang it. Columbia Records used the Wrecking Crew* to do that single, and the flip side. Those were the only two songs that we didn't play on. A lot of people say to this day, "Well, they didn't play on their first album." Well, if you listen to the first album, you know it's us playing. And sometimes I wished we had played on the single, John, because it was so slick! The Wrecking Crew were professional session guys. They were wonderful players. In fact, Leon Russell was on that date. Isn't that funny?

COWAN: Is "So You Wanna Be a Rock 'n' Roll Star" on that record?

HILLMAN: No. I think that's on the third record we did. That's when I started writing songs.

COWAN: Which you cowrote?

HILLMAN: I cowrote that, yes.

COWAN: Who'd you write that with?

HILLMAN: McGuinn.

---

* The Wrecking Crew was a collection of some of the greatest studio musicians ever assembled. They played backing instrumentals in LA on hundreds of Top 40 hits in the '60s and '70s. There's a cool documentary about them by the same name.

COWAN: You know, that song, to this day, is used as a catchphrase in modern culture, so that's got to be flattering to you.

HILLMAN: [*laughs*] Yeah.

COWAN: It's such a great song.

HILLMAN: Thank you. We were only twenty-four years old and had already been around the block for a couple of years and were sort of jaded! So, we wrote this song, and it was great. We had Hugh Masekela playing on it, and it had that groove to it. That's because Crosby and I had worked sessions for Hugh, and it was all these South African musicians. I came out of there, and it was so . . . it just opened up the doors.

COWAN: I always wondered, why the trumpet?

HILLMAN: [*laughs*] Yeah, yeah . . .

COWAN: I would never want to hear it without it, but it's such a strange instrument for that song.

HILLMAN: And in the key of G! [*both laugh*] For a horn player to play in G is tough!

COWAN: Whose idea was that?

HILLMAN: Well, it's because of the groove of the song. [*sings*] da,da,da,bum, chh, da,da,da, bum—really came out of the session I did with Masekela. So, I thought he would be great on this, so he came and played on it.

COWAN: That is so cool.

HILLMAN: Yeah, and the screams on the record, those were real girls who were screaming at our concerts in England.

COWAN: By the second or third Byrds album, you guys were hugely popular all over the world. How old are you at this point?

HILLMAN: Twenty-three. Twenty-four.

COWAN: What was that like for you?

HILLMAN: [*exhales*] It was pretty nice! [*both laugh*] I don't want to say, "If only I'd been smarter." Well, obviously that's a given. But it was very exciting. The early part of the '60s, when we went to London in the summer of 1965, and the Beatles came around and hung out, it was quite the thing. I always look at the early '60s—that was the time. It started to get a little dark as the decade wore on, and it got to be a little edgier and sketchier. But initially, it was wonderful. Also, what was interesting is that you had some freedom if you did get signed to a label. They would keep you around for a long time, like two or three albums. You had a lot of freedom, *creative* freedom, in the studio. Even in the pop situation, where they just wanted to sell product, you had a lot of freedom.

COWAN: As the Byrds went on, now up to the Notorious Byrd Brothers, you started having more and more input as a writer and a singer.

HILLMAN: Right. I wasn't a good singer, but they put up with me. Man, I could sing in tune, but just no passion. I was a shy guy. Really, a shy kid. But there's one song I wrote, "Have You Seen Her Face?" David Crosby came in, and he laid on some harmony, and he saved it. He made that song so good. Not because I wrote it, but because his voice was so good.

COWAN: Tell me about Gram Parsons coming into the band. Did you bring him in?

HILLMAN: Yeah, and that's the story. I literally met Gram in a bank in Beverly Hills. I'd heard about him, but I didn't know him. I met him when we were in the process of getting some new people in the band. Roger and I were the last guys holding the flag. And I said, c'mon down, and I told him we'd rehearse. And Gram came down. Roger said, "We thought we were hiring a keyboard player. But what we got was George Jones in a sequined suit." [*both laugh*] But here's the good part. Gram was young, ambitious, he had a couple of great songs, "A Hundred Years from Now" and, good lord, "Hickory

Wind." Fantastic. We hit it off right away, because he had a love of country music, and he actually said, "I had a copy of the Squirrel Barkers album!"

COWAN: Wow! [*laughs*]

HILLMAN: Gram said, "I always wanted to be in that group." That was done in '63 when I was eighteen years old, so he was a couple of years behind me. But we had a good time, and he helped. I had an ally as far as country music. We'd go down to Nashville, and we'd do the *Sweetheart of the Rodeo* album. Very well received critically. The worst-selling record we made, because it was such a departure from what we were doing. But it's still looked upon as a monumental record.

COWAN: Yeah, that record looms large today. There's been so much written and said about it. The intention, obviously, was to do what was done with it, right? So, now Gram is in the band, and you have an ally who's a complete country music freak, perhaps even a bluegrass freak. Did Roger just go, "Oh this is great, let's do a country record. Let's go to Nashville." Was everybody was on board?

HILLMAN: Everybody was on board. And remember about Roger, it wasn't a stretch for him.

COWAN: No, he recorded "Pretty Polly," for goodness' sake.

HILLMAN: Yeah, he knew the music and had been the most seasoned guy in the Byrds. He'd been an accompanist to all these people. He had arranged Judy Collins's album before I ever met him. He knew folk music, and he knew bluegrass. And he played banjo, OK? We didn't hold that against him.

COWAN: [*big laugh*]

HILLMAN: He had a big long-necked Pete Seeger banjo. He still plays that thing. So, everybody's on board. We went down to Nashville and made great friends. John Hartford was on it, and Lloyd Green, bless his heart—what a great guy he is. I just saw him a couple of years ago.

COWAN: And he still plays great.

HILLMAN: Yeah, what a nice guy. And Junior Huskey. What a nice time.

COWAN: So, was making that record just a whole lot of fun?

HILLMAN: A lot of fun and in Columbia Studios. Of course, you know the story. Columbia gets us on the Opry at the old Ryman when it was a radio show, and we had a little bit of a problem there.

COWAN: Well, let's talk about that.

HILLMAN: It was 1968, and it was just radio. Live, of course, and we were on the Tompall & the Glaser Brothers segment as guests. We had told them that we were gonna do "Sing Me Back Home," which Haggard had a hit with that year, and some Byrds song, either "Tambourine Man" or "Turn, Turn, Turn." Just a couple of tunes. Little did we know that as we get up there to do "Sing Me Back Home," and Tompall says, "Fellas, you gonna do 'Sing Me Back Home,' Merle Haggard's big hit?" Gram says, "Nope, not tonight! We're gonna do "Hickory Wind" for my grandmother!" And, man, you coulda heard a pin drop. Well, we did it, and Gram sang it really well. People liked it. But Tompall didn't like it. And after that, we were off the stage, and we got yelled at quite well by him. I don't blame him. You know, if I look back now, it was unprofessional. You don't do that. With Gram, I should've known that would happen. [*big laugh*]

COWAN: So, that was a surprise to you guys as well?

HILLMAN: Pretty much, yeah. We just sort of went with it.

COWAN: He hadn't said . . .

HILLMAN: No, he didn't. Like I say, I should've known better. I did have some great times with him for about two years. But that night, it was tough. When we did sort of scoot out of the Opry back door, the only person who was really sweet was Skeeter Davis, and she says, "Hey, you Byrds! Don't listen to what these people say!" I loved that.

COWAN: [*laughs*] You Byrds!

HILLMAN: So, moving up twenty years in the future, when Desert Rose Band was on the Opry, Skeeter was there. I said, "Skeeter, remember that night?" And she says, "Oh, yeah." I said, "You were our only friend." And she said, "I was ready to get you in the car and take you over the state line!"

COWAN: So, after *Sweetheart*, is that when Gram departed the Byrds?

HILLMAN: Well, after we went to England with Gram, we had a little problem. Mick Jagger and Keith Richards were our friends from the old days, and they came to see us, and they invited us out that night to go drive to Stonehenge. So, Gram met them, and he was just *enamored* with that whole deal. And Roger and I were thinking, *hmm*. They're great guys and we had a great time. But then along comes this tour six months later where we're going to South Africa. We had no idea what was going on down there. We just decided to do it for the money and play concerts outdoors. Gram, at the last minute, said, "I'm not going. I'm not going to go with you guys. I'm not going to get on the plane tomorrow." He'd been listening to Keith about apartheid. "Don't go down there, it's bad" and all this stuff. We didn't know it was that bad. But for Gram to let us down like that—we went and did the tour, and it was terrible. He stayed behind in England and hung out with Keith Richards. I should've known then that he was not a standup guy. He made a commitment, and he broke it.

COWAN: Right.

HILLMAN: Then I came back, and the Byrds were sort of floundering. I decided to talk to Parsons about the Burritos. I said, "Look, I'll do the Burritos with you," and he said, "Yeah, c'mon, let's do this band!" And I said, "I'll do it, but don't pull that stuff again." Little did I know! I had a year and a half of *really* good work with him, OK? We wrote a lot of songs. We started the Burrito Brothers. It was a great idea. But one thing in hindsight: we were a very loose band. Here I am coming from playing "Eight Miles High" with the Byrds when the Byrds got to be a tight musical band. And the Burritos were sloppy. We couldn't get arrested back then. We couldn't get on country radio, we couldn't get on rock radio. Of course, now it's the greatest thing in the world. Everybody *loves* the Flying Burrito Brothers. And it was good. But here's the deal: to end the story, Gram and I had our problems again, and I said, "That's it buddy. We're done." I loved him dearly, John. I loved him like a brother. We were very close. But it became Cain and Abel. Obviously, I wasn't Cain. I mean, I loved the guy, but I said, "You're out. You're out of the band." I put the band together, I kept the band together, and made a good live band. I hired Rick Roberts.

COWAN: I want to put a bookmark in that, because one thing I want to mention, which I think is important, is, are you responsible for getting Clarence White into the Byrds?

HILLMAN: I am.

COWAN: But you weren't there when he was there, right?

HILLMAN: I was there for about two or three shows. I sometimes regret not sticking around with the Byrds for a while because of Clarence.* I loved the guy. I knew him since we were sixteen. I had used him on sessions in the Byrds, and he was the only outside guy we used other than that Wrecking Crew deal with "Tambourine Man." I brought Clarence in to play on this song, "Time Between" that I had written. To this day, the most awesome solo you'll ever hear on a Tele, without his string-bender and all that stuff. Just right out of the amp. He plays a solo that would knock you over to this day. I said, "Roger, let's get him in the band," and Clarence jumped in there. There are a couple of photos of us playing onstage, but darn it, I should've stuck around longer.

---

* If you are unfamiliar with Clarence White, please check him out on YouTube. He was an innovative, bluegrass flat-picking giant who influenced everyone from Tony Rice to Albert Lee. You'll understand why Chris was wistful about not playing with him more than he did. Clarence was tragically killed at age twenty-nine by a drunk driver.

COWAN: I guess everybody has a favorite Flying Burrito Brothers record. Actually, mine is the one you made after Gram left, when Rick Roberts came into the band. One of the reasons for that is that I have always been so enamored with your singing. I love "To Ramona" on that record. "White Line Fever" is on that record, too. It's just so good.

HILLMAN: I appreciate that. I like that record. I thought Rick was and is a great songwriter, and he came in at the right time. He sang great harmony with me. Oh, my gosh, he was locked in. We built that band up. Bernie Leadon was in that band for a while and stayed in it till the end.

COWAN: I feel like that part of the Burritos, for my money, was really solid. Part of the charm of the early Burritos was that is *was* sloppy.

HILLMAN: [*laughs*] That's right!

COWAN: But this version of the Burritos was not.

HILLMAN: No, it was musical.

COWAN: It was Bernie and you and . . .

HILLMAN: It had a groove. The old Burritos were, as you say, very loose. It had soul to some degree, but it didn't have cohesiveness. You couldn't really move to it. It was too loose. It was well intentioned, but we were not taking care of business.

COWAN: He's gone now, but I don't want to miss mentioning Sneaky Pete Kleinow, who was a wonderful pedal steel player.*

HILLMAN: [*laughs*] Fantastic!

COWAN: Who ended up playing on a Stevie Wonder record.

HILLMAN: He did! You know what was interesting about Sneaky? Every steel player I've ever worked with, and I've worked with Jay Dee Maness and Tom Brumley and Lloyd Green and Greg Leisz, every one of these guys is so meticulous with their instruments. Everything is perfect with the instrument

---

* Sneaky Pete played pedal steel on so many other records, too, including Little Feat, Little Richard, Linda Ronstadt, and Harry Nilsson. Amazingly, when he was not playing on records, he was also a top-notch special effects animator in Hollywood, working on *Gumby*, *Davey and Goliath*, and *Land of the Lost*.

and the approach. Sneaky would come into a gig, and his steel was always real funky. And I'd say, you gonna tune up? And he'd say, "I'll tune up later." [*both laugh*] And some nights, he would be orchestral. He would be so good. Other nights, he would be like one of Lawrence Welk's band members. [*sings*] Do too doot to doot, doot to doo. But John Jorgenson worked with Sneaky in a band, too, and we all loved him. He was a real character. A great guy.

COWAN: He does this stuff on "To Ramona" with the volume pedal that's just so crazy and wonderful on this song.

HILLMAN: [*laughs*] It's weird.

COWAN: So, what was the last Burritos album?

HILLMAN: *The Last of the Red Hot Burritos.* It was a live album, and it's kickin'. Al Perkins replaced Sneaky. Bernie was gone, so it was Al playing steel and lead guitar. Phenomenal player. We were doing rock 'n' roll stuff, and in the middle of the show, we had a bluegrass thing with Byron Berline and Roger Bush from the Kentucky Colonels, and Kenny Wertz from the Squirrel Barkers and myself in the middle of a Burrito Brothers concert doing bluegrass, right? We taped it. We made a live album, which was really interesting, because I loved the rock 'n' roll. We were doing "Ain't That a Lot of Love" and stuff like that.

COWAN: Then came Manassas.

HILLMAN: Yeah.

COWAN: Manassas was a band that Stephen Stills started, at the peak of his success. Crosby, Stills & Nash had made one record that was hugely popular. Then they made the Crosby, Stills, Nash & Young record, *Déjà Vu*, which was also hugely popular and then, Manassas. Go figure.

HILLMAN: Stephen had two hit singles on his own. "Change Partners" and "Love the One You're With." I know only that I ran into him somewhere. We had a night off, I think it was Cleveland, and he was on the road with his big band and horn section.

COWAN: Did you know him?

HILLMAN: Yeah, I knew him in the Buffalo Springfield, in '65, '66. We were good friends. So, a month later he calls me. "I'm doing an album in Miami, and I want you and Byron Berline and Al Perkins to come down here for a couple of days. I said OK. We weren't doing anything. We fly down there to do sessions and out of that came Manassas, where he just says, "Hey, listen, why don't you and I start this band up?" Now, the Burritos at that point, John, were really starting to work a lot, working huge concerts and colleges. All of a sudden, after struggling all those years, we were becoming a band that was being sought after, and I had to make that decision. Musically, I felt like it was time to move on. I'd stuck with that thing for three years or four years, and working with Stills was fun. It was a great band and it kept me on my toes. These guys were top musicians.

COWAN: And the first record you make as Manassas is a double album!

HILLMAN: Yeah.

COWAN: Which is kind of crazy. [*laughs*]

HILLMAN: Yeah.

COWAN: And you have a song on there that you cowrote.

HILLMAN: A couple of 'em. It was fun working in that band.

COWAN: Did you go straight from there to Souther, Hillman, Furay?

HILLMAN: Absolutely. After about two years of Manassas, Stephen was getting pressure to get back with Crosby, Stills & Nash. Then, somebody comes up with the idea of putting Richie, another old friend, J. D. Souther, and myself together. I didn't know J. D. then, but when we got in the band, I got to know him, and he's one of my dear friends now, a very talented songwriter. And we had a band! Souther, Hillman, Furay.

COWAN: Just so people will know, Richie Furay was in the Buffalo Springfield, one of the lead singers, with Stephen Stills and Neil Young.

HILLMAN: Yes, he was.

COWAN: Then he started Poco, with Jim Messina, Rusty Young, and Randy Meisner.

HILLMAN: [*laughs*] It's all funny, right? They're going in one door and out the other. Of course, Randy Meisner comes out of Poco and goes with Rick Nelson and then the Eagles. Bang! As did Bernie Leadon. The Squirrel Barkers, Flying Burritos, Eagles . . .

COWAN: For those of you who don't know, J. D. Souther was a great songwriter and singer who's made wonderful records himself, but most people probably know his music because he cowrote so many of the Eagles' hits.

HILLMAN: He did.

COWAN: So now you're in a band with J. D. Souther and Richie Furay. Let's talk a little bit about that.

HILLMAN: It was an incredible idea, a great idea on paper. But it was three singer-songwriters that never quite jelled as a band. It didn't have a sound. It didn't have a distinct sound. We had Jim Gordon, a great drummer. I brought Al Perkins along, and Paul Harris, a Manassas alum, on keyboards. Musically, it was great band.

COWAN: Is your next thing your Sugar Hill solo albums?

HILLMAN: No, I got together with McGuinn and Gene Clark.

COWAN: Oh, that's right.

HILLMAN: The '70s were interesting. I was in two bands that sounded like law firms. Souther-Hillman-Furay, and McGuinn, Clark & Hillman. It really took a lot of time naming those bands! [*laughs*] But McGuinn, Clark & Hillman did have a Top 20 hit with "Don't You Write Her Off." We were on Capitol Records, and we made about three records. Then Gene took off again, and it all fell apart. It wasn't meant to be. After that, I went back to square one, in the early '80s and started playing mandolin again and playing bluegrass festivals with Al Perkins as a duo. He played guitar and Dobro, and I played guitar and mandolin. At that point, we did *Ever Call Ready*.

COWAN: That's you, Al Perkins, Bernie Leadon, Jerry Scheff, David Mansfield. It was a gospel record?

HILLMAN: It was. And it was pretty darned good. We did a lot of shows together. Jerry was in Elvis Presley's band. Great bass player. And David Mansfield, of course, did a lot of movie soundtracks. Whenever I'm in New Jersey, I call David up and hope he comes down and plays with me. He's such a good guy. I was really back in the acoustic mold. I worked on Dan Fogelberg's album, Herb Pedersen and myself, and Dan wanted us to put a band together to go out on the road with him.

COWAN: Was this the *High Country Snow* album?

HILLMAN: Yes. Excuse me. Dan did a *bluegrass* album down in Nashville, as a matter of fact, with Norbert Putnam. So, we put a group together with Bill Bryson and this young guy named John Jorgenson, who I'd never met.

COWAN: [*laughs*]

HILLMAN: And I meet him. And I hear him play. And I go, "Oh, my gosh." This guy could burn on the mandolin and the guitar.* I mean, he was just fantastic. And young, just twenty-three years old or something. So that's it, we were a quartet, Herb, me, Bill Bryson, and John Jorgenson. We opened for Dan, and we backed him for about a one-month tour. We came back, and John wanted to put a band together. I said, "No, I'm done with that. I'm done with plugging in." But he talked me into it. And you know, there's an old saying that when you're least searching for something, it will come right to you. John. It's like you and I, we run down to the mailbox to see if our check came in. It's never going to be there. It'll be there when we're not looking for it.

COWAN: For sure.†

---

* John Jorgenson also burns on the electric guitar, mandocello, Dobro, pedal steel guitar, piano, upright bass, clarinet, bassoon, and saxophone. John tours these days with his bluegrass supergroup J2B2.

† For the record, Chris Hillman's royalty checks are considerably bigger than mine.

HILLMAN: So, I wasn't looking for it, but we put a band together, which ended up with J. D. Maness on steel, Steve Duncan on drums, and the four of us, so it's a six-piece band. All of a sudden, we're playing the Palomino one night, and we get a record offer. I'm like, "I don't get this."

COWAN: Was the band named at that point?

HILLMAN: No, not really. But it became the *Desert Rose Band* after an album I'd done, called *Desert Rose*, and a song I had written. And we got a record deal. Paul Worley, who is still making lots of hits, a very successful fellow in Nashville, produced us. We put a single out, "Ashes of Love," a Johnny and Jack song from the '40s, and it got to number eighteen or something like that on the country charts. And I thought, well, OK, whatever. The second song we put out was a song I had written called "Love Reunited," and I get the phone call. "Hey, your song's number six next week." And I said, "What?" And Paul said, "Number six with a bullet!"* I was used to this sort of sublevel of existence. But it's not supposed to happen with me singing a song I wrote. But it started, John, and Desert Rose had an eight-year run. That was a good band. I mean, as far as all those bands we just talked about, that was the most consistent band onstage. Ninety percentile.

COWAN: Plus, you were making country music and for the first time, you actually succeeded in having hit records on country radio.

HILLMAN: That's right. And you know what the best part was? Most of the people who became our fans did not connect the dots. It didn't matter who was in the Byrds or who did what before. They accepted us for what we were doing. They liked the music they heard. We didn't have to draw on anything like, "Well, he used to be in, fill the name in here."

---

* Paul Worley was an A-list studio musician when I met him in 1983, one of the few "Nashville Cats" who was actually *born in* Nashville. His production, publishing, management, and playing credits became like a who's who of the last half century of country music, from the Nitty Gritty Dirt Band and Willie Nelson, to Lady A, Blake Shelton, Martina McBride, The Chicks, and more. In 1983, I made *Soul'd Out*, an album of soul and R&B classics, which Paul produced, and that began a lifetime friendship.

COWAN: Here's a little philosophical, geographical aside for you. Our friend John McPhee had a band called Southern Pacific, from California.

HILLMAN: Right. Same time.

COWAN: You had Desert Rose Band.

HILLMAN: Yes.

COWAN: Now, if we go back to Bakersfield, we go to Merle Haggard, Buck Owens. Dwight Yoakam. Has there always been a little bit of a problem between country music that's made in California versus Nashville? Not with the success so much, but do you think there's been a little bit of a rough patch between California and parts east of the Mississippi?

HILLMAN: [*laughs*] *That* is a loaded question, but I'll tell you my opinion on that. I think you really did have to live in Nashville to be completely accepted in the business. Mind you, Haggard and Owens were never made Opry members.

COWAN: Exactly.

HILLMAN: And neither was Dwight Yoakam.

COWAN: I think that we Southerners think that country music is about us, and we forget what we were talking about earlier.

HILLMAN: Yup.

COWAN: There's a hotbed of country music, from Cliffie Stone in the late '40s, that you were exposed to. We weren't getting that stuff.

HILLMAN: It's like I said earlier. These people were transplanted Southerners and Midwesterners. They came out with the music they loved, and there was a marketplace for it. Buck Owens was from Texas. Haggard was from Oklahoma. Rose Maddox and the Maddox Brothers, they came out during the Depression and the Dust Bowl from Oklahoma.

COWAN: People forget that Loretta Lynn, though she was from Kentucky, her career started in the state of Washington.

HILLMAN: That's right. She did.

COWAN: Thanks to Buck Owens.

HILLMAN: Right. And the California guy who I think was really the architect of that Bakersfield sound was Wynn Stewart.

COWAN: Oh, yes.

HILLMAN: It was interesting because everything goes in cycles. Here we were, Southern Pacific and Desert Rose Band. We did what we could do. And Dwight Yoakam, too.

COWAN: It's always been curious to me to hear someone say, "Oh, they're from California." I mean, I've heard that a lot.

HILLMAN: Oh, yeah. Oh, yeah.

COWAN: Like somehow it denigrates the music, when the reality is country music owes a lot to the state of California.

HILLMAN: Yeah, I used to hear, "Well, they can't really play bluegrass out there. They're from California." I'd think, really? Clarence White and Byron Berline started his career out there and grew up there, as did Don Parmley, who really got it going.* He was from Kentucky but came to California when he was a young man. It didn't really matter where you lived if you understood the music and where it came from and how to express it, how to sing it, and how to perform it. Even if you lived in Alaska.

COWAN: What's true about the rock 'n' roll bands of the '60s, including you and your own personal history, or the Beatles, or the Eagles, these guys are all young men who are deep. You look at the first Beatles records, and they are full of American R&B covers, and with the Byrds and some of the aforementioned bands, it seems like musicians were super aware.

HILLMAN: I would agree—but in another sense, California was the edge of the continent. People came out there to get a new start. People who weren't born there. I was third generation. My great-grandfather came out in

---

* Don Parmley played banjo in the legendary Bluegrass Cardinals. He also did all the background banjo work for the TV series *The Beverly Hillbillies*.

the 1880s. And that's where it stopped! You couldn't go any further west. People took chances. So, when I say, reinvent, I mean they took chances on whatever they were doing, whether they were in acting or music or business. It was like—here it is, this is it, make it or break it. That permeated the soul out there. Once again, not saying that anything is better than any place else, but . . .

COWAN: When you look at all the people who came out to escape the Dust Bowl, they were starting their lives over.

HILLMAN: Most of Woody Guthrie's career was in California, up and down the state.

COWAN: Absolutely. Chris, before we go, you mentioned Herb Pedersen. You've had a relationship for fifty years with him. Can you talk a little about the joy and friendship and the musical experience?

HILLMAN: [*laughs quietly*] Herb is a phenomenal musician and singer. I must've used that word a lot in this talk, but he's the guy who makes us all sound good. And he's a very low-key fellow. Here's a guy who I met in 1963, a great banjo player, an incredible tenor singer . . .

COWAN: One of the best singers, period.

HILLMAN: I've got to tell you, he's one of the great, open-chord, rhythm guitar players ever. He's like Tony Rice or Jimmy Martin with his rhythm. We go back so long, we were kids. We both have a similar sense of humor, and we've been through every facet of knowing each other. We've wanted to strangle each other, but he's like a brother. We get along great. My gosh, you look at his pedigree. Emmylou Harris's first big single was "If I Could Only Win Your Love." That's Herb singing the duet with her. It's beautiful. And all the stuff he did with Linda Ronstadt, Dolly Parton . . .

COWAN: . . . James Taylor.

HILLMAN: James Taylor. Yeah, if you want to get the job done, you call Herb, to this day. He still gets calls to go in and do it. Not as much as it used to be, because it's a different business.

COWAN: I have a few friends like that, who I've know that long, who I've played music with that long. There's something so sweet about that, having a lifetime friend to share the experience.

HILLMAN: Yes, and he'll go and do other things. I'll do other things. Then we'll get back together and go out, do dates, and have a great time. We're just old guys now. The biggest thing we care about when we get on the road is, let's find a good restaurant!

COWAN: Exactly. [*both laugh*]

HILLMAN: But let me tell you, I'll get up there, and I'll take a big cab ride on the mandolin, on a solo, and he's always there on the downbeat. I'll look over, and there he is. Wherever I go, he's there with me, and you can't beat that. And, of course, his singing. It's great. When we sing, and you know this, John, when you've worked with people you know so well, you know where he's gonna go.

COWAN: You get to be like siblings.

HILLMAN: Right, you know exactly where he's gonna go. It's like siblings without the baggage.

COWAN: You know I've known you and certainly been a fan of yours as long as I've been a musician, since I was thirteen. From where I'm sitting, to paraphrase Frank Capra, what a wonderful life you've had.

HILLMAN: I really have. I'm truly blessed. And I always say if it stops tomorrow, I had a great time. But I don't think it's gonna stop. Whenever it happens, it's not my call. But I truly have had a blessed life. I finally figured out, John, that the worst exercise to engage in is looking over your shoulders and saying, "If only I'd have . . . If I had just . . ." That doesn't count. Because it's divine in a sense. You do things for a reason, and we're presented with choices. I didn't make good choices all the time. Who has? None of us do. But, man, thank God I didn't make drastic ones. I think that's another discussion. I had two good parents and was taught values and responsibility. But we also had tragedy in the family. Things like that happen. But I've enjoyed a great life. And it's funny, I never went after being the star. I didn't want it. I was a band guy. When that finally changed, I said, "Well, I've had a long apprenticeship." With Desert Rose, I was singing lead and emceeing the show, and I had a great time.

COWAN: Well, sometimes we just find ourselves with the reins in our hands and not by our own intention.

HILLMAN: That is wonderful! I like that. I might use that in a song.

11

GOD'S OWN SINGER OF SONGS JUST MIGHT BE BERNIE LEADON

As far as we both can recollect, Bernie and I met each other in 1987, after he agreed, somewhat tenuously, to go back on the road as a member of the Nitty Gritty Dirt Band. Our band, New Grass Revival, had been opening for the Dirt Band since I had joined in 1974. That in itself was still a pretty big deal for us and, suddenly, so was meeting Bernie Leadon. Bernie and I both lived in West Nashville then and ran into each other frequently. I'd been around him enough that I finally felt like a peer, rather than an embarrassing fanboy.

I'd followed Bernie as a musician and fan since he joined Doug Dillard and Gene Clark for *The Fantastic Expedition of Dillard & Clark*, right on through his tenure with the Flying Burrito Brothers. I'd gone down the country rock rabbit hole from Poco (I was obsessed), to Graham Parsons, the Burritos, Mason Proffit, Ozark Mountain Daredevils, Amazing Rhythm Aces, Linda Ronstadt, Emmylou Harris, Clover, Pure Prairie League, and Cowboy. Somehow, Moby Grape was right in there, too. So, when I bought the first Eagles album, Bernie was the only Eagle I honestly knew anything about.

Beyond their technique, gifted musicians like Bernie are able to make simple, indelible contributions to music that we remember when we hear it. Think of B. B. King's three-note guitar bends, Eddie Van Halen's tapping, the beauty of Bonnie Raitt's phrasing, Earl Scruggs's three-finger, five-string banjo roll, Doc Watson's flat-picking and voice; I could go on. Next time you

Photo by Henry Diltz/Corbis via Getty Images

hear "Peaceful Easy Feeling" or "Take It Easy," go ahead and sing along and know that every note of those guitar solos that you know by heart is Bernie. If you journey down the path of his musical legacy, what you'll find is a conscious commitment to playing the appropriate thing sought by the composer, vision for how to put the pieces together in a coherent way, and a simple hard-fought beauty in every damn note. This visit with Bernie was conducted in the kitchen of his farmhouse southwest of Nashville.

JOHN COWAN: All right, Bernard Matthew Leadon III.

BERNIE LEADON: Hey, John.

COWAN: I want to know a little bit about your family. You had nine brothers and sisters? How long did you live in Minneapolis?

LEADON: Till I was ten.

COWAN: Were you the first person to have a musical instrument in your home?

LEADON: Other than my mom had a piano. We always had a piano, and she played wonderfully. She played music in the choir, and Dad sang baritone or bass in the choir. I'd sit in the choir loft, in this old wooden building, and listen to them sing three- and four-part harmony. I started piano at six. Then trombone when I was eleven or twelve.

COWAN: When did you move to San Diego?

LEADON: We moved to San Diego when I was ten. When the folk thing started, I discovered the Kingston Trio in maybe '61, and Dave Guard on banjo.

COWAN: So, you weren't necessarily aware of Elvis and that wave of rock and roll?

LEADON: No, I wasn't an Elvis guy, and I wasn't a Bill Haley and the Comets guy. I wasn't really aware of Chuck Berry, either. The first pop group that nailed me personally was the Kingston Trio. I need to explain this. I had an internal business plan from that point on: I'm going to do music professionally. I was like, thirteen. [*Cowan laughs*] I'm going to do music professionally. I will make a lot of money. And I will be famous. That was my business plan. [*laughs*] So, I discovered a bluegrass group in town . . .

COWAN: In San Diego.

LEADON: In San Diego, called the Scottsville Squirrel Barkers. They had a store called The Blue Guitar Shop where they did repairs and lessons and did gigs on the weekends, and I started hanging in with those guys and ditching school when I was fifteen. They were a great band. They did all these Jimmy Martin songs, and they sounded right. And they were funny, you know? I just was bitten. Of course, the mandolin player was Chris Hillman, who later on ended up in the Byrds. Then we moved to Florida when I was almost seventeen. By the time I moved to Florida, I was really a good banjo player already, technically, at sixteen. I found some bluegrass people to play with, and I started a Top 40 rock band.

COWAN: Were you enamored with the Beatles?

LEADON: Yeah, yeah, I loved the Beatles. They had a lot of folk in there, four chords and stuff. A lot of folkies could relate to the Beatles, you know? Anyway, I had a Top 40 band in Gainesville, playing college fraternities and stuff. Don Felder was in that band, who ended up in the Eagles. Me and Felder were kind of like the senior band at that point. My brother was playing with Tom Petty in *his* band, and they were five years younger, so they were in junior high. So, Felder and I would be in my bedroom practicing, and Petty and my brother would be in the other bedroom practicing.

COWAN: So, you go to Florida, and you're still playing the banjo, and you're still playing bluegrass.

LEADON: I think it was after I got to Florida that the Dillards had started playing in LA around '62 or whatever. Those albums were notable. I had them. I was fascinated by Doug Dillard. So, I just did the same slowing of his records down and learning his parts. I had learned a lot of Doug's music, and then in '67, I was in the army reserve, and I went to basic training. When I got back from training, I got a couple of phone calls from LA from two of the guys who had been in the Squirrel Barkers. They had each moved to LA and *each* was either in a band or managing a band that had a major record deal. They both offered me a slot to come and join their band for their second album. And I picked Hearts and Flowers because they were on Capitol Records. I did that for maybe a year. I think we did two albums, or one album, and we played the Troubadour, and that's about it. Then that band fell apart, and I had nowhere to stay. So, I met Doug Dillard somewhere, probably at the Troubadour bar, and I was like, "Man, you're like my banjo hero, y'know," and he invited me to come and stay on his couch. I was living with Doug and sleeping on his couch, and he was at loose ends, and so we would just sit around and pick way into the night. Some other people came over, and we started writing instrumental tunes. Then Gene Clark, who had been in the Byrds, started coming over. And he'd come back the next day with a complete set of lyrics. Whoa! Those are good lyrics. Let's sing that. So, we'd sit around and sing that in four-part harmony. And every day we'd have something new, and Gene would come back with another set of lyrics the next day. So within about two or three weeks, we'd written all the songs on the first Dillard & Clark album. We were rehearsing by ourselves for, like twelve hours a day. We were tight already. We were singing four-part harmony. So, we went in and recorded the whole album in about a week.

COWAN: Who wrote "Train Leaves Here" with Gene?

LEADON: I did.

COWAN: You did?

LEADON: Yeah.

COWAN: Aha. That's how it appeared on the first Eagles record.

LEADON: Yeah.

COWAN: So, you made the record. Then what happened with the expedition, so to speak?

LEADON: Dillard & Clark was kind of a fragile chemistry. I mean, there was really great chemistry, but there was a lot of volatility in Gene and, basically, it fell apart.

COWAN: I want to circle back to the Burrito Brothers and your entrée into the Burritos.

LEADON: OK, well, in '68 there were several groups that did sort of what now could be called country rock albums in LA. There was Dillard & Clark, the one we did. There was *The Wheatstraw Suite* that the Dillards did after Doug left. Poco started around that time, I think. And then the first Burrito album. They all sort of happened around the same time, '68 or '69. Actually, I was also playing on the side with Linda Ronstadt, who was also doing country rock.

COWAN: Right.

LEADON: She was doing Waylon Jennings's songs and stuff like that. So, it was kind of just all happening. The Burrito Brothers, both guys had come out of the Byrds, and there were no hits on that first album, so they didn't have a hit either. Dillard & Clark fell apart. I was working with Linda Ronstadt when the original bass player in the Burritos quit. We were all on the lot—we would see each other on the A&M lot—rehearsing, and I knew Chris Hillman from the Squirrel Barkers. So, their bass player, Chris Ethridge, quit. Hillman moved from guitar back to bass, which he played in the Byrds, and they said, "Hey, Leadon, you want to join?" [*laughs*] And I went, "Sure, I'm not making any money over here. I won't make any money with you, either, but it sounds like fun." What happened next is that they had an advance for their first album, and they had done a train tour and had spent all of their money. So, I joined a band that didn't have a hit on their first album, they had spent all their advance and had no money to give me *at all*. No support money. I mean we had no salary, nothing. So, Hillman and I got a place together.

COWAN: And at that time, the band was Gram Parsons . . .

LEADON: Chris Hillman . . .

COWAN: . . . Bernie Leadon, Michael Clark . . .

LEADON: . . . and Sneaky Pete Kleinow on steel.

COWAN: That's a pretty damn good band.

LEADON: The Burritos made a second album, which was kind of a classic sophomore album. They had brilliant songs on the first album, but then they had no more songs.

COWAN: This was the *Burrito Deluxe* record?

LEADON: Yeah, so we tried to write songs for that, but if you listen to that album, we were struggling to write good songs.

COWAN: Except, there are two songs on here, one that you wrote yourself, and the other is "Man in the Fog" that you wrote with Gram. But "God's Own Singer" is an amazing song. To me it should be in the canon of classics, and maybe it will be, who knows? Could you just tell me a little bit about writing that song? Had you already written it?

LEADON: I wrote it before I got in the band.

COWAN: You did?

LEADON: Yeah, I wrote it in probably '69 or something like that.

COWAN: Was it just fiction or was there a person you were thinking about who had his career for forty-nine years?

LEADON: No, no, it was fictional. I was aware of some of the older country artists and stuff. But I also had this idea of—maybe it was because I had just been in three bands and hadn't made any money—[*laughs*] that this could be a trend, and if this trend continues, I'll be this guy who basically did this music his entire life because he loved it and because he saw it as being service in a way, which I think, John, it is. Ultimately, what we've done our entire lives is be of service.

COWAN: Absolutely.

LEADON: To be an artist is to be of service to people. Shall I explain that briefly?

COWAN: Yeah, you should.

LEADON: OK, here's what an artist is. It turns out that everybody feels the same emotions about life. But most people don't know how to express it. So, the artist says, this is what happened to me, and it felt like this. And people go, "That's how I feel. Now I don't feel alone." That's the sum total of what artists do, I think, that's of service to people. And you got to have somebody do that, and that's what artists do. The guy in that song did it because he loved it. That's the deal.

COWAN: We probably should talk about Gram Parsons at this point.

LEADON: I don't know if people know anything about Gram Parsons. He's kind of considered the godfather of country rock, I guess. [*laughs*] He grew up in Florida and south Georgia, into what was a well-to-do family. His father was an alcoholic and committed suicide near Christmas Day when Gram was twelve, which had to have been really rough. Gram was a trust-fund baby.* He had been in folk groups in north Florida. He went to Harvard for one term, where he basically started a band in Boston, called the International Submarine Band, quit Harvard, moved to LA, somehow met the Byrd guys, and fell into that. They made *The Sweetheart of the Rodeo* album, which was too much country, I guess, for Roger McGuinn and the rest of the Byrds, so Gram left, and Chris Hillman left the Byrds, and then they did the first Burrito album, which I think has brilliant songs on it. So,

---

* What Bernie is referring to here is that the immensely talented Gram, whose given name was Ingram Cecil Connor III, was born into a fruit-packing empire. At one point, his family owned a third of Florida's citrus crop.

as I said, I joined for the second album. They'd run out of money, but Gram was a trust-fund baby, so he had plenty of money. He had new Harleys and whatever. Hillman had a little bit of money. I had no money, except for the session money that I was doing. Gram had the ability to move about the planet differently than most people. He was an extremely charming, southern gentleman kind of a guy. A tortured soul probably related to his father committing suicide while he was in the house. And, Gram, I guess it's no secret, got into drugs and alcohol. He was self-medicating more and more, but when I first met him, it was possible to hang out and have conversations and work and write and whatever. But it became less and less easy to do that.

Then what happened is that the Rolling Stones came to LA and spent the summer a couple of times, and Gram met them. And once he met those guys, he was just off to the races in that circus. Ultimately, Gram was fired from the Burrito Brothers, by Chris Hillman, for not showing up because he was trying to be part of the Stones, which didn't work out either. Around that time, Gram was going to leave to go live in the south of France to live with the Rolling Stones, and he asked me to go with him. I didn't go. My answer to him was, "It sounds like fun, but you have money, and I don't. [*laughing*] I can't afford to go to the south of France, man."

COWAN: Let's talk about your transition from the Flying Burrito Brothers into the Eagles, and how that all went.

LEADON: So, one weekend I was home, and I went down to McCabe's Guitar Shop in Santa Monica and ran into a lady. I expressed that I was less than thrilled about being in my current situation, and she said, "You know you should call up Linda Ronstadt's manager, because Frey and Henley are putting together a group. Why don't you call up those guys?"

COWAN: Did you kind of already know them?

LEADON: Yeah, I knew them from the Troubadour.* Not Henley so much, but, as the Burrito Brothers morphed after the Blue album, Sneaky Pete the steel player left, and we hired Al Perkins, who had come to LA with Don Henley's group, Shiloh. So, I was rooming with Al Perkins, and he kept talking about this great singing drummer named Don Henley, who's unbelievable, so I had my Don Henley radar on. When I went to McCabe's that day and that girl, Carol, said, "Don Henley and Glenn Frey are starting a group. You should call 'em," I called them up and said, "Hey, I'm thinking about leaving the Burritos. What are you doing?" And they said, "Come to our rehearsal." So, I went down to a place called Studio Instrument Rentals. The Jackson Five were in the next room.

COWAN: [*laughs*]

LEADON: Their costumes were in the hallway. We went into a little room and played for two hours. And we all went, "This is pretty good."

COWAN: The three of you, or was Randy already there?†

LEADON: Randy was already there. I'm not sure if Randy had ever hit a lick with them. So, we all sat in this one room, four original Eagles, and we thought it was pretty good. I remember that they came down to see me play at the Ash Grove, sitting in with Clarence White and those guys.

COWAN: The Kentucky Colonels?

LEADON: [*laughs*] Probably. So, I was sitting in with the Kentucky Colonels at the Ash Grove, and Frey and Henley came down and saw me play. I'm sitting there playing banjo, and they saw me rip a solo or something

---

* This isn't the first time in these interviews that the name Troubadour has come up. There's a reason for that. The legendary Troubadour, which opened in 1957 in West Hollywood, was (still is), a club that became a launching pad for the very biggest names in rock, folk, and comedy, including Elton John, Joni Mitchell, Neil Young, Kris Kristofferson, The Byrds, Tom Waits, Pearl Jam, Vince Gill, and Steve Martin.

† Randy, of course refers to the late Randy Meisner, a founding member of the Eagles and their original bassist. He wrote and sang lead on "Take It to the Limit," the Eagles' first number one hit in 1975, and also "Try and Love Again" from the album *Hotel California*. He quit the Eagles in 1977 for what was said to be "exhaustion" but also some private artistic differences that eventually became pretty public. He was replaced on bass by Timothy B. Schmit from the band Poco. Schmit had replaced Meisner in that band, too.

and thought, good, and the next thing we all go, "Hey, let's be a band." Glenn Frey and J. D. Souther were in this group called Longbranch Pennywhistle, and they were signed to David Geffen management, and Geffen was about to drop Glenn because he didn't want Glenn. He only wanted J. D. Glenn was desperate to come up with something and not get dropped by Geffen. We had entrée to his office and called up Geffen and said that we wanted to have a meeting. We went in and said, "OK, we're a band. You want us or not?" Geffen said, "I want to come to a rehearsal," so he came to one rehearsal and said, "OK, you're signed to management." We said, "We want to be on Atlantic Records." He said, "OK, I'll get you on Atlantic. I just started a label called Asylum with Atlantic, so you'd be distributed with Atlantic." And we say, OK. So, we get with Geffen, we're immediately on his own label. The first three acts were Jackson Browne, Joni Mitchell, and we were the first band. They sent us to Aspen, Colorado, to "woodshed" in ski season. We went up there and played two weeks at a time in a ski lodge. Four sets a night.

COWAN: Were you doing cover music?

LEADON: A lot of cover music. We had "Witchy Woman" already, and we were starting to work up stuff. Doing some J. D. Souther song . . .

COWAN: You wrote "Witchy Woman" with Don Henley.

LEADON: With Henley, yeah.

COWAN: Do you remember how that happened? Who did what?

LEADON: I had the music, and then he'd add the lyrics. Before the Eagles started, I had the music to "Witchy Woman."

COWAN: What did it start with? [*sings a melody*] Doo doot. Doo Doot . . .

LEADON: No, it was [*singing*], Da da, da da da, da da dah, da dah da. I mean, it really sounds like a Florida State football fight song!

COWAN: [*laughs*] Yeah, it's like, where's the Appaloosa?

LEADON: [*laughs*] So, we woodshedded for two weeks at a time twice in Aspen.

COWAN: Was that fun?

LEADON: Yeah, it *was* fun. We would start at nine and end at one in the morning, and we became a band because we did a lot of Chuck Berry songs. What else are we gonna do? We did every Chuck Berry song. And we'd just practice, and we became a band. So, then it was time to make an album. We'd wanted to hire Glyn Johns, the English producer who had worked with the Who and the Stones. Famously, he came and heard us at a rehearsal in Denver and said, "No, I don't think so." He thought the band was pulling in two directions. He thought Frey was pulling it Detroit rock, I was pulling it country, and the guys in the middle were being pulled both ways. He didn't think it had jelled, didn't think we were a good rock band, and sort of didn't really hear it.

COWAN: Did you have all the songs already for the first record?

LEADON: No, we had maybe half of them. So, famously, he went back to England, and we famously said, no, you made a mistake. Come back. So, he came back and came to another rehearsal in LA and again said, no, I don't hear it. So, we said, well, let's go to lunch. But before we go to lunch, let us sing you this song we just did acoustic, just four-part harmony with one acoustic guitar. So, we stood around, put our heads together, and did a song in four-part harmony, full voice. And then Glyn Johns said, "Aha!"*

COWAN: So, let's look at the first two records. I'm just curious about the band. Do you remember there being an intention about what it is you were doing or wanted to do?

---

* Glyn Johns is a member of the Rock & Roll Hall of Fame and was one of the most in-demand producers in rock history. He produced, engineered, or mixed bands like the Rolling Stones, the Who, Led Zeppelin, the Beatles, Eric Clapton, the Clash, Crosby, Stills & Nash, Emmylou Harris, and the Eagles, of course. In an interview with the BBC in 1982, he described the "aha" moment that Bernie mentions: "I don't think I'd been as excited since Led Zeppelin. . . . They were amazing. And they didn't really know what they'd got."

LEADON: Absolutely. In fact, I've been thinking about that a lot. We talked about that, and we stated our intention. Our business plan was simply to make excellent music that everyone loved, become world famous, and make a lot of money. That was pretty much it. That was my business plan from the time I was thirteen when I discovered the Kingston Trio, and then later the Beatles, and still later the Rolling Stones and whomever, and went, wow, it's possible to have it all. That's what we saw.

I think I mentioned before that that summer "Take It Easy" went up the charts, and you could not listen to a big station anywhere in the United States and not hear it every hour. And as we traveled around and landed in new towns and would hear ourselves, in that same hour in every town that same summer you would hear "Listen to the Music" by the Doobie Brothers.

COWAN: Which also has banjo in it.

LEADON: [*laughs*] Which also has banjo halfway through it!

COWAN: Though he doesn't play in double time.

LEADON: No, but I was like, "Yes! Banjos are rising!" [*laughs hard*]

COWAN: This can be the new thing.

LEADON: And actually, thirty-five years later, it did become the new thing in country music. Somebody explained that every country single has to have a banjo on it.

COWAN: Not so much now, I don't think.

LEADON: Yeah, it faded.

COWAN: There was the credibility scare in the '80s.

LEADON: Yeah, the banjo scare.

COWAN: "Early Bird."

LEADON: Oh, yeah.

COWAN: You got some crazy sounds playing under the bridge. Is there anything else in particular that you want to say about that song?

LEADON: Yeah, sure, so we're in England. It's November something. It's cold and rainy, and we're in a damp and cold studio, and we're drinking tea constantly trying to stay warm. We had a certain number of songs we came over with. "Take It Easy," "Witchy Woman," "Peaceful Easy Feeling," a number of them. But we were short. And Henley wasn't really writing yet. He had written "Desperado," but that's it.

COWAN: He couldn't have just written that song.

LEADON: Well, he had also written the lyrics to "Witchy Woman," so I take that back. But anyway, we were short songs. I had already done "Train Leaves Here This Morning," which I had brought over from Dillard & Clark.

COWAN: Right.

LEADON: Glyn Johns was trying to create this equality where Randy and I would also be singing a couple of songs, or at least one. Whatever. So Randy and I went off to try to write a song, and so we made "Early Bird" up out of nothing. That's why the lyrics are a little weak. The concept's a little thin. We basically wrote that song in the studio, and I think Randy had gone down to Portobello Road and bought this little cuckoo clock, and that's where the idea for the bird came. Cuckoo clock. Bird. Early bird. Whatever. Somehow, we cobbled this song together. But it's a cool track. And it's another excuse to play banjo.

COWAN: I love it.

LEADON: Music is a vocabulary, and it's a language. If you know how to speak music, you're going to speak in phrases just like you are in conversation. Somebody who is younger, who learns a lot of licks, even if they're just stringing licks together, you can hear that. They're not saying anything.

COWAN: That's the thing about those solos on "Take It Easy" and "Peaceful Easy Feeling." They were very melodic. It didn't sound like some guy . . .

LEADON: Noodling.

COWAN: It was very thoughtful. That's the word I would use about it. And it's everlasting. Anything else you'd want to say about "Peaceful Easy Feeling"? I've always thought, from the get-go of that track that the atmosphere of that song tells you what the lyric is going to be about.

LEADON: Well, good on Jack Tempchin, who wrote the song, and good on Glenn Frey to realize that was a good song.

COWAN: Do you know what form Glenn heard that song in at first?

LEADON: Glenn used to go down to San Diego County and do some shows with Longbranch Pennywhistle, and he ran into Jack Tempchin. So, they must've been sitting around backstage playing acoustic guitar. I imagine Glenn heard it as a singer-songwriter demo, live, just guitar and voice from Tempchin.

COWAN: So, how did it make its way on the record? Did Glenn just say, "Hey, I've got this song that Jack wrote. Here's how it goes"?

LEADON: Yeah, he would just play us the song. Glenn would write "Lyin' Eyes" or "Tequila Sunrise" or whatever, and he would say, "I'm working on this song, and it goes like this."

COWAN: I'd like to talk about "Desperado." A landmark record and artistic statement. How intentional was that?

LEADON: It was intentional. One thing I want to point out was within a few years, artists would only put out an album every couple of years. But when we signed in 1971–1972, the standard record contract said you will—you *will*—deliver two entire albums every year.

COWAN: That's unbelievable.

LEADON: The Beatles had to do that. The Stones had to do that. And we had to do that.

COWAN: You made two records a year?

LEADON: We made two records a year. We almost made it that first year. We went out and toured behind "Take It Easy," "Witchy Woman," and

"Peaceful Easy Feeling." Within a month, we were scheduled to go back into the studio. So, the Eagles had four writers who were still kind of developing. Then there was Jackson Browne, Jack Tempchin, and J. D. Souther, who were outside writers, and we had access to some of their material. So, while we were out touring, Jackson Browne, J. D. Souther, Glenn Frey, and Don Henley were talking about the "Doolin-Dalton" thing. Somebody had gotten a book about outlaw gangs, and that gang was not very well known. Glenn Frey and Don Henley were thinking about the outlaw concept, and "Doolin-Dalton" was the first song. I think Jackson Browne and J. D. Souther were in on writing that. It was kind of them collaborating and thinking that maybe we could expand this. I use this analogy of the rock and roll band now, and outlaws then. It was a youth, devil-may-care, live for today and to hell with tomorrow kind if thing. Then "Desperado" got written, which I have to say is a phenomenal song. It was Henley's first kind of complete song.

COWAN: If he had only ever written that song, that would have been enough for most people.

LEADON: I mean that's a phenomenal piece of literature, really.

COWAN: Absolutely.

LEADON: Yeah. Then shortly after, Glenn Frey said, let's make a concept album around this. We'll take some other stories from the book and from the life of those people, and we'll try to write songs around it. And then he kind of handed out topics.

COWAN: [*laughs*]

LEADON: Like, he said, so there's this guy in the band, Bitter Creek Newsome, who was one of the characters in the actual gang. Anybody want to write about Bitter Creek Newsome? And I went, "I will!"

COWAN: So, then after you've assembled the songs that were going to be on *Desperado*, is Glyn Johns already aware that this is what you guys want to do? Or was he even a part of this?

LEADON: Yeah, he recorded it.

COWAN: I know, but was he part of the idea?

LEADON: No, not really. But Glyn Johns was quite keen on concept records that were based on historical ideas. Not too long after I left the Eagles, Glyn recorded two concept albums around American themes, one around the Civil War and one around the American West, song cycles, and he used people like Emmylou Harris on them. But those came a few years after *Desperado*, and you could view them as being influenced by *Desperado*. But Glyn Johns was fine with this idea. Basically, Glyn was OK with any expression by an artist as long as it worked.

COWAN: Did it take any longer to make that record?

LEADON: The first album took three weeks. But we had most of the songs. I wrote "Early Bird" in the studio. The second album, *Desperado*, took four weeks total, but it had a string section, so that took an extra few days. So, four weeks, mixed. Done. The first album cost $13,000 to record.

COWAN: [*laughs*]

LEADON: The second album cost $26,000 because it had London Philharmonic strings on it.

COWAN: Almost as much as *The Long Run*. [*laughs*]

LEADON: For one day! [*laughs*]

COWAN: You guys had this onus to go on the road forever and come back and deliver hit records. That seems like a lot of responsibility.

LEADON: It is. I tried to take time off. I lived out near the beach, and I would go down to the beach and go bodysurfing. I had another circle of friends out there. Don and Glenn lived in town and lived together at that time, and they were pretty much immersed in it. They didn't have an escape. They were living it 24-7. And that's why they were so productive, too.

COWAN: Who was the point man on the Eagles who had to get on the phone with the agents and the publicists, which takes up twelve hours in a day sometimes?

LEADON: I think Glenn Frey. I remember when *Desperado* came out, there was this big Top 40 station in LA called KHJ, and it was right in the industrial part of Hollywood. Glenn organized renting a stagecoach from a movie studio, and he and Henley rode to KHJ in the stagecoach . . .

COWAN: [*laughs*] I love it.

LEADON: . . . down Santa Monica Boulevard, which was just busy with traffic. So, they pull up, and here come the DJs to meet the Eagles in a stagecoach.

COWAN: So, next comes *On the Border*.

LEADON: That was the third album. We tried to make that album in London. Only two songs were finished. "The Best of My Love" and "You Never Cry Like a Lover," both Henley songs. I had only had a steel guitar for two weeks, and I figured out a steel guitar part and played it on "Best of My Love," and Glyn Johns said, "Double it!" So, it was one of the first doubled steel leads.

COWAN: Was that a Top 10 or was that a number one song?

LEADON: It was a number one.

COWAN: That was your first number one?

LEADON: Our first number one, yeah. But before that record got finished, as I said, we didn't have enough songs, so we spent six weeks with Glyn Johns in London and didn't finish anything *except* those two songs.

COWAN: Oh, wow.

LEADON: We gave up.

COWAN: So why did it take six weeks?

LEADON: Because we didn't have any songs. We showed up with no songs except those two songs. We tried writing some other songs in the studio, but we were tired and burned out. We just didn't have the energy. So, we finished those songs, stopped to regroup and go back to LA, and when we got back to LA, a management change had happened. Irving Azoff was now the manager, and all that disruption was going on. So, we fired Glyn Johns and went into the studio with Bill Szymczyk.* Almost immediately, the band wanted to hire Don Felder as an additional guitar player.

COWAN: He was a friend of *yours*.

LEADON: He was in my high school band in Gainesville, Florida.

COWAN: How were they even aware of him?

LEADON: He came to a show in Boston. I went to Hollywood. Felder went to the Berklee School of Music in Boston. So, while he was studying up there, the Eagles came through and played, and Felder came backstage and met the guys. Obviously, Felder's a great guitar player.

COWAN: Sure.

LEADON: But he was in Boston. So, he brought his family to LA. I introduced him around the management office. He started working for David Blue, then he started working for Crosby and Nash. Stephen Stills had been in one of Felder's high school bands, too, so he knew those guys. Felder was on the scene in LA when all these changes were happening. We changed producers, changed managers, and the band wanted to add Felder, and I didn't object. I actually thought I was going to leave the band at some point, and I thought, I'll get my friend in.

COWAN: Your song "My Man" was on *On the Border*, right?

LEADON: Correct.

COWAN: And it's your obvious tribute to Gram Parsons.

LEADON: Yeah, because, as I said, when we went to England to record the third album, which became *On the Border*, I had been in the studio only

---

* Bill Szymczyk was a legendary music producer who, years before helping to define the sound of '70s rock 'n' roll, was a U.S. Navy SONAR operator from Muskegon, Michigan, with practically no musical training. Along with his work with the Eagles, including "Hotel California," he was the producer of B. B. King's signature song, "The Thrill Is Gone," among many others.

a week before with Gram Parsons, overdubbing down at Capitol Records. A few days later we flew to England, went through our jet-lag comedown, and around that time I heard that Gram was gone.

COWAN: Did you have any inkling when you saw him that things seemed out of kilter or was everything the same?

LEADON: Everything was OK except, for those who don't know, Gram had a drug habit, and he was a trust-fund baby, so he had money. I did notice that Gram, who had always been skinny, had put on a lot of weight, so I saw that going on with Gram. Anyway, I flew to England, found out he was gone, and got quite depressed about it.

COWAN: It must've hurt.

LEADON: Yeah. He was one of the first peers who had passed away, and we were all only twenty-six. Ironically, one of my guitar heroes was Clarence White, who had been in the Byrds and who invented the pull-string guitar style that I was copying and was a bluegrass giant, and he had been killed only about four months earlier. I had gone to the funeral and stood next to Gram Parsons, and the two of us sang "Farther Along" at graveside for Clarence. And here, four months later, Gram was gone. The combination of those two guys, those peers leaving at twenty-six, was pretty devastating. So, I wrote the song "My Man" about it. I felt better afterwards for having written it.

COWAN: We're coming to the recording of the fourth album. This would be your last album with the Eagles.*

LEADON: Yes, *One of These Nights*. We went down to Florida and rented the same house that Eric Clapton had put on the cover of the record *461 Ocean Boulevard* and stayed in that house. We had a housekeeper.

COWAN: How long did you spend on that record?

---

* Bernie left the band in 1975 for artistic and personal reasons and was replaced by guitarist Joe Walsh. He reunited with the Eagles in 1998 for their induction into the Rock & Roll Hall of Fame. The Eagles' *Greatest Hits*, which was released shortly after his departure, covered Bernie's four years with the band and went on to become the biggest selling record in American history.

LEADON: *Months!*

COWAN: Really?

LEADON: Yeah.

COWAN: When you went to make *One of These Nights*, I'm guessing that all the songs weren't written yet.

LEADON: No, but my brother Tom and I had started "Hollywood Waltz." It wasn't called "Hollywood Waltz," but it had all the same structures. Henley and Frey rewrote that song into "Hollywood Waltz." And actually, it's kind of a precursor to "Hotel California," because it's talking about the disillusionment of the West Coast hedonistic lifestyle. "One of These Nights" was the big hit off that record. "Lyin' Eyes" was another one. "Lyin' Eyes" kind of harkens back to the first two albums.

COWAN: Same kind of groove as "Peaceful Easy Feeling."

LEADON: Or "Tequila Sunrise."

COWAN: I so appreciate your time, Bernie. Thanks for having me out to your ranch.

LEADON: You're very welcome, Johnny C.

Jim Messina "sittin' in" with Andrea Zonn (left), me, and the HercuLeons. *Courtesy Madison Thorn*

12

A PRODUCER. A PICKER. A PIONEER.

Pickin' Up the Pieces with Poco's Jim Messina

Evansville, Evansville, always Evansville. I suppose it's because it was the first place that I ever had an apartment of my own. I was nineteen years old, playing in a band, and it was a heady time of refining some personal, formative rituals: Practice. Smoke pot. Find a gig. Smoke pot. Play the gig. Then later, smoke more pot and listen to music into the night. One more essential rite at that time was to visit our local head shop/record store, The Funky Monkey, run by an ex-Vietnam paratrooper with the 101st Airborne, featuring bongs and paraphernalia in the front and the latest record releases in the back. *Hmm, what's this here?*, I asked myself one day as I lifted *Kenny Loggins with Jim Messina—Sittin' In* from the rack. I was a devoted Jim Messina fan then and, being a musician who combed through every credit on every record I bought, already knew Jimmy's name from the Buffalo Springfield *Last Time Around* credits [engineer and bassist], as well as his band Poco with Rusty Young, George Grantham, and Randy Meisner. I was *all in* on Poco, country rock pioneers, and subsequently bought every record they ever made, which, after the first one, included my hero on bass, Timothy B. Schmit.

Jim Messina is a musician's musician, with a career spanning five decades, three supergroups, landmark production credits, and a solo career bridging country rock, folk-rock, Latin, and jazz. I first met him in California at a festival in Sonoma that the Doobies' former manager, Bruce Cohn, used to put on every year at his winery. Jimmy was still living in the Ojai area, and when we'd play anywhere nearby, he'd come and hang out with us. This wide-ranging interview, a portal into '60s and '70s folk-rock history, exists because of Jim Messina's generosity and a radio show I once hosted called *I Believe to My Soul*. I was working with my Doobie Brother, John McFee, who was producing a solo record of mine called *Sixty* (which, of course, you own), at his Lizard Rock Studio in Solvang, California. We asked Jimmy if he'd do two friends a favor and come play with us on this record, then hang out and let me interview him afterward for the radio show. To everyone's joy, he agreed to both. This is the transcript from that afternoon together.

JOHN COWAN: We're going to get right down into it. Welcome, Jim. Thank you so much for being here.

JIM MESSINA: Thank you, John. I appreciate it.

COWAN: You were born James Melvin Messina.

MESSINA: I was indeed.

COWAN: On December 5th, 1947, in Maywood, California. Where the heck is Maywood?

MESSINA: Well, Maywood is somewhere near Southgate these days. Melvin. That's a name I've tried to avoid all my life. [*Cowan laughs*] Since I'm old enough now to be able to handle it, and I got my big-boy pants on now, I was given that name by my grandfather who was, I guess the proper word is, a vaudevillian entertainer. He played what he called the Hawaiian steel guitar, which basically was a Dobro. He also was a clown in the circus. He was a crazy guy.

COWAN: Was his name Melvin as well?

MESSINA: Part of his name was Melvin. That's why he gave me that name. He was born somewhere in Tennessee. He was a happy man, kind of a spiritual guy you might say, meaning he enjoyed drinking the spirits. [*both laugh*] So he was commonly found wiggling down the road.

COWAN: Was music then always a part of your life and your childhood?

MESSINA: My father was a guitar player, and he was very, very taken by Merle Travis. He could play the thumb-style finger picking better than I can to this day. He wanted to be a professional musician. He had a little group, a trio, with steel guitar and two other guitars. So the guitar was always around the house, and I was always watching my dad play. I was so inspired by it. As I look back, I know the feeling that I had when I was watching him play and hearing the music come out of his guitar and watching his fingers play, the rhythmic aspects of all of that, plus the melodies he was playing. Then, of course, I would see Merle Travis on TV and then I'd watch my dad, and I'd go, "Whoa! He can do that." My inspiration to this day has been what my father was able to give me in that short time that I was with him, because I was only with him three months out of the year.* That was the most inspiring aspect of it. Along with that came Merle Travis and musicians like Joe and Rose Lee Maphis. Spade Cooley. The Collins Kids. All of those musicians that we used to see on *Town Hall Party* every Saturday night on the TV. And I'm laying there with my dad watching them when I was five, six, seven years old.

COWAN: At what age did you actually pick up the guitar and put your fingers on it?

MESSINA: Probably at four.

COWAN: Wow.

MESSINA: At the time, I remember my dad made an electric guitar, and it was heavy, so I would have to lay it sideways in my lap and try to figure out how to remember what he did. If I showed any interest, he'd say,

---

* That's because as a kid, his time was split between his mom's home in Harlingen, Texas, and his dad's place in California.

"Here, here's how you do that." And then I did that. Of course, when he was at work, I'd lean it up against the couch and play it halfway up the neck trying to practice.

COWAN: If you started at four, when do you think you started feeling accomplished and considering yourself a guitarist?

MESSINA: As you bring this up now, I'm starting to recall that I used to buy 45 singles. The Champs were one of my favorite groups. The Torquays. And of course, the Ventures.

COWAN: So, super surf-guitar-oriented music.

MESSINA: Yeah.

COWAN: So, let's cut up from there to Jim Messina and the Jesters.

MESSINA: The first record I made was *Jimmy and the Jesters*. It was 1963. I was fifteen. By the time the Jesters came in, I was listening to people like Freddie King and Dick Dale.

COWAN: So, how did you get to LA, and how did you end up being an engineer for the Buffalo Springfield?

MESSINA: I went to work for Madeline Baker, who was Jimmy Webb's publisher. They had a studio called Audio Arts in LA. I was their engineer for a period of time. Then Tutti Camarata* at Sunset Sound heard of me. Gypsy, who was the studio owner, called me in one day and asked me if I'd be interested in a job. Of course, it paid twice as much as I was earning, which brought me up to $300 a week. [*laughs*]

COWAN: Well, that was a lot of money in 1966, '67.

MESSINA: Well, it allowed me to rent a house and to drive a car and to eat. And that was a joy.

COWAN: There you go.

---

* Years before Tutti Camaratta worked at Sunset Sound Recorders, he was a trumpet player and arranger for big bands like Jimmy and Tommy Dorsey, and Benny Goodman. He also arranged and produced recordings by Duke Ellington, Louis Armstrong, and Billie Holiday. In a diverse and remarkable career, he also produced more than three hundred records for Disney, including the soundtracks of *The Jungle Book* and *Snow White*.

MESSINA: Bruce Botnick was the chief recording engineer there.* Then one day, Gypsy came to me and she said, "I need you to do a session for me. The engineer we have in there is a little old for the folks that we have in there. They're not really relating to one another. Would you be interested in doing that?" *It would require a lot of time*, is what she was saying. *I'd be up late.* I said, "No, I'll give it a try." Then she said, "Before you do that session, there's one other thing we need you to do for us. A guy named David Crosby has got some time booked in here. Would you do that? It's just a demo." And I said, "Oh sure, I'll do it. Is that Bing Crosby's son?" [*both laugh*] She said, "I don't think so." So anyway, I went in, and I did this session with David Crosby. There was a young woman with him who we were actually working with. I was just enamored by this singer-songwriter. At the end of the session, I asked David, "Who's the producer?" And he said, "I'm the producer." And I said, "Who do I put down as the artist?" And he said, "Joni Mitchell."

COWAN: And so the next project, I'm guessing . . .

MESSINA: Was Buffalo Springfield.

COWAN: Tell me a little bit about that. You show up for the session . . .

MESSINA: Well, I showed up for the session, and the person I meet is Neil Young. My first impression, of course, was that he was the producer, because usually when you walk into the studio, and there's a pile of tapes, and there's a guy there, he's the producer, right? [*both laugh*] We began working together and sorting out whatever was happening at that moment in time. I found Neil to be really pleasant. He was a hard worker and very considerate. But Springfield were very separate, these guys. Neil and Stephen Stills, and, of course, Richie Furay. There was nobody there to help Richie. Later on, once I'd finished the record with them, we started what was to become the *Last Time Around* album. We had just gotten started on that when Neil quit. He

---

* Producer Bruce Botnick was best known for his work on the Doors last album, *LA Woman*, and coproduced the Rolling Stones' *Let It Bleed*. His résumé includes work with the Beach Boys, Eddie Money, and Kenny Loggins.

decided that he just didn't want to be there anymore, which threw everything into a tailspin. So, I had bits and pieces from Stephen because he would go out and do his thing. And I wasn't sure what Neil was going to do because nothing had shown up. Richie was not a reader. He was not a chart man. He was a very vulnerable singer-songwriter.

COWAN: Tell me about how you and Richie decided to have this country rock band and call it Poco?* [*laughs*]

MESSINA: Well, on the last Buffalo Springfield tour, we were touring with the Beach Boys. Martin Luther King has been assassinated three days before, so we were in hell out there on the road. Some gigs were being canceled. Everybody was packing a gun. We were longhairs, and it was not a fun time to be there. Richie was kind of down, and I was feeling the same way, like, what are we going to do? Having engineered "A Child's Claim to Fame" and "Kind Woman," and all these songs that Richie had been a part of, I told him, "Why don't we do something different? We've been doing folk-rock. Why don't we do country rock? I mean, I grew up on it. You grew up on it." He said, "Ah, I just don't know. We'll see." So we went back to California, and I was finishing up the Springfield record, and we brought in a guy by the name of Rusty Young.

COWAN: Rusty was from Grand Junction. Pedal steel guitar player.

MESSINA: Exactly. That was the moment where I looked at Richie, and he looked at me and said, "Maybe we can do this country rock thing."

COWAN: Now I have a little bit of bone to pick, not with you, but with musical history. Here's my issue. I think the Flying Burrito Brothers were great. But as a rock and roll kid who started off playing Beatles songs in Kentucky, my first exposure to country rock music was not Gram Parsons; it was Poco. I don't know if they happened at the same time, but I've always felt like

---

* The original name of the band was Pogo, after the famous comic strip character, but the band changed their name to Poco when the comic's creator, Walt Kelly, not a fan of their idea, hit them with a cease-and-desist order.

you guys didn't get enough credit. For so many people I know, Poco was our first exposure to country rock.

MESSINA: In the process of trying to create Poco, we had me, Richie, Rusty, and drummer George Grantham. We needed another person in the band. We knew we were going to get a bass player, or I would be playing bass. We brought in Gregg Allman. Gregg came in and was not the right match. Then we brought in Gram Parsons. Gram Parsons wanted to take over the band. He wanted to fire me and bring in somebody, and Richie and I are looking at each other going, "Who *is* this guy?" [*both laugh*] We bring him into an audition, and he wants to fire you and you. So we both decided that that wasn't the right case. Then we got Randy Meisner, who came in and began performing with us. Gram would come to the Troubadour and watch us play. So, what I think happened is that it all kind of formed around the same time. Richie and I were thinking "country rock," and that's what we were telling the guys who were showing up. This is what we want to do.

COWAN: OK, so Poco starts, and the whole idea between you and Richie Furay is that you're going to have a country rock band. You certainly pulled that off.

MESSINA: Growing up, I was a big Buck Owens fan. With all the history I'd had and, in terms of what I liked to listen to, it was *Buck Owens and the Buckaroos Live* album that was one of the most influential albums of my life, because it really was the essence of energy, of harmony, of great country, and, as I saw it, rock and roll.

COWAN: They cut "Johnny B. Goode" on that record, and it's a darned good version.

MESSINA: See, I didn't tell you about this, but before going to Audio Arts and all that stuff, I helped build a studio called Universal Audio. It was owned by two Texas gentlemen, brothers, whose sister was married to Hank Williams and then to Johnny Horton. They had a lot of friends out in

Louisiana. One was James Burton.* Joe Osborn.† Roger Miller was a part of their scene. Keith Allison.‡ Jerry Allison.§ So, I was doing sessions there as an engineer with all these great rockabilly players. I had an opportunity to take what I learned from my father and apply it to this whole other step before I ever got involved with the Springfield. So, to suddenly one day hear Buck Owens and the Buckaroos was like hearing James Burton up there playing, or Keith Allison in the place of Don Rich. You had these rich harmonies coming out of Buck, and the steel was so inspiring to me. I think that is part of what made me pick up the Telecaster.

COWAN: I want to talk about the Telecaster. You mentioned James Burton, who we all know, and we think about Don Rich with Buck Owens, and we think about Roy Nichols with Merle Haggard. They all were Telecaster guys.

MESSINA: Yeah. I worked with Burton before Springfield doing sessions, and I brought him in to do "A Child's Claim to Fame." He played Dobro on all of that stuff. I've known James over the years, and I'm still good friends with him. I do benefits with him.

COWAN: Your tone on the Telecaster, as I look back on this music, is framed around your Telecaster. So many of your guitar intros and your overall style.

MESSINA: When I started out, Stephen Stills was also an influence in my life. I would play the way he would, with two steel picks and a thumb. For some reason, whatever it's made out of, would cause my cuticles to burn

---

* James Burton, "master of the Telecaster," performed with everyone from Elvis and Sinatra to Johnny Cash. He was inducted into the Rock & Roll Hall of Fame by Keith Richards. Three lines about him here are hopelessly inadequate.

† Joe Osborn was a legendary bassist and member of the famed Wrecking Crew. He played on hundreds of hits, such as "Bridge over Troubled Water," "California Dreaming," and, according to *Variety* magazine, fifty-three number one country hits. When asked why he never changed his bass strings for seventeen years, he replied, "No one told me I was supposed to."

‡ Keith was a guitar player with Paul Revere and the Raiders, among other achievements.

§ Jerry Allison was Keith Allison's cousin, three years older, and the drummer with Buddy Holly and the Crickets.

and cut. I was playing a Gretsch [guitar] one night when we were opening up as Poco at the Troubadour, and the first song was [*sings*] bonk-doodle-oo-dee-do, right? And I went, bonk-doodle-oo . . . , and I picked up like this, and the string, like a bow and arrow, took the finger pick and shot it out into the audience and hit somebody right in the head! [*both laugh*] It just messed up my groove from that moment on, you know? I couldn't play the parts, and I couldn't get rid of the picks, and I couldn't grab another one. After that set, I never used picks ever again.

COWAN: Did you just use these three fingers?

MESSINA: I just used these three fingers, because I was never going to do that again.

COWAN: Which is not unlike a banjo roll.

MESSINA: Oh, really?

COWAN: Yeah, the Scruggs three-finger roll is built on that same principle. Thumb, first finger, middle finger. I'm kind of curious whether that was conscious on your part or not.

MESSINA: Well, I got rid of them, and after that, I couldn't play the Gretsch. It was too cumbersome. So, then I bought a Telecaster. When I plugged it in and tweaked it out, I liked it and found out that the pickup was microphonic. If you got too close to an amp, it would feed back. But that was also part of what the sound was. So as long as I stayed away from the amp, it had this great, pop-y sound, which I think helped to contribute eventually to what people like.

COWAN: So, in 1968, if we look at the music business at that time, it's kind of infiltrated with psychedelia and British . . .

MESSINA: Tell me about it! [*laughs*]

COWAN: You've got everything from Led Zeppelin to Jimi Hendrix Experience . . .

MESSINA: And Creedence happening in there, too.

COWAN: OK, so how easy was it to go to a record label and say, "Well, we've got this idea. We're gonna fuse country music and rock and roll?"

MESSINA: Well, you have to understand that Ahmet Ertegun wanted to eat it up. But Ahmet wasn't willing to *pay*, meaning royalty rates at Atlantic records were really low.* And at the same time, Atlantic had Richie [Furay], but Epic had Graham [Nash]. So a trade went on. They traded Richie for Graham so that *Crosby, Stills & Nash* could be made, and Poco could now be at Epic Records.† We did our first concert showcase. There was Ahmet, Jerry Moss, all the major labels were there, to create this bidding war. Sadly to say, I think fate had it that for some reason we got on Epic Records instead of Columbia, because Clive Davis was the one who really wanted this act.

COWAN: And he was at Columbia.

MESSINA: He was at Columbia, and Epic was a subsidiary. And you just don't mess with the precedents, or the presidents you empower. But I don't think our president really understood what we were doing. He was more of an East Coast gentleman, and I don't think he got it. Who knows? Maybe he was forced to sign us for all I know. [*Cowan laughs*] Who knows what the politics really are?

COWAN: But you did get signed. My question is, were they hands-off? "Here, go make your record?" Or, did they try to A&R you to death?

MESSINA: No, they understood. Part of the deal was that I was the producer and also an engineer, and I knew what I was doing and where to take it. But the unions didn't get the memo on that, and they would not let me

---

* Ahmet Ertegun was a Turkish American businessman and musician who grew to become one of the most influential figures in American music history. As the founder of Atlantic Records, he helped to sign and develop the careers of artists like Ray Charles, the Rolling Stones, Led Zeppelin, John Coltrane, and, in partnership with Stax Records, Aretha Franklin, Otis Redding, Sam & Dave, Percy Sledge, Wilson Pickett, and many more. He was a founder of the Rock & Roll Hall of Fame and was eventually elected to it in 1987.

† Even by music industry standards, this was a pretty unique deal. When the newly formed Crosby, Stills & Nash lobbied hard to be on the Atlantic label, Ertegun at Atlantic worked out a trade with Clive Davis to move Poco to Epic Records.

touch the board. They would not let me do anything in that studio, otherwise I would be fined, because I was also an IBEW union cardholder,* but I was a recording artist as well, and there was a collective co-bargaining agreement that prohibited me from touching the board. So the first record, I had to use whoever they assigned, and they did not assign their A-team. I was literally having to educate them on where to put this and the baffle and the mics. Can you imagine someone, having never recorded your music before, and you have to hear that coming through the speakers? It was quite a disappointment for me. And that was sort of the tone that took off there. When you said earlier that you didn't understand why Poco didn't seem to make it, we just didn't have the direction. A lot of that was our fault. I don't think we had the right manager. I don't think we had the right people at Epic working for us. And as a result, it was just a lot of *work*. Unlike when I left Poco and went to CBS and started working directly with Clive, and I had somebody who understood what I was doing, I could then take a new act from the beginning, put all the pieces together, find the right players, press the right buttons, and it worked like a machine. Quite different.†

COWAN: Nevertheless, *Pickin' Up the Pieces*, the first record, is full of amazing songs and amazing music.

MESSINA: Thank you.

COWAN: So, on the second Poco record, which is just called *Poco*, Randy Meisner has been fired or quit, whatever.

MESSINA: Yeah, that's a story in itself.‡ [*laughs*]

---

* That would be the International Brotherhood of Electrical Workers.

† While it's true that you never get a second chance to make a first impression, history is looking a lot more favorably on this record than Jim is feeling right here. *Pickin' Up the Pieces* is the only Poco record to include members of the original Buffalo Springfield and future Eagle Randy Meisner. Although it never got higher than sixty-three on the *Billboard* charts, it's widely regarded as a groundbreaking classic and a milestone of country rock, alongside records by the Flying Burrito Brothers and the Byrds' *Sweetheart of the Rodeo*.

‡ The late, great Randy Meisner quit the band over artistic difference shortly before the album's release. If you look at the original cover artwork, you'll notice a cute little dog there on the left side. That dog used to be Randy.

COWAN: And Timothy B. Schmit, who most people would recognize as being with the Eagles since *Hotel California*,* was brought in as the bassist.

MESSINA: Absolutely.

COWAN: How did that happen? How did you guys know Timmy?

MESSINA: There was a woman we knew named Kathy Patrick who said, "Hey, I know a bass player." So she brought him in, and we auditioned him, and he was perfect. He was just energetic. He looked like he might've played football at one time.

COWAN: He looked like he was sixteen. How old was he at that point?

MESSINA: Sixteen. [*both laugh*] No, I had no idea.

COWAN: Was he even in his twenties?

MESSINA: I don't know. Is he older than me?† I was probably twenty or twenty-one, so he was probably twenty.

COWAN: Well, let me interject this, as a guy who's made his living singing tenor and playing bass. There are not a lot of these people out there. So the first guy in the band was Randy Meisner, who's an amazing bassist.

MESSINA: That's right.

COWAN: An amazing tenor singer. And then you find Timothy B. Schmit? For God's sake, the stars must've been aligned. I mean, for somebody to say, "Hey, I know a bass player," and this kid comes in, and he sings like an angel and plays as great as well, lucky you.

MESSINA: Tell me about it! [*both laugh*] I'm looking for a bass player today.

COWAN: As a listener, I loved the *Pickin' Up the Pieces* record, but it seemed like with the *Poco* record, everything jelled.

MESSINA: It did.

COWAN: Everything was more coherent. You've got the medley at the end with "Nobody's Fool." That record, to me, was kind of definitive

---

* Timothy replaced Meisner in the Eagles, too.
† They're both the same age. Schmit is older than Jim by one month.

MESSINA: I agree with you. That was the first time I felt, after I heard the playback, "Wow, I finally got onto tape what I was trying to do." Thank you. I'm glad you heard that, too.

COWAN: Eventually, you left Poco. What was behind your decision to leave the band? It was *your* band.

MESSINA: I didn't want the drama. One of the things that happened was that Richie was getting really upset or uptight. I think he felt that something should have happened sooner. I think he saw Stephen Stills's success and Neil Young's success, and we were struggling. And it was very hard for me to give him any direction anymore, musically. I thought that before this turns into fussing and fighting and so forth, I decided that maybe it was time to be home and produce, which is all I wanted to do anyway. I didn't like being on the road all that much. So, I went to Clive, and I talked to him about the idea of working as an independent. We both agreed that the most important thing was making sure that Poco was OK. I said, "I'm happy to stay, I'm happy to work, I'll finish producing the record, and I'll find a replacement for myself or the band will. Once the album is done and delivered, I'd like to discuss the idea of working as an independent for Columbia Records," and he said, "Fine. Let's get it all done, and we'll do that." I finished the record on Halloween night, it was my last show in San Francisco at the Fillmore. That was the night that Neil Young came in and sat in with us. And that was it. [*both laugh*]

COWAN: Was your first assignment to produce Kenny Loggins?

MESSINA: [*laughs*] No! My first assignment was to produce *Andy Williams*!

COWAN: Wow!

MESSINA: And I said to Clive, "I have to respectfully decline. This man is a phenomenal singer, but I cannot relate to what he does as a professional. I think you'd be making a mistake."

COWAN: Yeah.

MESSINA: The next project that was presented to me was Kenny. Kenny never really had a band. He never really had an agent. He was really kind of a folk singer. The first songs he brought to me in my home were "Danny's Song" and "House at Pooh Corner." I can't remember the others, but they were really lighthearted tunes. And I felt like to go someplace with artists that I choose, they needed to be *competitors*. They needed to be competing in a world of rock and roll. This was no longer a period of folk music. We were out of that, as much as some people wanted to think we weren't. In spending time with Kenny, I realized that he had a voice, and that voice was not really showing in his demos. When he started talking about songs he had written, he say, "Well, I wrote this song," and he sounded like Elton John. Then he'd sing another one and sound like Leon Russell. And I thought, wow, he has this ability to go in these different directions. We just need to find the material for him. Based on that, and the fact that I had written some songs, I thought that maybe as a producer, I could give him some tunes, and we can take some tunes that he had and rearrange them, but that was taking time. And now CBS was saying, "When are you going to give us an album?" I had six albums a year to produce, and I hadn't done *one*, and we were probably about four months into it.

COWAN: [*laughs*]

MESSINA: So, I told Clive, "We have a good artist here, but it's taking a lot more time. If you seriously want to sign him, there's a lot of work to be done here. He has no manager. No agent. All that stuff has to be gotten. What's the point in making a record if there's . . .

COWAN: No follow-through.

MESSINA: No follow-through, exactly. So in the process of creating all that for Kenny, in the process of trying to pick the musicians, I just realized that he was not a leader yet. He didn't know what to say or what to do. So I offered my services and said, "Why don't we make a record together, like the old jazz artists, where I'm sittin' in with you? I'll help you with the band. I'll help you get it organized. I'll help you get the agent and the manager. Once we're in place, then we go in, and we make the record." Of course, no one is going to sign you at that point, but at least the contacts have been made. Then, I figured that once we made the record, then it's up to the label to help us—which they did. So, the purpose of that first record really was to introduce Kenny Loggins to *my* audiences, the people who heard the music that you had heard growing up, and hopefully that would help him to become successful, help me to start my career as an independent, and maybe get off the hook for the other five records that year. [*laughs*]

COWAN: So, hence the title of that record. Most people think it was *Loggins and Messina*. But the first record was called, *Kenny Loggins with Jim Messina—Sittin' In*.

MESSINA: That's correct.

COWAN: And then also, something that I think was a stroke of genius on your part, but probably because you are a great musician, you bring in, correct me if I'm wrong, Merel Bregante on drums. Larry Sims on the bass. Al Garth on violin and sax. Jon Clark, who played sax, oboe, and flute. And Michael Omartian.*

MESSINA: And Michael Omartian, who happened to be a friend of Kenny's.

COWAN: Got it.

MESSINA: Kenny had a multifaceted voice that hadn't been heard really yet. I knew he could do gospel if he wanted to. My vision was to give him a diverse palette to be able to pick the colors going forward. As a producer, I wanted to have a group of musicians where we could throw different types of music in there so that it made it enjoyable for me. As much as I loved

---

* Michael Omartian is a supremely gifted keyboard player, singer, and record producer. Across three decades, Michael has produced albums for everyone from the Jacksons, Whitney Houston, and Rod Stewart to Dolly Parton, Trisha Yearwood, and Clint Black.

the boys in the Buffalo Springfield, they never really recorded together as a group. Very seldom. I mean, "Bluebird" is the only one that I can remember where we were actually in the same room together. I hate overdubbing. I don't like it. It's not fun. I love being in the moment with a group, where everybody rehearsed, we're playing, there's energy happening, there's spontaneity happening, there's a script, but there's room to ad-lib. And that was the group that I saw Loggins and Messina becoming, and we eventually did, thank God.

COWAN: Having been in the business myself for a long time, you absolutely did your job as a producer. You brought in great musicians, and you helped him choose the songs. He was a great singer that nobody knew about, so the whole thing kind of worked on all levels.

MESSINA: Going back to your comment, there's a time to talk, and then there's a time to listen. Merel and Larry Sims worked in a group called the Sunshine Company that opened up for Poco. That's why I knew them. Al Garth lived below me in an apartment, and I'd hear him out there playing,

With Jimmy Messina at my house during rehearsals for a tribute concert for our friend the late Rusty Young. *Courtesy Madison Thorn*

you know, and I just remembered it. John Clark was somebody we auditioned in looking for the right player that could work with Al. And fortunately, Michael Omartian was a good friend of Kenny's and had worked with him on some other projects. He was just a phenomenal keyboard player at twenty-two. Yes, it's being able to pull all those people together and create an environment where everybody's having fun. There's nothing like being in a group of musicians where everybody just loves being with one another.

COWAN: This brings us to "Danny's Song" from this first record. To this day, it's perhaps the song that's most associated with Loggins and Messina, and certainly Kenny Loggins.*

MESSINA: That's true.

COWAN: This first record, *Kenny Loggins with Jim Messina—Sittin' In*, begins a long and healthy career. The second record, which came out in '72, is called *Loggins and Messina—now you're established*. Everybody knows it's Jim Messina from Poco, and now it's a duo. The hit from that record was, "Your Mama Don't Dance and Your Daddy Don't Rock and Roll." Can you talk about how things were different for you, and where you guys were at that point.

MESSINA: We were at a point where we needed something to get the crowd moving and get them up. We needed something to close the set. I've always been a great believer that you have to create a great set, and the sequencing of that set is important.

COWAN: It's everything.

MESSINA: It *is* everything. And something was still missing in what we were doing. We were waiting for the guys to show up one day and maybe we gave them the wrong time, but Kenny and I were there an hour, and they weren't there. [*both laugh*] So, I said to Kenny, "I have this idea for this song.

---

* Kenny Loggins wrote "Danny's Song" when he was a senior in high school. It was written for his brother Danny after the birth of his son. Anne Murray's cover in 1974 became a *Billboard* Top 10 hit, and she received a Grammy nomination for Best Female Pop Vocal.

It's not quite finished yet." And I gave him the hook, "Your Mama Don't Dance and Your Daddy Don't Rock and Roll." Now, I don't remember who did what or what happened after that but, in about fifteen minutes, the song was done, and everybody showed up. We started showing everybody this, and we just started playing it and, boom, it just sort of happened. We thought, hey, we can put this into the set. I mean, the next thing you know, people were having so much fun with it. We thought, wow, we've got a song we can close with now. When the record company heard it, they immediately thought it should be released. There was no concept of it being a single. No concept of it being a great song. In fact, I think it's probably one of the worst songs we could've ever had as a hit.

COWAN: Because it wasn't necessarily representative of what you were?

MESSINA: Exactly. It was an extension of our humor, not so much an extension of our artistic abilities. Now, I warn people about doing humorous songs, at least on the first one. Chris Rock said something the other night that actually turned on a light for me. He said, "Don't you think it's funny that I can come up with great joke, a really great joke. I say it, people laugh, and they don't want to hear it again? Once you've heard a joke, it's over. But, if you write a great song, people want to hear it forever!" And I thought to myself, that's an interesting correlation between creativity and how humor and emotions can differ in terms of what people want to hear again. I try to keep it in mind about writing funny songs. [*laughs*]

COWAN: At that time, FM radio was alive. And although that turned out to be a Top 40 hit for your band, most of us who were buying records were listening to the whole record.

MESSINA: Right.

COWAN: That was just the nature of it. It's much different today, as we know.

MESSINA: Absolutely.

COWAN: But back in those days, we'd put on a record and listen to an entire album of songs.

MESSINA: Yeah, you'd sit down and listen to the whole thing at one time, and if it was really moving, you'd turn it over.

COWAN: So, we knew that "Your Mama Don't Dance" was a hit, but we also knew the rest of the record. We knew that that one song was just a little snapshot of who you were as artists.

MESSINA: Well, thank God that "Angry Eyes" was on that same record!

COWAN: One of my favorite bass lines ever.

MESSINA: You know what's really interesting? Somebody asked me a question: "Poison recorded 'Your Mama Don't Dance,' didn't they?"

COWAN: They did, didn't they?

MESSINA: I said, "Yeah." And they said, "So, what'd you think?" And I said, "Well, it was an interesting recording." And they said, "Well, did you like it?" And I realized after listening to their music that that arrangement was the way they played their music, and it doesn't matter whether I like it or not. It has to do with their fan base and the style that a person plays. What I didn't understand is why they would record it in the first place. So, it was interesting to find out that the song said something much different than I ever thought it did when I wrote it. I didn't realize that I was speaking for a generation of people. I was thinking about my own situation and how my parents were that way. How, growing up as a stepchild, I had to be in at a certain time, and I couldn't do this, and if that happened, this would be taken away. So that's where all that came from. I was trying to be funny about something that wasn't funny. But I never realized that it had that impact until Poison did it.

COWAN: I think the point you're making is that that was the generational experience that every teenager has. Whether it's that you feel your parents are being restrictive, you don't have anything to do, and you're trying to form your own identity.

MESSINA: My son's doing it now with me. [*laughs*]

COWAN: There you go! [*laughs*] I want to talk a little about geography here. With "Vahevala" from the first record and "Watching the River Run," there's some Caribbean flavor that started to seep into your music.

MESSINA: Remember Hamilton, Joe Frank, and Reynolds?*

COWAN: Yeah.

MESSINA: Tommy Reynolds was a musician, born in Jamaica, and I had worked with him with Jerry Riopelle and Leon Russell on some projects. He did a song that went [*sings with a Jamaican accent*], "Day after day, mo' people come to LA," which was about the earthquake, and I was inspired by his ability on this drum. I like making records like you make movies. They should be a soundtrack to the lyric. So when we did "Vahevala," I thought, *What could we do to this particular song to create a performance?* You said it yourself: you like listening to albums. You like listening to the whole thing. Michael Omartian was a brilliant pianist, and I brought Tommy Reynolds in to introduce him to the steel pan. I said, "What do you think about this?" And Michael, being the genius he is, he can also play the xylophone, finally figured out how to make that lead pan work. The other instrument that we had was a tenor pan, which only had eight notes on it maybe, and one other pan that only had three notes in it, just one, four, and five. So I taught one of the sax players to play [*sings*] duh-duh-duh, duh, da, duh-duh, and Michael was playing all this fancy stuff. So, on "Vahevala," we brought those up onstage. But Tommy made all those pans for us. He showed the guys how to play them. He came in, we gave him the song, and he arranged that one little section. He taught us how to play it, we recorded it, and we took it out on the road. We brought the pans and stuff with us.

---

* They were a soft-rock trio from LA whose hits included was "Don't Pull Your Love" in 1971 and "Fallin' in Love" in 1975.

COWAN: I just want to thank you so much for your time today. It's really been a pleasure and an honor.

MESSINA: Are you kidding? Thank you so much for having me. And thanks for the memories. You made me dig pretty deep. Spade Cooley!

PROG AND PROGENY

Have you ever walked by a restaurant and found the smells so new and intoxicating that you had to stick your head in the door to find out what it was? Music, for me, works exactly the same way. Growing up, there were sounds that drifted out of my radio that made me think, *What is this? Who are these people?* As part of my pedigree, I always had a hunger to find out everything about what I'd just heard.

Robert Lamm, Justin Hayward, and John Carter Cash represent music that came before me that was, in their own distinct ways, so radical and unfamiliar and now essential to my life. We'd hear horns on R&B records, but never in a rock setting as part of the counterpoint of the song, sharing equal space with the words, piano, rock guitar, bass, and drums. Chicago blew my mind. Moody Blues, with their hypnotic fusion of rock music and classical music, pioneered a prog rock sound that was nothing like the prog bands I loved like Emerson, Lake & Palmer, Yes, and Gentle Giant. And how to explain that I grew up in Kentucky but didn't know bluegrass or country at all? It was a style of music I had no familiarity with, but when I joined NGR, mercifully, there were a couple of songs I knew from being introduced to Mother Maybelle Carter and the *Will the Circle Be Unbroken* album in 1971.

All music that I ever listened to and the artists who composed it, I consider my person mentors. Like every working musician, I am standing on the shoulders of people who introduced me to possibilities that I'd never been aware of before and, what's more, showed me how to do it. I'll never know all of them personally. But sometimes, I'm lucky enough to say I do.

Courtesy Anthony Scarlati

13

CHICAGO'S ROBERT LAMM KNOWS EXACTLY WHAT TIME IT IS

Being a musician at sixteen is like being a sponge. You soak the music in, then the act of squeezing it out is done by your head, hands, and heart. And, oh, man, what a time to be a sponge. In 1969, our band was trying to play everything we'd heard: Hendrix, the Beatles, Cream, Motown, Stax, and, of course, Chicago Transit Authority, the original "rock with horns" band, which came out in 1969, followed by the album *Chicago* in 1970. I knew those two records so well I could probably sing you every guitar solo, bassline, horn arrangement, and vocal, note for note. Who didn't try to sing "25 or 6 to 4" and "Beginnings"? I got to see Chicago at Freedom Hall in Louisville around that time, and they were just as amazing live, led by keyboardist and vocalist Robert Lamm and James Pankow's brilliant, orchestral horn arrangements. It would never have occurred to me then, a kid up in the 300 level, that one day Robert Lamm would ask me to join the band.

In the spring of 2010, I went back to work as a Doobie Brother and discovered that the Doobies would be sharing the bill with Chicago that summer. I was dually thrilled and nervous to finally meet a musical icon whose hits had influenced so much of my musical upbringing, but in the current climate of touring for seasoned bands, it was unlikely that there'd ever be much "hangin' out" going on. The Doobies would open the show, play for ninety minutes, then after a stage makeover, Chicago would play for ninety minutes.

The encore would be both bands joining onstage together with everyone playing "Listen to the Music," followed by "25 or 6 to 4," then "Takin' It to the Streets." Robert, whose songs I knew so intimately, really didn't know me from Adam beyond looking across the stage and seeing the high-singing, new dude playing bass with the Doobies every night. That was about it.

Or, so I thought.

As the years went by, and we continued to tour with Chicago, our relationship grew, until one remarkable day in 2018, Robert Lamm called me and offered me the job of bassist-singer for Chicago, after the sudden departure of then bassist-singer Jeff Coffey. I was flattered and slightly flabbergasted. Remember that Randy Newman song, "My Life Is Good," where, in a fantasy, he imagines Bruce Springsteen saying, "Rand, I'm tired. How would *you* like to be the Boss for a while?" And Randy replies, "Well . . . *yes*." Unfortunately, my fantasy didn't quite work out that way.

It was Thanksgiving, and Robert wanted me to start with the band in mid-January. Since I had an obligation to the Doobie Brothers, I asked him if we could try playing together first before making a commitment. I think he was a bit shocked that I asked that, considering his offer to take over lead singing duties in Chicago, for God's sake. I think I was a bit shocked to hear those words come out of my mouth, as well. But, if I had taken the gig, and it didn't work out, which can happen, I'd be out of *two* jobs, his and the Doobies. We went back and forth for a week or two about it and, after a few more days, they withdrew their offer as suddenly as it had appeared. I'll probably never know entirely what that was about. I eventually decided that it was one of those things that just wasn't meant to be.

One thing that *was* meant to be was this gracious interview with Robert, a conversation we shared in his suite at a Chicago hotel during our tour together. For the uninitiated, Robert Lamm is a founding member, keyboardist, singer, and composer of Chicago, a band that has sold more than one hundred million records. He wrote many of Chicago's biggest hits, including "Beginnings," "25 or 6 to 4," "Saturday in the Park," "Does Anybody Really Know What Time It Is?," "Dialogue (Part I & II)," "Harry Truman," and more. He and Chicago would go on to have twenty-one Top 10 singles, five consecutive number one albums, and ultimately land Robert into the Songwriters Hall of Fame. His songs have never left the air in more than half a century. I started this conversation with one of my musical heroes by talking about his days in college at Roosevelt University in downtown Chicago.

ROBERT LAMM: When I decided to go back to school, to Roosevelt University in Chicago, I wanted to study composition. I really wasn't a great player. I'm *still* not a great player, but piano was my instrument. So, this was like, the mid '60s. I remember, I think, the Buckinghams had had a couple of hits, and there was brass stuff on there.

JOHN COWAN: Oh, yeah. "Don't You Care?" and "Susan" and all that stuff.

LAMM: Exactly. And then in 1967, Jim Guercio, who ended up being Chicago's producer and manager and kind of brought us into the world, produced a seriously good album, *Time & Charges* for the Buckinghams, and it made some noise. I remember one of the other students, kind of a young rocker who was in some of the same classes as me, said, "Oh, man, I hope that brass thing doesn't end up being the Chicago sound!" [*both laugh*]

COWAN: Oops.

LAMM: Well, of course, there was no Chicago at that point.*

COWAN: When you were at Roosevelt, was your focus on any particular kind of music? Were you studying classical or jazz or composition? What exactly was it?

---

* The founding lineup of Walt Parazaider, Terry Kath, Danny Seraphine, Lee Loughnane, James Pankow, and Robert Lamm that came together in 1967 were originally called the Big Thing for no reason other than that there were so many of them.

LAMM: Well, the curriculum was based on classical music. I had the full plate, you know. Theory and history. Piano was my major instrument, but I studied upright bass. I chose that because I wanted to be able to read bass clef so I could read the piano pieces for it.

COWAN: How far into your undergraduate work did the band start to evolve? Did you eventually finish school, or did the band take you away from school?

LAMM: No, I never did finish. I dropped out. I think I was there a full year, and it was in the second year that [horn player] Walt Parazaider called me. I had also been playing in little bar bands, and Walt called me and introduced himself and said who he was and said what his idea was, you know, to put a band together with horns, and was I interested? He'd either come to see me play at some club or he heard that I played keyboards and sang. So I said, "Yeah, that sounds very interesting." So, we all met, and we jammed, and we decided, "Let's see where we can go with this." We got work almost immediately, basically playing Stax and Atlantic horn stuff. We were driving from Chicago to Milwaukee or Chicago to Madison to play every night. Wherever we could drive to after classes, play the gig, and then get back home to go to school the next day.

COWAN: Was the band at the time intact, the way we knew it later? With Terry Kath and Peter Cetera?

LAMM: It wasn't with Peter. It was before Peter. Peter came a year later. We were playing the same club.

COWAN: Still doing covers?

LAMM: Still doing covers. We had actually started doing arrangements. I had written a few arrangements with brass and that kind of thing. Strange arrangements. We did "Hey, Joe." We did "Purple Haze."

COWAN: Is that how "I'm a Man" came to be?

LAMM: Well, "I'm a Man" was just a cover. We were doing actual arrangements, à la Vanilla Fudge. Vanilla Fudge's approach was to take covers and really make them kind of psychedelic. We were doing that.

COWAN: Just working them.

LAMM: Yeah, so there were a handful of songs like that that we were doing. We were playing the same venue as the band that Cetera was in. I honestly don't know if he didn't like where his band was going, but his band was amazing. It was a band called the Exceptions. Everybody was just a great player and a great singer, and they could do *anything*. But there was something going on in that band, and he quit them. He heard us play. Then they played their set, and he quit that night. We heard that he quit, and called him. At that point, we really needed a bass player, and it was great to have that voice.

COWAN: I want to get a little history about this.* On the first two records, you were prolific. And you were also the lead singer on the first record, for all practical purposes. I think Terry and Peter only sang one apiece.

LAMM: I don't know.

COWAN: If you look at a listing of the songs on the first record, you'd written all of them but five. I'm curious, once you were managed by Jim Guercio, and he took you to LA, is that where the writing process began for you?

LAMM: Yeah, yeah. Actually, I had written "Wake Up, Sunshine" before Chicago was together.

COWAN: Wow.

LAMM: That was on the second album. Terry, Lee Loughnane, and I all shared an apartment here in Chicago for about a year before we went to

---

* When Robert wrote "25 or 6 to 4" back in 1969 for the album *Chicago II*, the exact meaning of that lyric became the subject of a lot of creative interpretation, including one by the government of Singapore, which banned the song believing that, "Should I try to do some more? 25 or 6 to 4" was a reference to LSD. According to Robert, it's a song about writing a song. "I looked at my watch while I was writing, and it was 25 minutes to 4 in the morning. Or maybe 26."

California. That was still a period where some of us were still trying to make classes. But I wrote "Questions 67 and 68" in Chicago. And I wrote "Does Anybody Really Know What Time It Is?" Then we moved to California, and I wrote "Beginnings." We were all living in a house in Hollywood. Actually, before we even lived in that house, we were crashing with a couple of girls we knew from Chicago who had already gone out to California. We had just arrived, and I went for a walk one night and walked down to where there was a club down on Santa Monica Boulevard, and I just wandered in, and Richie Havens was playing. He was playing his acoustic guitar with another acoustic guitar player and a hand-drum player, and that was it. I was just mesmerized by the sound of the acoustics with that sort of Afro-Cuban thing going on. So, not knowing how to play guitar, I immediately went home and picked up a guitar and tried to emulate that [*Cowan chuckles*], and that's how "Beginnings" was written.

COWAN: Back in those days, bands like yourselves or the Doobies, who were enjoying success, would play three hundred shows a year. I'm not talking about three hundred days on the road. You would almost do that many shows, right?

LAMM: Yeah.

COWAN: And you'd still have to fulfill your one record per year contract, is that right? Is that kind of how it was?

LAMM: Not that we were aware of. It was always like, "OK, it's time to make a new album." And it was pretty much one a year for a while. By 1972, we were working on *Chicago V*.

COWAN: Which is amazing. But, when did you find time to write? Or were you always composing all the time for your own artistry

LAMM: I *still* write all the time. For me, writing has always been a combination of "this is what I wake up hearing" and the sitting down to play as a form of exploration and figuring out music. So I use the writing to figure out music. Music is a curious thing. I think most musicians are curious. It inspires curiosity. It's a wonderful, honorable way of life. I've never been great, I mean, until really recently, at writing on the road. In those days, it was too cumbersome. We didn't have laptops, so you had to drag something around with you. It wasn't like I could write on guitar, although Terry always had a guitar. Actually, Terry and Lee would always room together, so the two of them were always playing. And I would come over to the room and pick up a guitar and play stuff. A few songs, I kind of worked out on guitar until I could get to a keyboard and figure out what it was. I guess I just wrote when I was home. Always had a piano.

COWAN: The notion of the songwriter in the '30s and '40s was really strong, whether it was Jerome Kern or Sammy Cahn or the Gershwins, you name it. But when the pop bands and rock and roll came along in the '50s and '60s, we never thought about who was writing the song, like Lennon and McCartney, until later. Then the songwriter tag came around again with Joni Mitchell and James Taylor and Jackson Browne. People in bands, like you, who have composed so much, rarely get recognized in the same way as songwriters. I've talked to many people known for being songwriters and said, "Robert Lamm, look at this body of work!" So many of your songs have become part of our culture, which, as a songwriter has to be really gratifying to you. I think it would be equally important to be recognized in that same vein.

LAMM: The songs that I wrote early on, up to my first solo album, *Skinny Boy*, all those songs I wrote for Chicago. What I was writing was not just songs. What I was writing were musical pieces, so I didn't really think of them as songs. And sometimes, they don't hold up as songs. A song like "Does Anybody Really Know What Time It Is?" is the closest thing to a classic ABAB type song with a chorus and the whole thing. I didn't really understand the structure of a song then, because I just didn't. So, I didn't really think of myself as a songwriter until later, for *Skinny Boy*. I knew that was going to be a solo album, and I approached it as minimalist as I could. I tried to have the songs be songs. By that time, I *was* listening to Cole Porter, and I *was* paying attention to structure. I don't know if you've heard me onstage when I introduce the band, but the first thing I say is, "I'm Robert Lamm, and I'm a songwriter who got lucky."

COWAN: OK, so does that mean, with your touring schedule in those days, through your first few albums, when you guys were just crazy busy, that when it was time to make a record, you'd just hole up somewhere for six weeks and write? Or were you writing on the road a little bit?

LAMM: I really didn't write on the road, except for a song like "Dialogue." I woke up with that. I woke up in the middle of the night and wrote down the lyrics. I heard the changes already. So then, once I got to a piano, I was like, OK, that's what that is. I wish it happened more. But other than those kinds of things, for me, I wrote when I was home. I wrote when I had the two or three weeks or whatever between the tour. Then I was like, "OK, we're gonna record, so bring your stuff." I got into the habit of charting everything. I would show up at the first prerecording rehearsal, and I'd have a half dozen songs already, and we would just play ' em down, and they would develop into whatever they developed into. But I did not write on the road.

COWAN: I noticed on the first couple of records that it sounded like perhaps you were casting. Since it's a bit of a democracy in a band . . .

LAMM: Yeah.

COWAN: . . . it's like, "OK, Peter's gonna sing this."

LAMM: Yes. That was so much fun for me. It's crazy, but I didn't ever think about the keys. I mean, whatever key I happened into in the process of writing the song, that was the key that it was.

COWAN: [*laughs*] Then, would they change with the singer or would they not change?

LAMM: Not too much. No, not at all.

COWAN: [*falsetto*] You'll sing this up here. [*both laugh*]

LAMM: I mean, nowadays, I can kinda almost sing "25 or 6 to 4." I have done it. But I've had other guys say to me, "Aren't you sorry you didn't write it in G?" [*both laugh*] Yeah! I am. But Cetera was just always such a great singer. It was really fun for me to write something in five or seven and say, "Can you sing this?" He could. He did. He made himself do it.

COWAN: Would the melodies change much with each person's personality, or would it kind of stay close to what you had written?

LAMM: No, they were pretty close. I always said though, that whether it was the vocal or the various parts, in this band, the recorded versions of the songs I wrote always improved once I put it in their hands. Here are the parts. Let's play it. And if somebody said, "What if I tried this?," we'd absolutely try that. It always made the song better to let people be who they are.

COWAN: I got right involved with the first record, the CTA record. I think I was sixteen or seventeen. Did you have any sense, other than we're doing something really cool, and we're really enjoying this, that you were having such a great effect on people?* To this day, there are people in my age-group who think about you with such reverence for the body of work that you've done and its influence on so many people like me. And I went on to being in the world of bluegrass for God's sake [*Lamm laughs*], but I took that with me. I took the things that you guys created. Did you have any sense whatsoever of the effect you might be having out there?

LAMM: No. [*laughs*] Not really, no. I mean, it's really taken me most of my life, really until the last few years, where I can actually hear that when

---

* In 1969, Chicago Transit Authority was originally signed to perform at Woodstock. But promoter Bill Graham, who had contractual influence over the band's gigs, decided to move CTA to his iconic San Francisco club, the Fillmore West, on the same date. In their place, he helped to book another band that he managed, Santana, to perform that Saturday, August 16th. Santana was the only band to play Woodstock without a recording contract.

somebody says that to me. I just couldn't hear it before, if they were saying that to me.

COWAN: The funny thing is, I've tried to be cognizant in my own little artist's space over the years, not to deflect when people say things like that. I don't know why that's so hard to internalize and to let it get into your heart. And it's equally hard to express that it means a lot to you back to them. It's tricky, isn't it?

LAMM: It is. I had a guest in Atlanta and, you know, he was just kind of saying similar things. He said, you must know that you've had such an effect on the culture, etcetera. And I wasn't trying to be modest, and I wasn't saying, oh, I knew that. I was just listening to what he said, and I said, "Thank you for everything you've said, but . . . it's not the reason I live!" [*both laugh*] I'm really just more concerned with the next batch of songs or whatever. Whatever process it is, you know? The sauce has been boiling down on the next batch of songs, and I'm just waiting for it to become the ragu! [*laughs*]

COWAN: Because after all, we're working. Forty-five years, right?

LAMM: Yeah.

COWAN: You guys have managed to hold on and continue to do what you do.

LAMM: It's been really tough.

COWAN: I'm sure. But here you are, man. Any comments about what's different?

LAMM: Well, I have a few comments. One is that it's gone by really, really quickly. I'm sort of in that stage of my life where I'll just remember something from some distant past and just shake my head, or wonder, *Whatever happened to that guy?* or, *Why did I say that?* or *What a jerk I was.* [*both laugh*] All that stuff, you know? I'll just groan out loud when I have those thoughts. The main thing is that it's just perplexing that I'm the age that I am, and that I've been doing this for as long as I have been. I never knew—it took me a long time to realize—that this, indeed, is my life. And this is going to be my life, and it's OK. You know, after the *Chicago Transit Authority* album came out, and I actually had it in my hand, and I put it on the player for the first time, I just thought, *That's it. I'm done!*

COWAN: [*laughs*]

LAMM: *I've always wanted to do this, and now I've done it.*

COWAN: *How does it get any better from here?*

LAMM: Yeah. I was still of the age where I thought, *Now I'll figure out what I really want to do, or what I really am supposed to do with my life.* It's really taken me the better part of thirty-five years to figure out that this *is* what I'm going to do for the rest of my life, God willing. And more and more, I feel like I'm running out of time for all the things I want to do, which I think is a good place to be. I'm not panicked, but I'm feeling the squeeze a little bit.

COWAN: The impetus of urgency.

LAMM: Yeah. But the forty-five years has not been easy. I mean, it's been *luxurious* in many ways. In a material sense and an experiential sense. Certainly in a travel sense. I love to travel. I don't know if it's a conditioned response, but I love to travel. But I think the toughest part has been that, as we go on, there's the needing to compromise as a band, within the band, to do everything.

COWAN: You mean, on a political level, between each other?

LAMM: Yeah, between each other. Giving room to each other. Because, certainly as we get older, we get more self-directed, and not necessarily in the same direction as everybody else in the band or anybody else in the band. I certainly have a better handle on who I am than I did when I was thirty or twenty. I have to assume that Jimmy [James Pankow, trombone], Walter [Parazaider, saxophone], and Lee [Loughnane, trumpet], similarly are on their own paths, and they're not *converging* paths. We're growing further and further away from each other, so it takes more and more willingness to compromise to keep the whole thing on the rails, which is where it needs to be.

14

I'M JUST A SINGER WITH JUSTIN HAYWARD OF THE MOODY BLUES

I've loved the Moody Blues music since I heard Denny Laine sing "You'd Better Go Now" in 1965 when I was twelve, and the British Invasion was in full swing. I had pored over *Days of Future Passed* all the way through *Seventh Soujourn*, which included my first LSD trip for existential listening pleasure. Even so, when I got a call from my friend and wonderful mandolinist David Harvey, asking me if I'd be interested in singing on an acoustic bluegrass tribute to the Moody Blues, I really had to give it some thought. I mean, you can't just take any genre of music, play it in 2/4, throw some banjos, fiddles, and flat-pick guitar on it, and not have it sound a lot like a parody. But when Dave and his partner, Randey Faulkner, told me of the other artists who had signed on to the project—Alison Krauss, Sam Bush, Harley Allen, Larry Cordle, Russell Smith, Tim O'Brien, Jon Randall Stewart, and other bluegrass royalty—I enthusiastically agreed. The resulting record, *Moody Bluegrass, Vol. 1*, turned out to be one of the records I'm most proud to have been a part of in my career. It was also how I came to meet Justin.

After that record was released, David and Randey proposed performing that record in its entirety at the Ryman Auditorium in Nashville, inviting all the singers and players on the album, along with the Moody's Justin Hayward, John Lodge, and Graeme Edge. On October 23rd, 2005, to our delight, and theirs, as it turned out, the Moody Blues arrived at the Ryman for an iconic

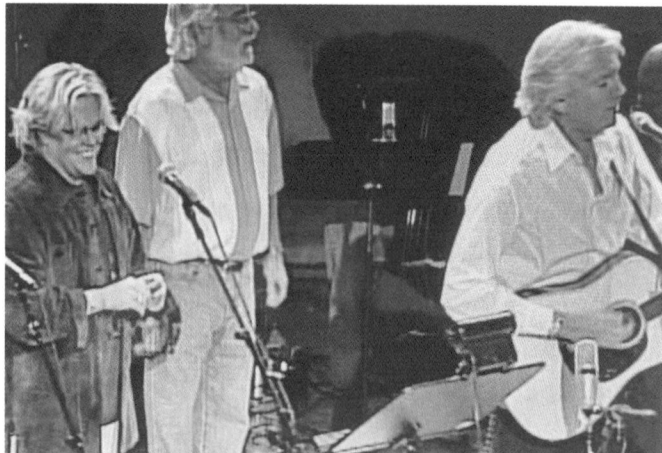

Singing "Tuesday Afternoon" with Justin Hayward of the Moody Blues, at the Moody Bluegrass Tribute Concert, Ryman Auditorium, October 23, 2005. *Courtesy of Randey and Cindyrae Faulkner*

evening of Moody Blues hits backed by some of the greatest names in country and bluegrass. One of the last numbers of the evening was "Tuesday Afternoon," which Justin and I sang together. (You can find it on YouTube.) After the show, I asked Justin to autograph my lyric sheet. He wrote, "Thank you, John. The best version of this song I've ever heard." —Justin Hayward.

Our interview was conducted just a few years later in Justin's suite in the Loews Vanderbilt Hotel on Nashville's West End.*

JOHN COWAN: You played last night at the historic Ryman Auditorium here in Nashville. I was so amazed at the love affair between the fans and the band. It's been a long time since I've seen people spontaneously get up for solos, for crescendos, and songs. Is that a common occurrence at a Moody show?

JUSTIN HAYWARD: Well, it is with a certain group of fans. I think it was strong last night because I think it was a bit of a fan fest. It was a very strong thing from the Moodys' fan community. But, yeah, it's a familiar pattern with us. I think that kind of music lends itself to it. The people who come to see us really know our music.

COWAN: I think a lot of us first became familiar with the Moodys with Denny Laine and "Go Now." Then there was a bit of a disappearance, and then I think "Tuesday Afternoon" was it for most of us.

HAYWARD: Yeah.

COWAN: How many years has it been in the Moodys?

HAYWARD: Well, since 1966. John Lodge [bassist] came at the same time, but we didn't know each other. I had my songs recorded with them earlier. There's a lot of stuff before "Tuesday Afternoon." It was really only after *Days of Future Past* when people started paying attention. That was about a year after I joined.

COWAN: I'm probably going to get this wrong . . .

---

* I once auditioned for a Viagra TV commercial at the Loews Vanderbilt. I didn't get it.

HAYWARD: OK.

COWAN: But the idea behind *Days of Future Past* originally was to record Dvorak's *New World* Symphony?

HAYWARD: Yes. We had a debt to Decca Records. They needed kind of a house band to make a demonstration record of stereo, because Decca had a consumer division that sold stereo units and mono record players. They wanted to demonstrate that stereo could be as interesting for rock and roll as it was for classical music. They had a special projects guy named Michael Dacre-Barclay who had this idea of putting a rock group side by side with an orchestra. They wouldn't play together because that would be meaningless. You would put them separately in stereo, one after the other, and the stereo sound would continue, and things would be still in the right place.

COWAN: Were you recording in eight-track at that time?

HAYWARD: Four-track.

COWAN: Wow.

HAYWARD: Yeah. Some of it was two-track. There was a two-track machine and a four-track. We were bouncing as we went, you know, so when you got a backing track, you'd bounce that with the vocals to another machine if you wanted to double-track vocals or something, or if you wanted to double-track anything. Backing tracks were never double tracked, of course.

COWAN: So, with "Tuesday Afternoon," you'd already come with that song. How did that work? You had the songs, and they wrote the orchestral charts to those songs?

HAYWARD: Right. Well, they had this idea that we should learn the commercial bits from Dvorak; and Peter Knight, who was a classical composer and arranger, would play the real Dvorak. Well, Michael Dacre-Barkley and Peter Knight came to see us. They saw our stage show in which we were already doing "Knights" and quite a few of the other things. "Another Morning" and another song of Mike Pinder's called "Dawn Is a Feeling." Then they came to us. Michael and Peter Knight sort of suggested, "What if we do it the other way around?" Then Michael said, "Well, that wouldn't be what Decca wanted." But the executive producer went along with it, and Peter became very determined that it should be the other way around, that he wouldn't do Dvorak but he would orchestrate. We would do our songs, and then he would do an orchestral version of them that told some kind of narrative, in the way that the orchestra played, to give you the story of a day in the life of one guy, which is what our stage show was already based on. Peter deserves a lot of credit for that, because there's probably only thirty minutes of us on the record, and the extra fifteen or seventeen is Peter Knight. So, we went in secretly. They'd given us the studio time but with only the executive producer, and without any others from Decca, and we recorded our songs in about three days. Then, on a Saturday when I was there, they did an orchestra session. They ran through it once, did one take, and then they went home. That was it. It was committed.

COWAN: When you heard the finished product, were you pleased?

HAYWARD: I knew what Peter was going to do. I'd heard the orchestra. I'd heard our stuff and how we'd done it. I was very pleased the way it segued, and I thought it was a delightful album. I assumed, right from the beginning until right through to the end and its release, that we were making a stereo demonstration record. It came as a bit of a surprise at the Monday meeting to Decca when Michael Dacre-Barkley played it to them, and they said, "This is not Dvorak." [*both laugh*] And he said, "Yeah, but we've spent the studio time, and it's a great stereo demonstration." So, they went ahead with it as a demonstration record at a budget price. Then, within about a month, they put it up to full price. I thought we were making kind of an arty thing that would have a limited appeal, and that I might meet some really intelligent ladies from *The Guardian* or *The Observer*, and we'd go to a nice little cocktail party, and that was about the limit of it. I could not imagine. It did not have any commercial appeal, in my opinion.

COWAN: And was that 1967?

HAYWARD: That was 1967. The album came out November 11th, 1967.

COWAN: Is it true that "Tuesday Afternoon" was a hit twice?

HAYWARD: The album finally got to number one in '72 in the United States. "Knights in White Satin" was a hit four times. "Knights" was a hit in '67 in the Top 20. Again in '72–'73. Again in '79. And then again in 2010.

COWAN: It seems like you found a home really early here in Nashville.

HAYWARD: We turned up here, you see, in the winter of '68 for Bill Graham in America. FM radio was just starting, and we were playing a lot of psychedelic clubs and that kind of stuff. We supported Cream on their farewell tour, and we were the support band for a lot of people. But for our album, its home was in FM radio, and they loved it. And the next album they loved just the same to the last chord. *Days of Future Past* was just perfect for those guys who just got stereo radio, and for those DJs who wanted it. It wasn't like the Beatles. I'll never understand why George [Martin] didn't do nice stereo. Beatles had the drums on the right and the vocals on the left. It was just truly awful.

COWAN: Almost like an old jazz record.

HAYWARD: It was awful. But our stuff had a beautiful stereo picture and, of course, when it came to the CD format, our stuff was perfect because it was recorded beautifully. Not like a lot of the '60s stuff that was just very much straight down the middle trying to get it onto a 45.

COWAN: Your records, all the way up to *Seventh Sojourn*, continued to feature a lot of symphonic music. Did you start thinking that way?

HAYWARD: That's a good point. I think it probably did influence us. The mellotron* and [keyboardist] Mike Pinder were so central to the Moody

---

* The mellotron was an electric keyboard-sampling instrument that appeared in the '60s and was the forerunner of the synthesizer. It looked a bit like an organ but was much trippier than that. The right-hand keys gave you a choice of about eighteen different prerecorded lead instruments. The left hand gave you choices of rhythms, background sounds, and voicings, all pre-fed onto hundreds of short tapes inside. For that reason, you didn't have to be a particularly gifted musician to make interesting music. But in the hands of artists like Mike Pinder, you could make music history. Other famous moments of the mellotron include the Beatles "Strawberry Fields," Bowie's "Space Oddity," and the flutes in Led Zeppelin's "Stairway to Heaven."

Blues. He was a great loss to the band when he decided that he didn't want to do it anymore. But his sound made my songs work. I mean, before, when he was just playing piano, I couldn't get anything to sound the way I really wanted it. When I wrote "Knights," I took it into the rehearsal room the next day. I had only written the song on the side of the bed the night before, and I played it to everyone, and nobody was really that impressed by it as a song. It was just one guitar and a voice. It's only with the connotations now that you can listen to it, with one guitar and voice now, and say, "Oh, yeah, I love this." But then, it was just like [*sighs*], "Oh, well, whatever." Then Mike said, "Play it again," and so I sang "Knights in White Satin," and Mike went [*sings the mellotron opening*], Duh duh duh da duh duh duh on the mellotron, and suddenly the rest of the group went, "That's nice," and everybody was into it. So the mellotron was huge in those first few years.

COWAN: You made a comment last night that the A&R people wanted to tell you what to do, but in the end, nobody ever told you what to do. But that's probably not right, is it?

HAYWARD: No, the first seven albums, nobody told us what to do.

COWAN: Oh, that's good.

HAYWARD: A lot of people told us, "I don't want to work with it because it's not commercial." Right at the beginning, there were people saying, "Oh, this is never gonna happen. I'm pulling out of it." A&R guys, or independent promo guys who said, "I can't do anything with that." But then, in the '70s, Sir Edward Lewis* was getting very old. He died in '79. Decca passed to Deutsche Grammophon,† and then we got guys saying, "You should be doing this and you should be doing that."

---

* Sir Edward Lewis was the founder of the Decca Records Company which for years was one of the two largest recording companies in England, EMI being the other. He was a pioneer of recording advancements and new technologies in sound engineering, including introducing the move from shellac 78s to more vivid-sounding vinyl LPs in the '40s. Like most of us, not every decision he made worked out for the best.

† Deutsche Grammophon was essentially a classical music label at the time. It was founded in 1898 and is still the oldest existing recording company.

COWAN: As I look at your body of work, it's so high-minded and artful. Your musicianship is really at a high level. It must've been wonderful at that time to not have any constraints, where you'd write a song and just let it go wherever it wanted to go.

HAYWARD: Artistically, there was a lot of freedom. Almost too much, insomuch as some albums took several months to make. I listen back to tracks now, and I think that if I had someone with maybe a bit more courage, even if the late Tony Clarke had had more courage, he'd have said, "Justin, you need to think about that word or maybe think about words lyrically that could make it stronger."

COWAN: When I look at all these songs that you've written, and John and Mike have written, there's a lot of great songwriting here. I wonder if you always thought of yourself as a songwriter?

HAYWARD: I thought of myself as a songwriter since the time I was with Marty Wilde* as a guitar player. I had played in bands in school and all that stuff and strayed away from school at seventeen to become a professional musician. Marty was a guy who was a rock and roll hero in the late 1950s and early '60s, and he told me then that to survive in the business, you've got to write your own material, and I started writing then. After the age of eighteen onward, I considered myself a songwriter. I came into the Moodys as a songwriter and a reluctant kind of a singer.

COWAN: In a rock and roll band.

HAYWARD: In a rock and roll band.

---

* Marty Wilde was a British singer and songwriter who was among the first English stars to copy the vocal chops of American pop singers. In the early '60s, Marty asked a seventeen-year-old Justin Hayward to join a new band he was putting together called the Wilde Three, along with Marty's wife, Joyce.

15

BY AND BY, JOHN CARTER CASH KEEPS THE CIRCLE UNBROKEN

In 1989, I had the opportunity as a member of New Grass Revival to participate in the Nitty Gritty Dirt Band's *Will the Circle be Unbroken Vol. II*, along with Johnny Cash, June Carter Cash, Helen Carter, Anita Carter, Levon Helm, Bruce Hornsby, Rosanne Cash, Vassar Clements, Jimmy Martin, John Denver, John Prine, Ricky Skaggs, Emmy Lou Harris, Michael Martin Murphy, John Hiatt, Radney Foster, Vince Gill, Bill Lloyd, Roger McGuinn, Earl Scruggs, The Whites, Rangy Scruggs, Gary Scruggs, Steve Wariner, Tracy Nelson, Wendy Waldman, and, of course, Bob Carpenter, Jimmy Ibbotson, Jeff Hannah, and Jimmy Fadden, the Dirt Band. Yes, that's an ass-load of name-dropping, but tying generations of music together, as the Carter Family once sang, is what surely made this album unique and was always the intended consequence.

A decade or so later, I met John Carter Cash (Johnny and June's only child together) at the International Bluegrass Music Association yearly conference. I, of course, knew of him. He had been carrying on the Carter-Cash tradition of rebellion by leading his own hard rock-metal band. Upon our meeting, he informed me that he was a New Grass Revival fan, as were his mother and father. He asked for my phone number and assured me that he had projects in mind for me to work on. I liked John right off the bat; he had a quiet, sturdy sense of self-assurance, a wicked sense of humor, and a big, old

John Carter Cash (left), in studio with his father, Johnny. *Courtesy Daniel Coston*

plowshare of heart. John called me over the years to work on all sorts of varied stuff as a vocalist and bassist.

John has a cabin with an overstocked 2.5-acre pond on forty acres that his dad, Johnny, constructed in 1979 as a place to get away, across the street from the Cash home, on the edge of Old Hickory Lake north of Nashville. It was eventually made into a nice recording studio. I've been an avid amateur freshwater fisherman since my father introduced my two brothers and me to the dharma of "a line and pole" early in our lives. John, a hunter and fisher of renown, has been very generous with me over the years. I've made some of my own records at the Cash Cabin, but just as important to me, he welcomed me out to throw in a line through every season, whether he was in town or not. All my stepchildren and stepgrandkids have caught many a bluegill, catfish, largemouth bass, and turtle at John Carter's.

As far as the "Cash dynasty" is concerned, the lineage looks like a master's thesis of Americana music. A. P. Carter, "Mother" Maybelle Carter, June Carter Cash, Sarah Carter, Anita Carter, Carlene Carter, Helen Carter, Janette Carter, Rosanne Cash, Nick Lowe, and Rodney Crowell are all part of this living, breathing, incandescent institution that has changed not only the music world but many of our lives.

You will find here in the interview that John Carter (as he is most often known), has taken on the daunting task of procuring and furthering the legacy of not only his father, Johnny Cash, and his mother, June Carter Cash, but all things Carter Family. He has embraced this stewardship soberly with vision, great heart, and humility. We recorded our conversation at WSM studios in Nashville.

JOHN COWAN: Where did we first meet? I'm not sure.

JOHN CARTER CASH: We met at the Galt House Hotel at the IBMA Awards. Do you remember that?

COWAN: [*laughs*] I don't!

CASH: Actually, we were sitting at the bar. You were having a Coke, and I might've been drinking something different.

COWAN: Oh. [*both laugh*]

CASH: And that was many years ago. Might've been fifteen years ago.

COWAN: As some of you will recognize, John is the son of Johnny Cash and June Carter Cash. I think it goes without saying that their imprint on what we know as country music is huge. I want to talk a bit about the Carter Family and some of the things you do.

CASH: I watch after the Carter Family, where I can, and I want to spread the word about the music. Of course, Peermusic has a whole lot to do with the music because the songs are still all copyrighted with Peer.* Dale Jett, who is A. P. and Sara Carter's grandson, and is a dear friend—he takes care of the image of the family heritage along with Rita Forrester, their granddaughter down there in southwestern Virginia. It's a matter of heritage. To me, the Carter Family represents the foundation of country music.

COWAN: Absolutely.

CASH: So many people know the songs, know the melodies, but don't exactly know where they came from. "Will the Circle Be Unbroken" or "Wildwood Flower"—these are Carter Family songs. If it had not have been for a young man named A. P. Carter, who decided to become a traveling salesman, explicitly to go door to door, front porch to front porch, and picking up people's songs, then we would not have country music as we know it. The Carter Family were not only the first country band inducted into the Hall of Fame, but they were also the first country band to be played in people's homes.

COWAN: And really, near the invention of the phonograph record, the Carter Family's first recording that they made went on to sell 300,000 copies.

CASH: In the *1920s*!

COWAN: That's phenomenal.

CASH: Yeah, in the '20s there were still a lot of record sales. But record sales went down significantly because of radio. It was groups like the Carter Family that, through the Depression, bridged the gap between phonograph

---

* Peermusic is the largest independent music publisher in the world. It was founded more than eighty-five years ago by the visionary record producer Ralph Peer, who some have called "the Father of Country Music." It was Peer who discovered Jimmie Rodgers and the Carter Family and recorded them and others for the legendary *Bristol Sessions*.

records and radio because they still continued to make records *and* they were on the radio, doing live radio shows and whatnot. So, radio nearly killed records back in the '20s just as the internet today knocked out CDs. But music lives on. That's the point. The Carter Family became my favorite band about ten years ago.

COWAN: I want to talk a little bit about this gentleman Ralph Peer, who I believe was from New York, and he is someone you might call an ethnomusicologist, and the journey he took to the state of Virginia. Do you know exactly how it was that he found A. P. and the Carters?

CASH: Well, he put out an ad in the newspaper, you know, to come for auditions to record a record. And it was the same week that A. P. Carter, Sara, and Maybelle Carter, who is my grandmother, got in the car—Maybelle was pregnant with her first daughter, Helen—and they drove down there.

COWAN: They drove to Bristol.

CASH: They drove to Bristol from Hiltons, Virginia.* It was like twenty-four miles to Bristol, and back then, twenty-four miles was an all-day affair. And Maybelle pregnant and everything.

COWAN: Yeah, there was no interstate.

CASH: [*both laugh*] No, but they made the auditions, and so did Jimmy Rodgers† that same week in 1927. Arguably, the most important week in the history of country music.

COWAN: So, they went and auditioned for Ralph. Did he have a portable recording device of some kind to capture them?

CASH: Yeah, I'm not going to describe what it was because there are historians out there who know exactly what it was. I don't know if it was a wire recorder or a wax recorder, but yes, he had a machine that he brought with him.

---

* Hiltons, Virginia, in Scott County, is the home of the Carter Family Fold and is the site of Johnny Cash's last public performance.
† Jimmie Rodgers, the "Singing Brakeman," was among the first nationally known country music stars. He died, tragically, of tuberculosis at age thirty-five. At the time of his death, his yodeling blues/folk recordings accounted for 10 percent of all RCA record sales. He and the Carters were the only performers signed by Peer that day.

COWAN: So, he captured not only the Carter Family at that time, A. P., Maybelle, and Sara, who was the lead singer. But he also captured Jimmie Rodgers. Did they possibly know each other previous to that?

CASH: I do not know. I know that Jimmie Rodgers actually auditioned once before and was turned down in, like, 1924. But I don't think they were friends. They may have been acquaintances at that point or they may have met that week. There's a wonderful book out there called *Will You Miss Me When I'm Gone*, about the history of the Carter Family, and I've read it, but I just can't remember if it was mentioned.

COWAN: It was such a fortuitous occasion for Ralph Peer to discover A. P. and Sara and Mother Maybelle and Jimmie Rodgers at the same time, because they went on separately but, of course, did so many things together to become the bedrock of what we know as country music.

CASH: And to country guitar. I mean, if it hadn't been for Mother Maybelle Carter's style, the fact that she was the main rhythm and the lead player, she had to figure out a way to play the lead melody and the rhythm at the same time. And in doing so, she played the melody on the big strings with her thumb and continued to play the rhythm at the same time. And it was simple necessity that made this something that she developed, this style, and it basically is country music guitar.

COWAN: It became known over the years as the Maybelle scratch.

CASH: Yes, the Carter scratch.

COWAN: So, if you jettison yourself up to the late '40s and early '50s, you have people like Merle Travis, Doc Watson . . .

CASH: . . . Chet Atkins, also . . .

COWAN: . . . and a little later, Norman Blake. They all openly attribute their being able to do what they do, and some of the ideas that they were able to bring themselves to the guitar, to Maybelle.

CASH: Earl Scruggs's banjo playing. He developed that style from listening to Maybelle.

COWAN: The story of the Carter family, your family, your grandparents, just that side of your family is just so unbelievable to me because they almost single-handedly created an art form.

CASH: Mm hmm, yeah.

COWAN: So, by the end of 1929, the Carter Family had sold 300,000 records. In a business sense, A. P. was a pretty smart guy.

CASH: Yes, he was.

COWAN: Was he smart enough to know, even at that time, to think, I need to copyright these songs? That we need to make this a revenue stream?

CASH: I think it was set up that way with Peer from the beginning. It was like a business partnership. And A. P. did the footwork, going around and collecting these songs, because the fact remains that A. P. didn't necessarily pen all of these songs. He *edited* them. He put them together, but "Keep on the Sunny Side" and "Will the Circle Be Unbroken," these are turn-of-the-century songs.

COWAN: Right, they were around.

CASH: They were around for a while. But he would go from front porch to front porch and pick up these songs. He would go from railroad yard to railroad yard listening to hobos, listening to black bluesmen and whatnot, and he would put all these songs together. He would edit them also. He would make them a certain length, speed them up, slow them down. He would make them a three-minute song or two-and-a-half-minute song, whatever it would have to be to fit on the record. And in doing so, he created modern music in some ways.

COWAN: This is something historically that's been done time and again. It's what Bob Dylan famously did with Woody Guthrie's catalog. And then strangely enough, there are some bootleg records out now where Bob took a Carter Family tune and rearranged it, exactly like A. P. would've done, changed the title, and called it his song. So, it's pretty common.

CASH: "The Great Speckled Bird" is also the same thing as "Honky Tonk Angels." And it's all, "Little Darling, Pal of Mine." It all came from the Carter Family.

COWAN: Yup. [*both laugh*]

CASH: So, we all borrow it. That's part of it.

COWAN: I don't know if you know the answer to this, but after 1929, the Carter Family went to Louisville, Kentucky, and made a record. So, I guess they were off and running at that point. Had they become full-time musicians? Is that what they were doing?

CASH: They did some performances. They did high-school gymnasiums, so I know they did travel around and do performances. I know that A. P. spent a lot of time on his own, seeking out songs. So, yes, it was their career and their life. It was what they were dedicated to. I think A. P. from the beginning was very serious about it. I think Maybelle and Sara weren't as serious right at the beginning, because no one had ever heard of country people becoming recording artists. It had never happened before. This whole idea was completely foreign to them. So, it wasn't as if they could have the dream to aspire to do something that had never been done.

COWAN: I have to say that I discovered Jimmie Rodgers before I started listening to the Carter Family. When I first heard Jimmie Rodgers, I thought, well, this is Robert Johnson. This is a white guy doing Delta blues. It's a little different in that, and I don't mean this in a derogatory way, it was hillbilly music.

CASH: Oh, yeah.

COWAN: It was the same blues-based music and of course, Jimmie Rodgers's singing was angelic. And he yodeled! And the thing that strikes me about the Carter Family's music is its soulfulness. A term was coined later about the "high and lonesome sound" that's so associated with Ralph Stanley and Bill Monroe. But you can just hear the mountains in the Carter Family.

CASH: Oh, you do. There's a specific culture. And you hear a lack of influence from the outside. But you also hear an amazing interpretation of what influences they did have. Maybelle heard mariachi bands at the Texas border in the 1930s, and it was through listening to this that she developed the guitar lick that's on "You Are My Flower." So, they were picking up stuff, but they were interpreting it their own way. They were listening to other people's work, but they were isolated enough to where it was pure. We're all influenced by so many things. today. Part of their purity was the limited amount of influence.

COWAN: From a generational standpoint, what generation of the Carters first came to the United States? Do you know where they were from?

CASH: They're from the British Isles. Maybelle, specifically, her last name was Addington. And there were Carters in the United States as early as the late 1700s. So, they've been here awhile. The Cashes have actually been here since the 1670s! [*laughs*]

COWAN: Do you know how or why music was part of A. P. and Maybelle's lives? Was playing instruments a tradition in their family?

CASH: I think it was church. I think that was the main thing, that they played music at church. But I don't know about the household or how Maybelle ever learned to play guitar.

COWAN: "Will the Circle Be Unbroken," which was originally called "Can the Circle Be Unbroken," "Wildwood Flower," "Keep on the Sunny Side," of course, which was a big part of the Coen brothers movie *O Brother, Where Art Thou?* Were the Whites the people who did it in the movie?

CASH: Uh huh.

COWAN: These are standards in music, not just in folk music or country music. I think you could say the words, "Will the Circle Be Unbroken . . ."

CASH: . . . and just about anybody would recognize it.

COWAN: It just astounds me really how this music has endured. I think it's so important in this day and age.

CASH: Oh, I agree.

COWAN: Because it's such an essential part of your biology and history, do you feel the onus, at all, to be the flame keeper of this stuff?

CASH: It's a passion. There's great passion there that drives me. In some ways, yes, it's about spreading the word of the music. It's about your showing appreciation for how we got where we are because of it. So, yeah, if it wasn't for the passion and the love for it, no, I wouldn't be feeling as if I had to keep the flame.

COWAN: This station where we're taking, WSM in Nashville, has been one of the torchbearers of country music. But that brings up another subject. As country music continues on, and this is not really a criticism more than an observation, what I worry about is the artists that WSM built their radio station on and country music was built on, which started with Jimmie Rodgers and the Carter Family, is kind of evaporating. Is that troubling to you at all?

CASH: Yeah, it really is. People will love what's good, there is no doubt. And people will appreciate what's good, because people are smart. Because people are understanding. Because people have taste.

COWAN: [*both laugh*]

CASH: I really do. I think the problem is that a lot of people aren't introduced to it. People know good music. And there's so much music that's still there. I listen to old music, a lot of old-time music.

COWAN: I do, too.

CASH: Because I think we're blessed enough to live in an age where we can learn about the very foundation of all music. Five hundred years from now, they're going to be looking at the music of the twentieth century as being like George Washington and Thomas Jefferson, in its own right, in the history of music. I mean, we're really lucky to be this close to it.

COWAN: Yeah. And since we're talking about the Carter Family, we need to start talking a bit about your father, Johnny Cash. The Carters brought us up to the string band years, like Uncle Dave Macon, and we're talking about the Opry now in the '40s and '50s with people like Lefty Frizzell and Hank Williams Sr. We had the emergence of amazing women artists like Kitty Wells, Loretta Lynn, Patsy Cline, even a little farther up with Lynn Anderson. I don't know what's going to happen to all of that.

CASH: People say, who's gonna fill their shoes? Or who's gonna be that great again? And the thing about it is, no one ever will be because you can't reroot a tree.

COWAN: No, you can't.

CASH: The tree is already there, and you can't change that. The best we can hope to do is forward on the flowers and the fruit. The foundation is already there, and we gotta appreciate it for what it is.

COWAN: It's really important that we know history. It's not that we want to repeat the Carter Family, because it already exists. But I guess, my biggest bone of contention is, in terms of contemporary country artists, is that I could go up to them and ask, "What's your favorite Bob Wills record?," and they'd say, "Who's that?" Actually, you don't even have to go back that far.

CASH: Lots of them know who he is and will go around saying he's their favorite, but that's when you ask them to sing something. [*laughs*]

COWAN: Well, that's something else I wanted to ask you. A few years ago, I turned on the Country Music Awards, and there was an artist performing, and they had these big neon signs, C, A, S, H, flashing behind them. Cash, flashing.

CASH: Cash.

COWAN: The deal was, I guess he was name-dropping your dad, Johnny, in the song, I think, I don't know, but as I watched it, [*laughs*], I thought, *Oh, my gosh, how gratuitous is that?* What I got from that is cash money. [*laughs*]

CASH: Well, that's really what it meant. He was using that name to sell records.

COWAN: We've seen a lot of that in the past ten or fifteen years where your parent's names are being dropped into songs. Who knows? It's an argument that doesn't necessarily go anywhere. But it brings us to your father, Johnny Cash. The thing about your mom, June Carter, and your dad, Johnny Cash, is that they were such bright people. Even though they both came from the country and an agrarian society, they were very worldly. They were very smart. You can see it in their songs.

CASH: Oh, yeah. Well-studied. My father was a well-studied man, as my mother was. They read all the time. My dad was a life student. He was a very intelligent man and a scholar.

COWAN: You gave me that book for Christmas, *The House of Cash*, last year, and I read it voraciously. I just loved it. And one of the quotes in there from a few years ago, somebody asked your dad, "What do you think of modern country music?" And he said, "I think modern country music is for people who hate country music." [*both laugh*]

CASH: That's exactly it. For people who hate country music. It's become something else. I think a lot of it is not really country music. It's just that our definitions have changed.

COWAN: One of the reasons I wanted to do this with you, besides being your friend, is that, what your bloodline and biology and legacy brings is just absolutely astounding. So, let's talk a little bit about your father, Johnny Cash. What was it like to grow up around that? You probably didn't think anything about it.

CASH: Yeah, you don't know any different. I think I knew from a very early age the great influence he was having on people and music. I saw it specifically on people, and how everyone looked at him differently. The energy, the charisma that a lot of people felt—he was just Dad to me.

COWAN: Right, of course.

CASH: But he had that great charisma and energy, and I became aware of it later in life, not so early on, because he was just my dad. I don't know, if he wasn't such a good-hearted, simple man, I think all the bigness of who he was would have been a lot harder to take. But Dad, he was not haughty. He had an ego. There ain't no doubt about it. But he wasn't a prideful man as if he was a rich man on a throne. He wasn't like that. He was a humble man from humble upbringings. He was a hardworking kid when he was growing up. He loved gospel music. He was just a good, simple southern man in his heart. And so that made all the fanfare a lot easier to take. But I struggled a lot trying to figure out who I was.

COWAN: I contend, and I've talked to Rodney Crowell about this, that there's such a thing as a natural-born songwriter. Did your dad always write music?

CASH: Yeah, he was writing poetry very early. There's a song that is probably one of my favorite compositions of his, "Big River." Bob Dylan says that my father was one of America's great poets, and he cited that song specifically.

COWAN: Oh, yeah.

CASH: And that's a natural writing process. You can tell, it's just pure poetry.

COWAN: There's so many examples of your father's songwriting. I listened to "Get Rhythm," and it's a movie.

CASH: Oh, yeah, yeah, the imagery.

COWAN: It was the same reason I loved Chuck Berry when I was younger. His songs were like little snippets. Not only "Big River" but "Get

Rhythm" and so many others. They were so descriptive. As a listener, when the words are coming at you, you can picture everything that he's trying to tell you.

CASH: Oh, definitely so.

COWAN: He always kept his eye on the prize, from my perception. He was always creating. He was always digging up stuff. He was always wanting to write something else. Things were always pouring out of him. According to your book, *House of Cash*, there's stuff from his later life where he's still writing . . .

CASH: [*interrupts*] He was always following his heart. He was always right there in the spirit. So, yeah.

COWAN: Beautiful poems. Do you think that's something that came natural to him, or do you think it was something he was conscious of?

CASH: Well, I think it's the kind of thing that can only come natural. I think he was conscious of turning it on and appreciating it and saying, "I'm gonna get creative now," and getting in that energy.

COWAN: That's what I mean.

CASH: But I think it was a matter of practice, too. He continued to do it throughout his life. He was always creative. He was always pursuing the next creative thing, whatever that may be. And some would say there were times where it faltered, and it wasn't as fruitful or it wasn't as good, or whatever. But he never stopped pursuing it. He never stopped pursuing what his heart told him to do next. And so, I think that's the beauty of it. Whether it was doing a silly record in the '60s or the early '80s that was more comical than it was anything, or whether it was doing the more serious-minded stuff like the records with Rick Rubin, he still pursued his creative spirit.

COWAN: What we know about marriage is that it's a really tricky dance to begin with. And you are married to an artist. And your father was married to June Carter. Did she ever feel overshadowed? Was she all good with it? Was she busy being supportive of John, raising the kids? Did she find time to still be a creative person herself? Was that available to her?

CASH: Yeah, she continued her creativity, and she continued to work in music, but it was by his side, and it was to back him up, for many, many years. When she married my dad, she became Mrs. Johnny Cash, and she got onstage as his partner. So, it was to support him creatively and to be a part of his show and to be a part of the family music and whatnot. It wasn't until later in her life, when she went into the studio and made her last two records as a solo artist, *Press On* and *Wildwood Flower*, that she really came back out and flourished again in her creativity, and that was right at the end of her life.

COWAN: I guess the question would be to you, as someone who was there, do you think that was OK with her? Was she happy?

CASH: Yeah, I think she was. I'd say at some point, every once in a while, she might've thought, *well, I coulda done this* or *I coulda done that*. I mean, I'm sure there were wishful moments, especially in the 1980s when things with Dad were really crazy, and his insanity and addiction was back, I'm sure it crossed her mind. But, in the end, their love endured, and the strength of that love was only stronger because of the hardships that it survived. So, I know she was happy with the life that she and Dad created.

COWAN: The thing that I've always found astounding, and I can look at this from my own reality, as a kid who grew up in rock 'n' roll, like yourself, Johnny Cash was *cool*. He was just *cool*.

CASH: Oh, yeah.

COWAN: And it didn't matter if I listened to Hendrix all day.

CASH: Oh, I know.

COWAN: It'd be like, Johnny Cash? Oh, he's cool. And the other thing is, as little as I knew about country music, I knew that your mom was June Carter Cash. That she was from the Carter Family. I didn't know anything about them, but she seemed to have her own identity.

CASH: A very unique identity. And such a powerful, gentle strength that the dark, foreboding man in black onstage was softened by her.

COWAN: You know, one of my favorite songs by your father to this day, and I've heard it done by a million people, is "I Still Miss Someone."

CASH: Oh, yeah.

COWAN: It such a beautiful, plaintive love song.

CASH: Just simple expression, but in a poetic way.

COWAN: Not only the words, but the melody and chord changes. It's just genius.

CASH: I know. He wrote that song with my first cousin, Roy Cash Jr.

COWAN: I didn't know that.

CASH: Yeah, Roy Cash was very young when he wrote that. I think he was like sixteen or seventeen. He was just a kid when he wrote it with my dad. A great song. Great spirit. "I Still Miss Someone" tells an amazing story of lost love and "where did she go?" I mean, we all feel that, right?

COWAN: Your sister Rosanne's book, which came out in 2010, I think it's called *Composed*, which I really enjoyed, talked briefly about the *Walk the Line* movie and how for her, and I'm paraphrasing here, she saw it as an invasion of privacy and really just a nuisance.*

CASH: Well, you know who really made that movie? My parents made it. I mean, they're the ones who set it up.

COWAN: So, they were all about it.

CASH: They were the ones who went in with the producers, worked with the screenplay writers on the script. They made the financial agreements and everything, together. My dad and mom both approved Joaquin and Reese. And Dad approved a final version of the script. So, he saw the script, and he was there, and it was their baby. They chose that. And it's a story of their love,

---

* Rosanne, a great singer and songwriter, is one of four half sisters that John has from his father's first marriage to Vivian Liberto. His half sisters are Rosanne, Kathy, Cindy, and Tara.

specifically. And it's not about Dad's love with his first wife, really. That's not the focus of it, you know. It was their choice to do it. [*laughs*] It really was. So . . . y'know.

COWAN: Well, I'm trying to put myself in your family's position where somebody made a movie about Richard and Cleo Cowan. [*both laugh*]

CASH: You know, it's like selling your soul, it really is. You just don't know what you're going to wind up with. [*Cowan laughs*] *Walk the Line*, specifically, could've been *a lot worse*. Reese was amazing. But if you're looking for more about Dad's *faith*, the depth of his character, as we were speaking of earlier, his knowledge, his wisdom, all these things, you're going to miss it. It's not there. It's about a love story. That's the only thing it is, really. It's a love story. It's a tale about two people's love, and how they struggled, and how they got together. And it does that very well. So, I just try to judge it on that.

COWAN: Right.

CASH: But I mean, man, there's always things that I wish were done differently. But there are a lot of worse biopics out there, so . . . [*laughs*]

COWAN: So, I want to talk about what *you're* doing, what you've been doing, and your vision for not only yourself but your family on down the line. So, let's talk about you! [*both laugh*]

CASH: OK! I'm creative. I love to make music. I make some of my own music. I do a lot of traditional music also. And sometimes my music is more rock 'n' roll. I really love producing records. I've produced a lot of records in the past fifteen years. I started working, of course, with my mother and my father. I've produced material for Marty Stuart, Billy Joe Shaver, and Loretta Lynn. Lots of different artists.

COWAN: As someone who has worked for you as a producer, you're a damn good producer.*

---

* John Carter Cash is a five-time Grammy winning producer. He's produced wonderful tracks for everyone from Loretta, George Jones, and Ralph Stanley to Elvis Costello, Chris Cornell, Sheryl Crow, John Prine, and more.

CASH: Oh, thank you.

COWAN: You are.

CASH: Well, thank you. Thank you. Well, John, you're a damn good singer!

COWAN: [*both laugh*] Thank you.

CASH: But I love to follow my spirit. I follow the creativity, and it's led me in different directions. I wrote a biography for my mother called *Anchored in Love*. It's about her life and my life with her. Three children's books out there that are on Simon & Schuster that are available on the internet or in bookstores. I have a novel coming out next year. Talking animals and stuff but lots of bloodshed. It's for young adults. I didn't write it thinking it would be "young adult," but my publisher says, "Oh no, sixteen and up" and I thought, well, OK. It's called *Lupus Rex*. And I wrote a book about my dad and the family, called *House of Cash*, that focuses on my relationship with my father.

COWAN: That is just an amazing book.

CASH: It's like a coffee-table book.

COWAN: It *is* a coffee-table book; however, it's just loaded with personal memorabilia. And what's so interesting to me is that you were able to copy in a way that it looks like these things were all original in the book. Poems. Recipes . . .

CASH: Yeah, I was worried that they wouldn't get it, but they nailed it. It's beautiful. It's like the real deal.

COWAN: I gave it to my son-in-law for Christmas.

CASH: Yeah, so I follow my creativity and spirit, man, but I want to continue to do things to carry that flame and to pay a special appreciation to heritage. I'll follow my creativity just like my dad did, wherever it may lead. It gets silly sometimes, but you know, that's OK, because I followed my heart. That's the way I figure it.

COWAN: I would be so remiss if I didn't publicly acknowledge the huge debt that we all owe to John McEuen, Jimmy Ibbotson, and Jeff Hanna and Les Thompson for making the *Will the Circle Be Unbroken* album. Because that album came out, once again, when I was just a rock 'n' roll musician, and somebody brought this record over to our house.

CASH: The Dirt Band set the standard, man. They really did.

COWAN: Yeah, I discovered Jimmy Martin. Mother Maybelle Carter. Doc Watson. Vassar Clements. Earl Scruggs. I mean, that was my first foray into real country music.

CASH: I know. And John McKuen and I are talking about doing some stuff together, actually.

COWAN: I thought that I heard rumblings that you guys were maybe doing some *Circle* shows of some sort.

CASH: We may be doing some shows, yeah, here together, doing some things, talking about the Carter Family heritage and about the Dirt Band's record, so, yeah, we're working on it.

COWAN: Awesome. Well, thank you so much for coming in today. Your friendship means so much to me, but especially you taking time out of your busy schedule to come in here and yak with me.

CASH: Thanks for having me, John.

EPILOGUE

Thanks to the twelve steps, I try to live in a "spirit world." I've always felt from an early age that music is a spiritual endeavor, as singing for me literally started in church.

My addictions started with food as a way to cope with my loss of control as a result of my being sexually molested for basically a summer when I was eight years old. As someone looking for outside relief to internal trauma, it was almost predetermined that drugs and alcohol would be my next form of refuge, and so it was. As I've gotten older, I have had to take stock or an "inventory" to make peace with myself, the people I've loved, the people I've harmed, and my Creator. It occurs to me that I have really accomplished

Courtesy of Madison Thorn

nothing on my own worth mentioning or repeating, especially the things I'm not proud of that I've had to ask forgiveness for. Every single action or interaction I've had with other people required collaboration, especially in my work life. All the notes, all the chords, all the singing required my intention to be a "part of" as opposed to be "apart from." Even if I'm sitting by myself playing or singing, I am hardly alone. There is spirit. For me, God is present, and I, whether or not I am cognizant, am praising him, albeit publicly or privately. Other humans have taught me well. Some things I wanted or needed to learn, a lot of things I didn't want to learn. I don't do well with taking credit for victory or failure. One puffs me up, and the other beats me down. I cannot successfully discount other people's contributions to my life. If I do or try to do that, then all the things I have claimed about my relationship with the God of my understanding are untruths. Just as the world must cease putting its foot literally and figuratively on the necks of God's children, so must I. So, I'm truly not alone, never have I been, nor will I ever be.

Thank you, and much love,

John C.

ACKNOWLEDGMENTS

As you may have just noticed, there's a lifeline of companionship that runs deep through my fifty-year musical career. From my parents, Richard and Cleo, supporting my love of music, driving me to high-school gigs and sewing clothes for the band, to old friends recommending me to new friends, to the loyal fans who stayed with us when the chair snappers left, helping to lift NGR into the Bluegrass Hall of Fame. I hate to think where I'd be without you. To borrow a phrase from my dear friend Leon Russell, "I mighta wound up selling in-surance."

Any notion of companionship must also include that black-and-white TV in our living room in Minerva, Ohio, and the AM radio in my car that first introduced me to Sam & Dave, the Beatles, the Byrds, Loretta, Delaney & Bonnie, Elvis, Cash, Chicago, Moody Blues, John Prine, and Motown, shaping me a little more with every song. Y'all know what I mean. The idea that many of these same artists are now, through the grace of God, *friends of mine*, is proof that some things in life are much harder to explain than others.

To my 1962 Fender Jazz bass "Whitey" that I've played consistently since 1975 and that has brought me a lifetime of joy without measure, this book is for you, too, buddy.

To everyone who has shone their light from every lighthouse and carried me this far, I know you, I love you, and I'm eternally grateful.

The fact that you're reading this memoir at all is thanks to the support and vision of Chris Chappell and his tireless team at Rowman & Littlefield Publishing Group who used their gifts to bring this five-year labor of love with Jimmy Schwartz to life.

As I've gotten older and the idea of a memoir first entered my mind, it became vital that I acknowledge some of the giant musical forces who helped shape any success I've enjoyed. I realize that not everyone can have a chance to sit and talk at length with artists they've spent so many hours of their life listening to with eyes closed, trying to soak up and channel everything they had to give. In that spirit, I hope you enjoyed these conversations with some of my friends and musical companions, many of whom I myself have paid money to see and who helped, in ways big and small, make me the artist and person I came to be. It would be hard for me to imagine twentieth-century music without them. Some people say that you can know a person better by the company they keep. You'll have to tell me later if you found that to be true.

Finally, the thing I can never forget is that none of us can make music for a living without people to support us. When ticket prices were $6, that was a lot of money, and fans spent that to see New Grass Revival. And when those tickets were $15, then $25, whatever it was like, it was always people whose support we needed and got. We create the music, but people create the bands. As I say in recovery a lot, I can never be sufficiently grateful for the life I've been given and provided, starting with the companionship of people like you who wanted to hear us play music. Thanks for listening, reading, and taking the time to hang with us. I wish God's grace to you all.

—JC

DISCOGRAPHY

Studio albums

1986: *Soul'd Out!* (Sugar Hill), as Johnny "C"
2000: *John Cowan* (Sugar Hill)
2002: *Always Take Me Back* (Sugar Hill)
2006: *New Tattoo* (Pinecastle)
2009: *Comfort and Joy* (eOne)
2010: *The Massenburg Sessions* (eOne)
2014: *Sixty* (Compass)

Live albums

1984: *Live From Toulouse* (Sugar Hill)
2009: *8,745 Feet: Live at Telluride* (eOne)

With New Grass Revival

1975: *Fly Through the Country* (Flying Fish)
1977: *When the Storm Is Over* (Flying Fish)
1977: *Too Late to Turn Back Now* (Flying Fish)
1979: *Barren County* (Flying Fish)
1981: *Commonwealth* (Flying Fish)
1981: *The Live Album* (Paradise) [with Leon Russell]
1984: *Live* (Flying Fish)
1984: *On the Boulevard* (Capitol)
1984: *Deviation* (Rounder) with [Béla Fleck]
1986: *New Grass Revival* (Capitol)
1987: *Hold to a Dream* (Capitol)
1989: *Friday Night in America* (Capitol)

As a member of the Sky Kings

1992: *From Out of the Blue* (Sony Entertainment)

2000: *From Out of the Blue* (rereleased, Rhino Handmade)

A FEW PERFORMANCES ONLINE

https://youtu.be/VvRdUz96WCA

"Dark as a Dungeon"

John Cowan and Sam Bush

https://youtu.be/JW7wCeUjFcA

"Can't Stop Now"

New Grass Revival, 1987

https://youtu.be/1AYl8VBfzH4
"White Freightliner Blues"
New Grass Revival

https://youtu.be/00AFX_2aDJ4
"Calling Baton Rouge"
New Grass Revival, 1989

https://youtu.be/WFfd2wLKV-U
"Reach"
New Grass Revival, 1987

A Few Performances Online 299

https://youtu.be/gBqcEO2gbCQ
"How About You"
New Grass Revival

https://youtu.be/p2s4UztLuTo
"Hold to a Dream"
New Grass Revival, 1988

https://youtu.be/PUd9sC3tMxM
"You Plant Your Fields"
New Grass Revival, 1989

https://youtu.be/ht8Ogm3wUDk

NGR's Final Show, December 31, 1989

Opening for the Grateful Dead

Oakland Coliseum Arena

INDEX

Acuff, Roy, 50, 51
addiction, Cowan, J., on, xx, 291–92
Aereo-Plain (album), 59
Aereo Plain Band, 58
Ahern, Brian, 130
Ain't Living Long Like This (album), 131
"Ain't Living Long Like This" (song), 124, 129
"Ain't That a Lot of Love" (song), 195
"Ain't That Peculiar" (song), 25
Akeman, David "Stringbean," 66–67
Akeman, Estelle, 66–67
Allison, Jerry, 234
Allison, Keith, 234
Allman, Duane, 140
Allman, Gregg, 233
Allman Brothers, 59
All Things Must Pass (album), 42
Ambrose (percussionist), 16
American Idol (TV show), 125
American Music Association, Lifetime Achievement Award in Songwriting from, 124
Ampeg B-12 Bass Amplifier, 3
Anchored in Love (Cash, J. C.), 288
Andy Williams (album), 239
"Angel Eyes" (song), 26
"Angry Eyes" (song), 245
Anita Kerr Singers (background singers), 154
"Another Morning" (song), 266
"Any Way the Wind Blows" (song), 26
"Anyway You Want Me" (song), 161
Apollo Delman, 14
"Are You Lonesome Tonight?" (song), 158
art, forging of new genres of, xi
Arthur Godfrey Show, 106

"Ashes of Love" (song), 199
Ash Grove (club), 179, 184, 214
"A Song for the Life" (song), 131
"A Song for You" (song), 42
Aspen, Colorado, 215–16
Asylum (label), 215
Asylum Choir, 20
Atkins, Chet, 157–58
Atlantic Records, 174, 215
Audio Arts (studio), 230, 233
Axton, Estelle, 175
Azoff, Irving, 223

"Baby, What About You?" (song), xvi
"Baby's Got Her Blue Jeans On" (song), 25
Bach, Johann Sebastian, 75
Baker, Kenny, 184
Baker, Laverne, 138
Baker, Madeline, 230
"The Ballad of Stringbean and Estelle" (song), 66–67
band, being part of a, 33
banjo, 190, 217; Bach played on, 75; in bluegrass music, 72; Fleck on, 70–72; West Africa originating, 80
banjoists, progressive, *73*
bass: Cowan, J., playing, *4*; Fender Jazz, 149; Plexiglas Dan Armstrong, xvii; Univox Beatle, 3; "Whitey," *xvii*, xx, 291
the Beach Boys, 232
the Beatles (band), 52, 133, 140, 184, 268; the Byrds emulating, 186; Cowan, J., first experiencing, 2; Leadon loving, 208
Beatles Songbook (book), 38
Beckham, Bob, 94
"Beginnings" (song), 256
Benson, George, 39, 41, 42

Berline, Byron, 195, 201
Berry, Chuck, 133, 283–84
The Best of Atlantic Jazz (record), 59
"Best of My Love" (song), 222
Between the Buttons (album), 53
The Beverly Hillbillies (TV show), 71, 201
"Big Bad John" (song), 154
"Big River" (song), 283
Big Thing (band), 253
Billboard R&B hits, 173
birth, of Cowan, J., 1
birthmark, of Cowan, J., 1
Black, Jeff, 65
Black, Michael, 163
Blake, Norman, 58
"Blame Me" (song), 177
Blank, Les, 60
Blonde on Blonde (album), 90, 91
Blue, David, 223
"Bluebird" (song), 242
"Bluebird Wine" (song), 129
Bluegrass Alliance (band), 54, 56, 57
Bluegrass Boys (band), 57
Bluegrass Cardinals (band), 201
Bluegrass Country Soul (movie), 57
Bluegrass Festival, 25
Bluegrass Hall of Fame, 8
bluegrass music, xii, xix, 10, 28–29, 184, 271–73; banjo in, 72; in LA, 185; post-, xiv–xv; skill required to play, xiii; traditional, 11–13
Bluegrass Unlimited (magazine), 18
The Blue Guitar Shop (store), 208
Boenigk, Michael, 6–7
Botnick, Bruce, 231
"A Boy Named Sue" (song), 114
Bradley, Owen, 110, 115–17
Bramlett, Bonnie (née Bonnie Lynn O'Farrell), 134–36, 139, 141–42, *143*; on helping younger musicians, 147–48; Mad Dogs and Englishmen tour impacting, 144–45; Presley listened to by, 138; on the Rolling Stones, 140; on singing, 137–38; "Superstar" discussed by, 146
Bramlett, Delaney, 141, *143*, 146
Bregante, Merel, 241
Breuster, Thomas, 172
O'Brien, Tim, 28
Britt, Tom, 7, 8, 16
Brooks, Garth, 24
Brownsville Road Car Wash, 7
Bryant, Boudleaux, 94
Bryant, Felice, 94
Bryson, Bill, 198
the Buckinghams (band), 253
Buck Owens and the Buckaroos Live (album), 233
Buffalo Springfield, 196, 227, 230, 231, 232, 242
Burch, Curtis, 9, *10*, *15*, 19, 46
"Burning Love" (song), 24
Burns, Jethro, 51–52
Burrito Deluxe (record), 211
Burton, James, 130, 156, 234
Bush, Charles Samuel "Sam," 8–10, *11*, *15*, 25, 45–47, 67; on Bluegrass Alliance, 54; *Bluegrass Country Soul* discussed by, 57; Burns on, 51–52; in The Bush Sisters and Sammy, 48; on Clark, 65–66; Cowan, J., and, xvii, 7, *45*; on fiddle, 49–51; improvising discussed by, 59; in NGR, 27, 63–64; on Rice, 55–56; on Russell, L., 60–61; Smith, K., discussed by, 62; songwriting by, 65
Bush, Kathy, 16
Bush, Lynn, 63
Bush, Roger, 195
The Bush Sisters and Sammy (band), 48
the Byrds (album), 212
the Byrds (band), 185; the Beatles emulated by, 186; Parsons departing, 192; White in, 193

California, 179, 185, 200, 201, 210
"Callin' Baton Rouge" (song), 24, 26

Camarata, Tutti, 230
Campbell, Glen, 58
The Cannery (venue), 28
"Can't Stop Now" (song), 22–24
Capitol/EMI records. *See* EMI/Capitol records
Carter, A. P., 274, 275, 277, 278, 279
Carter, Maybelle, 249, 275, 276–77, 278, 279
Carter, Sara, 274, 275, 278
Carter Cash, June, 273, 282, 284–85, 286
Carter Family, 271, 274, 276–77, 278, 279, 285, 289
Carter Family Fold, 275
Cash, John Carter, 271–73, *272*, 284–86, 289; Carter, M., discussed by, 279; on Carter, A., 277–78; on Cash, Johnny, 281–83; country music discussed by, 280–81; on Peer, 274–76; as producer, 287–88
Cash, Johnny, 114, 163, *272*; Carter Cash marrying, 284–85; on Cash, J. C., 281–83; Kristofferson on, 92, 95, 97–98; songwriting discussed by, 129
Cash, Rosanne, 124, 286
Cash, Roy, Jr., 186
Cash Cabin, 272–73
CBS Records, 240
Cetera, Peter, 254, 255, 259
Chance, Bobbie, 147
Charles, Ray, 174
Chicago (album), 251
Chicago V (album), 256
Chicago II (album), 255
Chicago Theatre, *xviii*
Chicago Transit Authority (album), 261
Chicago Transit Authority (band), 249, 251–53, 259, 261
"A Child's Claim to Fame" (song), 232, 234
Clapton, Eric, 43, 224
Clark, Gene, 185, 186, 205, 209
Clark, Guy, 65–66, 126, 127
Clark, John, 241, 243

Clarke, Tony, 270
classical music, 36, 39, 74, 254
Clayton, Sam, 26
Clem, Michael, 9, 46, 62–63
Clement, Jack, 97
Clements, Vassar, 58
Cline, Patsy, 106, 118
"A Closer Walk with Thee" (song), 154
Cocker, Joe, 39, 41, 144, 145
Coffey, Jeff, 252
Cohn, Bruce, 228
college, Cowan, J., in, 6–7
Coltrane, John, 58, 59
Columbia Records, 187, 236, 239
Columbia Studios, 90, 191
Combine Records, 94
Composed (Cash, R.), 286
concept albums, 221
Connor, Ingram Cecil, III, 212
Cooke, Sam, 169–70
Cooley, Spade, 183
Coolidge, Rita, 99, 146
Cordell, Denny, 37–38, 41, 144, 145
Cordell, Leon, 144, 145
Corea, Chick, 20
Costello, Elvis, 44
country charts, 107
Country Gentlemen (band), 57
country music, 39–41, 92, 184, 199–200, 217, 282; Cash, J. C., discussing, 280–81; mainstream, 22; rock and roll fused with, 236; women in, 106, 109, 113; WSM radio influencing, 280
Country Music Awards, 24, 281
country music business, xii–xiii
Country Music Hall of Fame, 22, 90, 94, 161
country rock, 181, 210, 212, 232, 233, 236
Country Style, USA (TV show), 47
"County Clare" (song), 23
"Cover of the Rolling Stone" (song), 114
Cowan, Blanche (grandmother), 1
Cowan, Cleo (mother), 1

Cowan, John, *viii*, *4*, *15*, *28*, *86*, *164*, *242*.
    See also specific topics
Cowan, Liz (wife), 16, 21, 45
Cowan, Richard (father), 1–2, 6–7, 8
Cowan, Richard Douglas (brother), xx, 1
Cowan, Steven (brother), 1
Cowan, Sue (sister), 1
Crary, Dan, 55, 57
Cream (band), 268
Crenshaw, Marshall, 26
Crosby, David, 185–86, 231
Crosby, Stills, Nash & Young (band), 195
Crosby, Stills & Nash (album), 195, 236
Crosby, Stills & Nash (trio), 236
Crossing the Tracks (album), 20
Crowe, J. D., 11, 56
Crowell, Rodney, 87, 93, 125, 131, 283; on Clark, Guy, 127; Cowan, J., playing with, *123*; Harris worked with by, 129–30; Kristofferson admired by, 126; as singer-songwriter, 124, 127–28
"Crying in the Chapel" (song), 159
CTA records, 259
Culberson, Rosetta, 139
The Cumberlands (song), 45

Dacre-Barclay, Michael, 266, 267
"Danny's Song" (song), 243
Davis, Clive, 236, 239
Davis, Skeeter, 191–92
"Dawn Is a Feeling" (song), 266
Days of Future Past (album), 263, 265–68
Dean, Jimmy, 154
"Dear John" (song), 109
"Dear Uncle Sam" (song), 113–14
Decca Records, 110, 266, 267
Déjà Vu (album), 195
Delaney & Bonnie (duo), 135–36
Delaney & Bonnie and Friends, 142–44
Desert Rose (album), 199
Desert Rose Band, 192, 199–200, 204
Desperado (album), 220–22
"Desperado" (song), 218–20

Deutsche Grammophon (recording company), 269
"Dialogue" (song), 258
Diamonds & Dirt (album), 124
Dickens, Jimmy, 104
Dickson, Jim, 185, 186
Dillard, Doug, 205, 208–9
Dillard & Clark (band), 209–10
The Fantastic Expedition of Dillard & Clark (album), 205
The Dirt Band, 289
"Does Anybody Really Know What Time It Is?" (song), 256, 257
"Don't Be Cruel" (song), 153, 158–60
"Don't You Write Her Off" (song), 197
Doobie Brothers, *xviii*, 181, 217, 228, 251–52
Doolin-Dalton outlaw gang, 220
the Doors (band), 231
Doo Wop Shop, xvii
Dowd, Tom, 174
Dr. Hook (band), 114
Drive (record), 75–76
"Dueling Banjos" (song), 71
Duncan, Steve, 199
Dunn, Duck, 174
Dvořák, Antonín, 266
Dylan, Bob, xii, 90, 91, 277, 283

the Eagles, 213, 214, 220, 238
Earle, Steve, 24
"Early Bird" (song), 217–18, 221
Ed Sullivan Theater, 2
Emery, Ralph, 24
EMI/Capitol records, 21–25, 38, 197, 209, 224, 269
Epic Records, 237
The Ernest Tubb Record Shop (album), 50, 111, 118
Ertegun, Ahmet, 174, 236
Ethridge, Chris, 210
Evansville, Indiana, 5, 227
Ever Call Ready (album), 197–98

Index

Exceptions (band), 255

Fairfield Four (group), 170
Farley, J. J., 171, 172
"Farther Along" (song), 224
"Fate Full of Shadow" (song), 182
Faulkner, Randey, 263
"My Favorite Things" (song), 59
Feeling Mortal (record), 99
Felder, Don, 223
Fender Jazz Bass, 149
Fender Precision, xvii, xix
fiddle, Bush, C., on, 49–51
Fillmore West (club), 259
"Fishing in the Dark" (song), xvi
Flatt & Scruggs (duo), 40
Fleck, Béla, 19–21, *25*, *32*, 63–64, *68*, *73*; on banjo, 70–72; on classical music, 74; on *Drive*, 75–76; Grammys won by, 69–70; musicians found to play with by, 83; NGR left by, 25–27, 77–78
Flecktones (band), 27, 64, 76, 78, 79
Flying Burrito Brothers (band), 192–95, 205, 209–10, 212, 213, 232
Flynn, Pat, 20, *25*, 26, 102
"Fly Through the Country" (song), 20
FM radio, xii, 244
Fogelberg, Dan, 198
Fogelsong, Jim, 25
Foggy River Boys (quartet), 151
Foley, Red, 154
"Fool Such as I" (song), 159
football, Cowan, J., playing, 3–4
Forrester, Rita, 274
Foster, Fred, 94, 96
Foster, Paul, 171, 172
Franklin, Aretha, 177
Franklin, C. L., 177
Frey, Glenn, 213–15, 219–22
Friday Night in America (album), xv, 26
"Friday Night in America" (song), 26
The Funky Monkey (store), 227
Furay, Richie, 196, 197, 231–32, 239

Gaither, Bill, 153
Galt House Hotel, 273
Garcia, Jerry, 29–30
Garrett, Snuff, 41, 141
Garth, Al, 241, 242
Gaye, Marvin, 22, 25
Gayle, Crystal, xvi
Geffe, David, 215
"Get Rhythm" (song), 283–84
gherm (slang), 168
"Ghetto Song" (song), 37–38
Gibson, Mac, 54
Gillespie, Gerry, 3
"Ginseng Sullivan" (song), 58
"Girl from the North Country" (song), 92
"God's Own Singer" (song), 211
"Gone" (song), 154, 163
"Go Now" (song), 265
Goodman, Steve, 27
"A Good Woman's Love" (song), 17
Gosdin, Vern, 185
gospel, 39, 177
gospel music, 153
gospel singers, 137
Graham, Bill, 268
Grammy Awards, 38, 39, 69–70, 90
Grammy Lifetime Achievement Award, 90
Grand Ole Opry, 39, 50, 66, *101*, 104, 111
Grantham, George, 233
The Grateful Dead, xiv, *29*, 53–54
"Great Balls of Fire" (song), 58
Greatest Hits (album), 224
"The Great Speckled Bird" (song), 278
Green, Johnny, xx
Green, Lloyd, 190
Greengrass Group, 185
Gretsch guitar, 235
Griffith, Nanci, 23, 24
Grisman, David "Dawgfather," 78
groupie culture, 146
Gruhn, George, xix
Guard, Dave, 207
Guercio, Jim, 253, 255

guitar, 183; Gretsch, 235; Kristofferson on, 90; Lynn, L., discussing, 103–4; Messina playing, 229–30; Sears Silvertone, 3; Telecaster, 234–35. *See also* bass

Guthrie, Woody, xii, 202, 277

Hall, Tom T., 93
Halsey, Jim, 22
Haney, Carton, 57
Hank Wilson (album), 39
Hank Wilson's Back Vol. 2 (album), 35, 39–41
Harris, Emmylou, 64, 123, 129–30, 221
Harrison, George, 43
Hartford, John, 58, 59, 60
Harvey, David, 263
Havens, Richie, 256
"Have You Seen Her Face?" (song), 189
Hawkins, Hoyt, 159
Hayes, Isaac, 175, 176
Hayward, Justin, 265–67; Cowan, J., singing with, *264*; on "Knights in White Satin," 268–69; as songwriter, 270–71
Hazel (crew member), 16
Hearts and Flowers (band), 209
Heaven's Gate (album), 99
Hee Haw (TV show), 66
Hendrix, Jimi, 285
Henley, Don, 213–14, 215, 220, 221
HercuLeons (band), *viii*, *226*
"Hey, Loretta" (song), 114, 116
Hiatt, John, 26
High Country Snow (album), 198
The Highwaymen (supergroup), 99
Hillman, Chris, 179, *180*, 191–93, 204, 213; on California, 201; country rock pioneered by, 181; on Crosby, 185–86; Desert Rose Band discussed by, 199–200; "Have You Seen Her Face?" written by, 189; Jorgenson met by, 198; Kleinow discussing, 194; on Leadon, 182, 184; on Manassas, 195–96; McGuinn discussed by, 190; Pedersen complimented by, 202–3; on Poco, 197; on "Sixty-Minute Man," 182–83; "So You Wanna Be a Rock 'n' Roll Star" cowritten by, 187–88

Hiltons, Virginia, 275
Hits 1979–1989 (album), 124
"Hold On, I'm Comin'" (song), 167, 175–76
Holiday Inn, 45
Holler, Butcher, 103
Hollyridge Strings (orchestra), 38
"Hollywood Waltz" (song), 225
Holt, Culley, 151
"Honky Tonk Angels" (song), 109, 278
"Honky Tonk Girl" (song), 105, 107–9
Hopkins, "Lightnin'," 185
Hot Band, 64
The Hot Band (band), 129
"Hotel California" (song), 225
Hot Rize (band), 27
"Hound Dog" (song), 159
Hourglass (band), 140
The House of Cash (Cash, J. C.), 282, 283, 288
The Houston Kid (song), 129
Hubbard, Bob, 151
Huskey, Junior, 191
Husky, Ferlin, 109, 154, 163
Hut, Quonset, 154
Hutton, Danny, 141

"I Am a Pilgrim" (song), 35
Ibbotson, Jimmie, 20
I Believe to My Soul (radio show), 228
IBEW. *See* International Brotherhood of Electrical Workers
IBMA. *See* International Bluegrass Music Association
"I Don't Want to Set the World on Fire" (song), 170
"I Fall to Pieces" (song), 106

"If I Could Hear My Mother Pray Again" (song), 103
"If I Could Only Win Your Love" (song), 202
"If I Didn't Care" (song), 170
"If Something Is Wrong" (song), 177
"I Go Out Walkin'" (song), 106
"I Hate Your Ugly Face" (song), 91
Ikettes (trio), 139
Illinois State Fair, xvii
"I'm a Man" (song), 254–55
improvising, Bush, C., discussing, 59
"I'm So Lonesome I Could Cry" (song), 47
Indiana State University, Cowan, J., attending, 6
Ink Spots (band), 170
International Bluegrass Hall of Fame, 47, 70
International Bluegrass Music Association (IBMA), xix, 271–73
International Brotherhood of Electrical Workers (IBEW), 237
International Submarine Band, 212
"I Owe You One" (song), xvi
"I Still Miss Someone" (song), 163, 286
"I Take What I Want" (song), 176
"It's Been So Long Darlin'" (song), 104
"It's Only Make Believe" (song), 117
"I Want You, Need You, Love You" (song), 158

Jackson, Mahalia, 17
Jackson Five, 214
Jacobs, Gene, 141
Jagger, Mick, 192
James, Etta, 138, 183
James, Sonny, 154
jazz, xii, 84
Jefferson Airplane, 53
Jennings, Waylon, 210
"Jesus Gave Me Water" (song), 170
Jett, Dale, 274
Jimmy and the Jesters (record), 230
"Jody Rider" (song), 175

Joey Bishop Show, 52
John, Elton, 44
John Duffy and the Country Gentlemen (band), 51
"John Henry" (song), 51
"Johnny B. Goode" (song), 233
Johnny Cash Show (TV show), 95
Johnny Otis Show (TV show), 183
Johns, Glyn, 43, 216, 218, 220–21, 222–23
Johnson, Courtney, 8, *10*, *15*, 46, 56, *61*; Fender Precision borrowed by Cowan, J., from, xvii; house owned by, 9; NGR left by, 19
Johnson, Hazel, 9
Johnson, Robert, 278
Jones, Danny, 55
Jones, George, 40, 178
Jordanaires (band), 157, 158, 163; in Nashville, 161; records appeared on by, 149; songs with appearances from, 151; Stoker, G., discussing, 152
Jorgenson, John, 195, 198

Kaye, Carol, xix
Kelly, Walt, 232
Kennedy, Bill, 46
Kennedy, John F., 2
Kenner, Bill, 16
Kenny, Bill, 170
Kenny Loggins with Jim Messina—Sittin' In (album), 227, 241–43
Kentucky Colonels, 195, 214
Kerr, Anita, 154
KHJ (radio station), 222
King, Albert, 139–40
King, B. B., 205, 223
King, Freddy, 42
King, Martin Luther, Jr., 232
King of Hearts (club), 169, 171, 173
Kingston Trio, 207
Kirby, Beecher Ray "Bashful Brother Oswald," 50

Kirkham, Millie, 163–64
Kleinow, "Sneaky" Pete, 194
Knight, Michael, 267
Knight, Peter, 266–67
"Knights in White Satin" (song), 268–69
Koller, Fred, 26
Kristofferson, Kris, 87, *88*, 89, 91, 94, 99–100; on Cash, Johnny, 92, 95, 97–98; Crowell admiring, 126; on guitar, 90; as singer-songwriter, 92–93; on singing, 96
Kupka, Doc, 42

LA. *See* Los Angeles
Laine, Denny, 263, 265
Lamm, Robert, *250*, 251–52, 259–60; arrangements by, 254–55; *Chicago Five* discussed by, 256; on Chicago Transit Authority, 253; on compromise within a band, 261–62; *Skinny Boy* discussed by, 257–58
LaPuma, Tommy, 38
"The Lark Ascending" (song), xv
The Last of the Red Hot Burritos (album), 195
Last Time Around (album), 227, 231
Law, Don, 154
LA Woman (album), 231
Lawson, Doyle, 57
Lawton, Oklahoma, 36
Leadon, Bernard Matthew "Bernie," III, 63, 194, 205, *206*, 214; the Beatles loved by, 208; "Desperado" discussed by, 218–20; on "Early Bird," 217–18; in Flying Burrito Brothers, 209–10; Hillman on, 182, 184; on Johns, 216, 221; *One of These Nights* discussed by, 224–25; *On the Border* discussed by, 222–23; Parsons discussed by, 212–13; "Witchy Woman" written by, 215
"Leaving Louisiana" (song), 129
Lee, Albert, 130
Leon Russell & the New Grass Revival, Rhythm and Bluegrass (tour), 15

Let It Bleed (album), 231
"Let's Make a Baby King" (song), 26
Levitan, Ken, 24
Levy, Howard, 27, 78
Lewis, Edward, 269
Liberto, Vivian, 286
Lifetime Achievement Award, Grammy, 90
Lifetime Achievement Award in Songwriting, from American Music Association, 124
Linde, Dennis, 24, 26
"Listen to the Music" (song), 217
"Little Darling, Pal of Mine" (song), 278
Lodge, John, 265
Loews Vanderbilt Hotel, 265
Logan, John "Juke," 16
Loggins, Kenny, 239–42
Loggins and Messina (duo), 243
London Philharmonic, 221
"Lonesome and a Long Way from Home" (song), 135–36
"Lonesome Fiddle Blues" (song), 58
The Lonesome Pines Special (TV show), 78
Lonesome River Band, xx
"Long Distance Runaround" (song), xv
The Long Run (album), 221
Los Angeles (LA), California: bluegrass music in, 185; country rock in, 210; music scene in, 179
Louisville, Kentucky, 45
"Love Reunited" (song), 199
Lovett, Lyle, 24
Lowery, Donnie, 26
Lupus Rex (Cash, J. C.), 288
"Lyin' Eyes" (song), 225
Lynn, "Doolittle," 103, 105, 106, 112–13
Lynn, Loretta, 87, *101*, 105, 117, 200; Bradley discussed by, 110; Cline met by, 118; "Dear Uncle Sam" discussed by, 113–14; on Grand Ole Opry, 104; guitar discussed on, 103–4; "Honky Tonk Girl" discussed by, 107–9; movie on, 102, 119; NGR opening

for, 101–2; singing discussed by, 115–16; songwriting discussed by, 104, 106, 112; on Tubb, 110–11; Twitty discussed by, 118; *Van Lear Rose* by, 120–21; on White, 120–22

Mad Dogs and Englishmen (record), 39
Mad Dogs and Englishmen tour, 144–45
"Mama Stewart" (song), 100
Mammoth Cave Opry, 54
Manassas (band), 195–96
mandolin, 51, 183–84
Maness, J. D., 199
"Man in the Fog" (song), 211
Mansfield, David, 198
Marley, Bob, 22
Marlin, Sleepy, 50
Martin, George, 268
Martin, Jimmy, 13
Masekela, Hugh, 188
"Masquerade" (song), 42
Matthews, Bill, 151
Matthews, Monty, 151
Matthews, Neil, 155, 159
Mayer, John, 128
MCA Records, 108–9, 167
McCabe's Guitar Shop, 213–14
McCabe's Pub, 26, 179
McCoury, Del, 55, 184
McCreary, Scotty, 125–26
McDaniel, Mel, 25
McFee, John, 181, 228
McGraw, Tim, 125
McGuinn, Clark & Hillman (band), 197
McGuinn, Jim Roger, 185, 187, 190
McKuen, John, 289
McMichen, Clayton, 50
McPhee, John, 200
"Me and Bobby McGee" (song), 90, 94–95
Meisner, Randy, 214, 218, 233, 237, 238
mellotron, 268
Mercury Records, 94
Meredith, Bud, 54

Messina, James Melvin "Jim," *226*, 227–28, 236–37, *242*, 243–44, 247; Burton worked with by, 234; guitar played by, 229–30; Loggins produced by, 239–42; on picking, 234–35; on Poco, 232, 239; Reynolds inspiring, 246; Schmitt discussed by, 238; Universal Audio built by, 233; Young met by, 231; on "Your Mama Don't Dance," 245
Meyer, Edgar, 65, 74, 85
A Mighty Wind (mockumentary), 185
Miles, Buddy, 144
Miller, Roger, 95–96, 234
Mitchell, Joni, 125, 231
"Molly and Tenbrooks" (song), 57
Money, Bob, 151–52
Monroe, Bill, 12–13, 17–18, 40, 51, 57, 122
Monroe's Bluegrass Boys, 13
Montgomery, Robbie, 139
Monument Records, 94
Moody Bluegrass, Vol. 1, 263
Moody Bluegrass Tribute Concert, *264*
The Moody Blues (band), 249, 263, *264*, 265, 270
Moore, Joyce, 167
Moore, Samuel David Moore "Sam," *166*, 167–68, 173, 177; Cooke on, 169–70; on "Hold On, I'm Coming," 175–76; Prater met by, 169; vocalists inspiring, 178; Wexler signing, 174; on Wilson, 171–72
The Motel Shot! (album), 144
Motown, 133, 175
"Mr. and Mrs. Used to Be"? (song), 110
"Mr. Tambourine Man"? (song), 186–87
MTV (TV channel), 23
Munde, Alan, *73*
Murray, Anne, 243
music, as spiritual endeavor, 291
music movements, xi
music scene, in LA, 179
"My Life Is Good" (song), 252

"My Man" (song), 223, 224

Nash Ramblers, 64
Nashville, Tennessee, xii–xiii, xiii, 40, 89–90, 108, 126, 190; California contrasted with, 200; Jordanaires in, 161; Old Hickory Lake near, 272; WSM radio out of, 47, 136
Nashville Banner, 66
The Nashville Network (TNN), 23–24
Nashville Now (show), 24
Nashville Songwriter's Hall of Fame, 115
Nelson, Gunnar, 156
Nelson, Ken, 163
Nelson, Kris, 156
Nelson, Matthew, 156
Nelson, Ricky, 155–56, 162
Nelson, Sam, 156
Nelson, Tracy, 156
Nelson, Willie, 14
Neville, Aaron, xvi
New Bethel Baptist Church, 177
Newbury, Mickey, 95, 126
New Grass Revival (NGR), xiii–xvi, xvi, 7–12, *29*, 46, 54, *61*; at Apollo Delman, 14; bands opened for by, 22; break up of, 27, *28*, 63–64; Burch leaving, 19; Bush, C., in, 27, 63–64; crew for, xvii–xviii; EMI/Capitol records signing, 21–22, 24–25; fan base of, 23; Fleck leaving, 25–27, 77–78; good-bye show of, 28–29; in International Bluegrass Hall of Fame, 70; Johnson leaving, 19; Lynn, L., opened for by, 101–2; for Nitty Gritty Dirt Band opened for by, 205; at Perkins Palace, *41*; on radio, 76–77; Russell, L., opened for by, *17*, 35, *41*, 59–60; start of, 56; voice of, 18; *Will the Circle be Unbroken Vol. II* participated in by, 271
New Lost City Ramblers (band), 183
Newman, Randy, 252

Newsome, "Bitter Creek," 220
NFL Football, 2
NGR. *See* New Grass Revival
Nicholson, Gary, 25
Night Beat Club, 171
Nitty Gritty Dirt Band, xvi, 10, 46, 205, 271
"Nobody's Fool" (song), 238
Notorious Byrd Brothers (band), 189

O Brother, Where Art Thou? (movie), 279
O'Connell, Maura, 23
Old Hickory Lake, near Nashville, 272
Olympic White Fender Jazz Bass, xvii
Omartian, Michael, 241, 243, 246
One of These Nights (album), 224–25
"One of These Nights" (song), 225
"One's on the Way"? (song), 114
"One Tin Soldier" (song), 57
"Only Make Believe" (song), 118
On the Border (album), 222–23
Opryland Hotel, 89–90
orchestras, 84–85
Osborn, Joe, 234
Otis, Johnny, 183
Owens, Buck, 106, 201, 233, 234
Oxford (university), 89, 97

Pankow, James, 251
Parazaider, Walt, 254
Parker, Charlie, 27
Parmley, Don, 185, 201
Parsons, Gram, 181, 189–90, 233; the Byrds departed by, 192; Leadon discussing, 212–13; passing of, 224
Patrick, Kathy, 238
Paul Revere and the Raiders (band), 234
"Peaceful Easy Feeling" (song), 218–19
pedal steel, 194
Pedersen, Herb, 130, 198, 202–3
Peek, Billy, 139, 140
Peer, Ralph, 274–76
Peerce, Lonnie, 54, 56

Index 311

Peermusic (publisher), 274
Pennell, John, 65
Pennywhistle, Longbranch, 215
Perkins, Al, 195, 213–14
Perkins Palace, NGR at, *41*
Phillips, Stu, 38
piano, 36, 152, 207, 253
Pickin' Up the Pieces (album), 237
"Pieces of the Sky" (song), 123
Pierce, Webb, 107
"The Pill" (song), 113
Pinder, Mike, 266, 268
"Please Remember Me" (song), 125
Plexiglas Dan Armstrong bass, xvii
Poco (album), 237–38
Poco (band), 227, 236; Hillman on, 197; Meisner in, 214; Messina on, 232, 239
A Poem Is a Naked Person (documentary), 60
Pogo (character), 232
Poison (band), 245
popular music media, xi
Porter, David, 175
post-bluegrass music, xiv–xv
Prater, Dave, 167, 169, 170, 173
Prater, J. T., 173
Presley, Elvis, 24, 130, 183, 207; Bramlett, B., listening to, 138; Kirkham singing with, 163; Stoker, G., with, *150*, 155, 157, 159–62
Press On (album), 285
"Pretty Polly" (song), 190
"Prince of Peace" (song), 57, 60, *61*
Prine, John, 27
producer, Cash, J. C., as, 287–88
progressive banjoists, *73*
prog rock, 249
psychedelia, 142, 144, 235
Putnam, Norbert, 198

Quartet, John Daniel, 152
"Questions 67 and 68" (song), 256

radio, 47, 249; EMI/Capitol records focusing on, 24–25; FM, xii, 244; NGR on, 76–77. *See also* WSM radio
Radle, Carl, 60–61, 62
Raitt, Bonnie, *29*, 205
Rancho Santa Fe, in San Diego County, 182
RCA records, *150*, 158, 275
record contract, standard, 219
Reeves, Jim, 40
Reynolds, Tommy, 246
Rice, Tony, 55–56
Richards, Keith, 192, 234
Riopelle, Jerry, 246
Robbins, Butch, 50, 60, 62
Roberts, Marcus, 84
Roberts, Rick, 193, 194
Robertson, Robbie, 144
Rock, Chris, 244
rock and roll, 12, 52–53, 92, 184, 223, 236
Rock & Roll Hall of Fame, 22, 216, 234; Burton elected to, 156; the Eagles inducted into, 224; Russell, L., inducted into, 35, 43
Rodgers, Jimmie, 274, 275, 276, 278
the Rolling Stones, 43, 53, 140, 213, 231
Ronstadt, Linda, 210
Roosevelt University (Chicago), 253
Roulette records, 173
Rounder Records, 20
Rowan, Peter, 50
Roy Acuff Museum and Exhibit, 50
Russell, Leon, xvii–xviii, xix, 14–15, 21, *34, 41*; "A Song for You" written by, 42, 125; Bush, C., on, 60–61; on classical music, 36, 39; on Cordell, 37–38; on *Hank Wilson's Back Vol. 2*, 39–41; Harrison working with, 43; on John, 44; NGR opening for, *17*, 35, *41*, 59–60; Rock & Roll Hall of Fame inducting, 35, 43; touring with, 18–19; voice and phrasing of, 16–17
Russell, Nancy, 120
Ryman Auditorium, 166, 263, *264*, 265

Sam & Dave (duo), 173, 174
San Francisco, 53
Sangaré, Oumou, 81
Santana (band), 259
"Save the Best for Last" (song), xvi
Scheff, Jerry, 145, 198
Schmit, Timothy B., 214, 227, 238
Scott, Darrell, vii
Scottsville Squirrel Barkers (band), 184, 195
Scruggs, Earl, 70–72, 205, 235, 277
Sears Silvertone guitar, 3
Seeger, Mike, 183
The Seldom Scene (band), 64
Sensational Hummingbirds, 173
Sessions, Bristol, 274
Seventh Sojourn (album), 263, 268
Sgt. Pepper (album), 142
"Shame on the Moon" (song), 124
Shampsi (percussionist), 16
Shelor, Sammy, xx
The Shelter People (album), 37–38, 59
Shepard, Jean, 109
Shields, Tom, 3
Shiloh (group), 214
Shindig! (television music show), 141
the Shindogs (band), 141, 142
Sholes, Steve, 161
Silverstein, Shel, 114, 116
Sims, Larry, 241, 242
Sims, Merel, 242
Sinatra, Frank, 28
singers, xv, 133, 137, 167
singer-songwriter: Crowell as, 124, 127–28; Kristofferson as, 92–93; movement toward the, xii
singing, 152; Bramlett, B., on, 137–38; Kristofferson on, 96; Lynn, L., discussing, 115–16
"Sing Me Back Home" (song), 191
"Sinister Minister" (song), 78
Sixty (album), 181
"Sixty-Minute Man" (song), 182–83
Skaggs, Ricky, 18

The Skillet Lickers (band), 50
Skinny Boy (album), 257
Smith, Emily, 14
Smith, Jessie Mae, 139
Smith, Kenny Lee, 8, 59, 62
Smith, Russell, 26
Smokey Mountain Boys, 50
solo artist, 33
"Some Old Day" (Crowe), 11
"Song for a Life" (song), 126
"A Song for You" (song), 42, 125
songwriters, 87, 130, 257–58, 270–71
songwriting, 41, 92, 115, 129, 146, 283; by Bush, C., 65; Cash, Johnny, discussing, 129; Lynn, L., discussing, 104, 106, 112
Sony Classical, 81–82
Soul'd Out (album), 199
"Soul Man" (song), 176
the Soul Stirrers (band), 169–71
The Sound of Music (movie), 59
Souther, Hillman, Furay (band), 196
Souther, J. D., 197, 215
Southern Pacific, 200
"So You Wanna Be a Rock 'n' Roll Star" (song), 187–88
"Spain" (song), 20
Spectacle (album), 44
Spectrum (band), 20
Speer, Ben, 158
Speer, Brock, 158
The Speer Family, 158
spirit, Cowan, J., on, 8, 291–92
spirituals, 153
Springsteen, Bruce, 252
Stanley Brothers (band), 57, 185
Staples, Mavis, 167
Starling, John, 64
Stax records, 175
Stevens, Barry, 59
Stewart, Jim, 175
Stewart, Wynn, 201
Stills, Stephen, 195, 223, 234

Index

Stoker, Alan, 150; at WSM radio, 152
Stoker, Brent, 150, *164*
Stoker, Gordon, 149, 158, *164*; Cowan, J., meeting, 153; "Don't Be Cruel" discussed by, 159–60; Jordanaires discussed by, 152; on Kirkham, 163–64; Nelson, R., met by, 155–56; Presley with, *150*, 155, 157, 159–62; on Twitty, 164–65
Strawberry Music Festival, 24
Stuart, Marty, 167
Stubbs, Eddie, 26
Studio Instrument Rentals, 214
Sullivan, Ed, 52
Summer Lights (festival), 24
Sunset Sound Recorders, 230
Sunshine Company, 242
Super Sport Chevelle, 8
"Superstar" (song), 146
Sure-Fire Music Co. (label), 111
Swan, Billy, 95
Sweeney, Joel, 80, 81
The Sweetheart of the Rodeo (album), 190, 212
Szymczyk, Bill, 223

"Take It Easy" (song), 218
"Tambourine Man" (song), 193
Taylor, James, 202
Taylor, Johnny, 171
Taylor, Sam, 171
team sports, Cowan, J., playing, 33
Telecaster guitar, 234–35
Telluride Bluegrass Festival, xiii, 20, 24
Tempchin, Jack, 219
tenor singers, 167
"There He Goes" (song), 107
"This Masquerade" (song), 39
Thompson, Bobby, *61*
Thompson, Verlon, 66
Three Dog Night (band), 140
Throw Down Your Heart (documentary), 80–82

"Till I Gain Control Again" (song), 126
"Time Between" (song), 193
Time & Charges (album), 253
TNN. *See* The Nashville Network
Tompall & the Glaser Brothers, 191
Tom Petty and the Heartbreakers, 145
"To Ramona" (song), 195
Tottle, Jack, 18
Tower of Power (band), 42
Town Hall Party (TV show), 229
"Train Leaves Here" (song), 209
"Travelin' Man" (song), 155, 156–57
Travis, Merle, 35, 229
Tri-Cities area, Illinois, 136, 137
Trischka, Tony, 20, *73*
Troubadour (club), 179, 209, 214
trumpet, 188
Tubb, Ernest, 104, 109–10, 117
"Tuesday Afternoon" (song), *264*, 265, 266, 268
Tulsa, Oklahoma, 14
Turner, Ike, 139
Turner, Tina, 139
Tutt, Ron, 145
twelve steps, 291
"25 or 6 to 4" (song), 255
Twitty, Conway, 115, 117, 118, 164–65

Ulrich, Nicky, 3
"Uncle Pen" (song), 122
"Unconditional Love" (song), 25
The Union (album), 42–43
Universal Audio (studio), 233
Univox Beatle Bass, 3

"Vahevala" (song), 246
Van Halen, Eddie, 205
Vanilla Fudge (band), 255
Van Lear Rose (album), 120–21
Van Zandt, Townes, 126–27
Vietnam war, 113–14
vocalists, 178

"Wake Up, Sunshine" (song), 255
WAKY (radio station), 167
Waldman, Wendy, xvi, 26
Walker, Ebo, 56, 60
Walker, Ray, 159
Walk the Line (movie), 286–87
Walsh, Joe, 224
Was, Don, 99
"Watching the River Run" (song), 246
Watkins, Sara, 99
Watson, Doc, 205
Webb, Jimmy, 230
Webb, Ted, 107
"The Weight," 167
"Welcome to Sweetie Pie's?" (song), 139
Welk, Lawrence, 195
Wells, Corey, 141
Wells, Kitty, 106
Wernick, Pete, *73*
Wertz, Kenny, 195
West Africa, banjo originating in, 80
Western Kentucky University, 54
Western swing, xii
West Point (academy), 89, 97
Wexler, Jerry, 174
The Wheatstraw Suite (album), 210
White, Clarence, 193, 201, 214, 224
White, Jack, 120–22
"Whitey" (bass guitar), belonging to Cowan, J., *xvii*, xx, 291
Whitlock, Bobby, 145
"Why Are You Crying?" (song), 181–82
Wilburn, Doyle, 109, 111
Wilburn, Teddy, 109, 110–11
Wilburn Brothers (TV show), 111
Wilde, Joyce, 270
Wilde, Marty, 270
Wildwood Flower (album), 285
"Wildwood Flower" (song), 274
Williams, Hank, 40, 47, 92, 124

Williams, Ralph Vaughan, xv
Williams, Vanessa, xvi
Wills, Bob, 183, 281
Will the Circle Be Unbroken (album), 10, 46, 249, 289
"Will the Circle Be Unbroken" (song), 274, 279–80
Will the Circle Be Unbroken Vol. II (album), 271
Will You Miss Me When I'm Gone (album), 276
Wilson, Jackie, 171–72
Winchester, Jesse, 26
Winwood, Steve, 43
"Witchy Woman" (song), 215
Woodstock, 259
Wooten, Roy "Future Man," 26, 27, 79
Wooten, Victor, 27, 78
Worley, Paul, 199
Wrecking Crew (supergroup), 187, 234
WSM radio, 150, 168, 273; country music influenced by, 280; out of Nashville, 47, 136; Stoker at, 152
Wyman, Bill, 43

Yes (band), xv, 45
You (band), 45, 46
"You Are My Flower" (song), 279
"You'd Better Go Now" (song), 263
"You Don't Know Like I Know" (song), 176
Young, Curtis, 163
Young, Neil, 231
Young, Rusty, *242*
"Young Love" (song), 154
the Young Turks (band), 5
"You Plant Your Fields" (song), xvi, 26, 27
"Your Mama Don't Dance" (song), 243–45

Zero Records, 107
Zonn, Andrea, *226*

ABOUT THE AUTHORS

John Cowan is an American soul, gospel, progressive bluegrass vocalist, and bass guitar player. In 1974, he became the iconic lead vocalist and bassist for influential bluegrass pioneers the New Grass Revival. He was elected to the Bluegrass Music Hall of Fame in 2020 along with bandmates Sam Bush, Courtney Johnson, Curtis Burch, Béla Fleck, and Pat Flynn. John's singing credits include fourteen albums with New Grass Revival, eight studio albums, and vocal and bass sessions for multiple well-known country, folk, and bluegrass artists, including Garth Brooks, John Prine, Steve Earle, Alison Krauss, Leon Russell, Ricky Skaggs, Reba McEntire, Mark O'Connor, Zac Brown, and the landmark *Will the Circle Be Unbroken* albums. He

Photo by Jeremy Denton/Courtesy Karim Karmi, Full Stop Management

is currently a singer and bassist for the American rock band the Doobie Brothers, the HercuLeons, and the John Cowan Band. Mr. Cowan lives in a suburb of Nashville.

@johncowan.com

IG: johncowanmusic

FB: johncowanmusic

Jimmy Schwartz is a contributing writer, editor, and longtime friend of Mr. Cowan's. He worked for more than three decades as an advertising writer and creative director in Chicago. He first met Mr. Cowan during the production of a radio commercial thirty-five years ago in Nashville. In 2018, a single comment from John over stuffed spinach pizza in Chicago, "We should work on something together," kindled the spark of this project for which Jimmy, a lifelong Americana music fan, is unspeakably grateful. Mr. Schwartz is a devoted husband and awestruck father of two, currently living in the western suburbs of Chicago.